Contemporary Perspectives on Science and Technology in Early Childhood Education

A volume in
Contemporary Perspectives in Early Childhood Education
Olivia N. Saracho and Bernard Spodek, *Series Editors*

Contemporary Perspectives on Science and Technology in Early Childhood Education

Editorial Advisory Board

Contemporary Perspectives on Science and Technology in Early Childhood Education

Edited by

Olivia N. Saracho
and
Bernard Spodek

INFORMATION AGE PUBLISHING, INC.
Charlotte, NC • www.infoagepub.com

Library of Congress Cataloging-in-Publication Data

Contemporary perspectives on science and technology in early childhood
education / edited by Olivia N. Saracho and Bernard Spodek.
    p. cm. – (Contemporary perspectives in early childhood education)
  Includes bibliographical references.
  ISBN 978-1-59311-635-4 (pbk.) – ISBN 978-1-59311-636-1 (hardcover)
  1. Science–Study and teaching (Early childhood) 2. Technological
literacy–Study and teaching (Early childhood) 3. Educational technology.
I. Saracho, Olivia N. II. Spodek, Bernard.
  LB1139.5.S35C66 2007
  372.3'5–dc22

                                                              2007037873

CONTENTS

INTRODUCTION

THE RECIPROCITY BETWEEN SCIENCE AND TECHNOLOGY

Olivia N. Saracho and Bernard Spodek

INTRODUCTION

For at least three decades, many leaders (e.g., politicians, business leaders) have been concerned about the quality of education in the United States. A major issue is that American children may not be competitive on international tests of mathematics and science. This issue has also become important for early childhood education. Fifty percent of the children between the ages of three and five are enrolled in preschool programs in the United States today. Unfortunately, there are no state, federal, or national standards for science or technology in preschool or kindergarten programs (Bowman, 1999). Many professionals foresee new requirements in science and technology in our postindustrial world. New knowledge is rapidly being developed and disseminated, demanding that students acquire a wider range of skills and knowledge in these areas.

The notion that scientific and technological knowledge should be a part of every individual's education has become apparent. Students in our society need to become literate in many subjects, including science and technology (Scherz & Oren, 2006). The literature in these areas also shows ways to enhance young children's scientific thinking and problem-solving

Contemporary Perspectives on Science and Technology in Early Childhood Education, pages vii–xvi
Copyright © 2008 by Information Age Publishing

skills as well as their technological abilities (New, 1999). The attention to
these prominent areas has motivated the creation of the present volume,
although the chapters in these areas are independent of each other. The
purpose of this volume is to present a critical analysis of the review of
research on science and technology. These two areas overlap with each
other while also being independent of each other. The first part of the volume will include contributions by leading scholars in science, while the second part will include contributions by leading scholars in technology.

SCIENCE AND TECHNOLOGY

Science and technology have been perceived as the indispensable foundation for economic advancement (e.g., Lewis, 2006). The *National Science
Education Standards* (National Research Council, 1996, 2000) on scientific
literacy includes both science content knowledge (declarative facts and
conceptual knowledge) and reasoning knowledge (e.g., analyzing data,
building explanations from evidence, engaging with scientific questions).
These standards apply to science education for all age groups and include
a major feature of scientific literacy (Bransford, Brown, & Cocking, 2000;
National Research Council, 1996, 2000). In addition, technology and its
relationship to science became part of the *Benchmarks for science literacy*
(American Association for the Advancement of Science, 1993).

Researchers within the science education community perceive technology to serve as an entrance to children's understanding of scientific concepts (e.g., Benenson, 2001; Crismond, 2001; Kolodner, 2002). They relate
science and technology based on studies that include pedagogic
approaches that simultaneously enhance both scientific and technological
literacy in children. Benenson (2001) maintained that systemic reforms in
science are the result of technological demands in the society, and he demonstrates the way "everyday technology" can serve as the context to promote both scientific and technological literacy in children. Crismond
(2001) used novice and expert designers to examine and redesign tasks.
The results indicated that expert designers were better at linking tasks with
scientific principles. Kolodner (2002) used a "Learning by Design" technique to teach scientific concepts. Her design tasks were used to prompt
students in learning scientific principles. These researchers studied the
prospects of design as science pedagogy to predict the recognition of cooperation with technology education.

Young children need to understand the technological world as the
objects are developed with sophistication. Society requires that education
change in the areas in science and technology. The effects of scientific and
technological change need to undertake issues of conflicting social priori-

ties. Scherz and Oren (2006) suggest that science and technology education be related to authentic scientific research and technological developmental practice, allowing students to explore real questions. Two current terms that have surfaced in the literature are *scientific literacy* and *technological literacy*. In the first chapter titled, *Scientific and Technological Literacy Research: Principles and Practices*, Olivia N. Saracho and Bernard Spodek describe the research on the principles and practices of scientific and technological literacy. They offer the different meanings and rationales for scientific and technological literacy. They also provide recommendations on what knowledge about the nature of technology is required for scientific literacy and emphasize ways of thinking about technology that can contribute to using it wisely. Saracho and Spodek use this chapter on scientific and technological literacy to connect the first section on science and the second section on technology of the volume.

SCIENTIFIC RESEARCH

Over the last five decades, it has been argued that "developmentally appropriate" activities provide young children with opportunities to develop their cognitive understanding in science. While programs for young children should be developmentally appropriate, they also need to be content appropriate. That is, the content of these programs should not only provide achievable goals for young children, but they should also reflect legitimate areas of knowledge that are of value to our society (Spodek, 1991).

Research has focused on investigating the role of cognitive factors in early childhood science education. In the last few years there also seems to be an increasing interest in the role of affective factors in science education (e.g., wonder, excitement, enthusiasm, emotion). In the chapter titled, *Affect and Early Childhood Science Education*, Michalinos Zembylas reviews recent research on affective issues in early childhood science education that have been published in journals and books within the last ten years (1996-present), focusing on the theoretical and practical accomplishments of this work. According to this review, early childhood science educators have begun to acknowledge the importance of affect and its implications for teaching and learning science to young children. However, more systematic research needs to be undertaken to document the rich and reliable ways that the emotional experiences of young children and teachers in the classroom as well as advance the development of multi-dimensional theories in the affective domain that has had an impact on early childhood science education.

Developmental considerations influence the teaching of the process skills of observation, classifying, measuring, communicating, estimating/

predicting, and inferring. Classrooms can be organized to provide opportunities for children to develop these skills. Exemplary early childhood science teaching strategies engage all learners and rely on dynamic social interactions. Children's use of decontextualized language enables them to reflect on the meaning of their science experiences. Communicative roles of the teachers and students as co-participants in a classroom community shape the children's understanding of science concepts. Within this sociocultural perspective, the dialectic relationship of interaction and context leads to the social construction of shared understanding. The quality of peer relationships and teacher child relationships are related to the types of social exchanges and oral language use that can lead to conceptual understanding. To improve the quality of interaction during science activities, more emphasis needs to be placed on teaching the skills associated with effective interaction and collaborative learning skills. In their chapter, *Early Childhood Science Concepts and Process Skills: Social and Developmental Considerations*, Ithel Jones, Vickie E. Lake, and Miranda Lin discuss the science process skills that should be taught and developed in the early childhood years with reference to the children's cognitive development.

In the next chapter, *Knowledge Acquisition as Conceptual Change: The Case of a Theory of Biology*, Grady J. Venville explores and reviews the literature on young children's understanding and development of a theory of biology. A conceptual change in the theoretical perspective is adopted through which to view and analyze the literature. The body of the chapter is structured around a series of questions posed by Chinn and Brewer (1998) as a framework for understanding and evaluating theories of knowledge acquisition. These questions result in a discussion of the nature of the knowledge change, regardless of the intermediate stages in the knowledge change and the factors that initiate and influence knowledge change. Venville concludes with a discussion about the implications for research and practice, which we ultimately assume is related to technological research.

TECHNOLOGICAL RESEARCH

Presently, all facets of American life depend, to some extent, on technology. Technology is increasingly being used in early childhood classrooms and the development of software for young children continues to flourish. It is essential that researchers examine the effect of technology on children and identify ways for young children to take advantage of the use of technology. The National Association for the Education of Young Children (1996) published a position statement where it addresses a number of concerns in relation to technology's use with young children. This position statement includes the following guidelines:

- the essential role of the teacher in evaluating appropriate uses of technology;
- the potential benefits of appropriate use of technology in early childhood programs;
- the integration of technology into the typical learning environment;
- equitable access to technology, including children with special needs;
- stereotyping and violence in software;
- the role of teachers and parents as advocates; and
- the implications of technology for professional development.

In this position statement, the National Association for the Education of Young Children (1996) mainly refers to computer technology. However, this term also includes related technologies (e.g., telecommunications, multimedia), which have become incorporated into computer technology. The next chapter initiates the second section of the volume, which focuses on technology with young children. There have been a wide variety of technology-enhanced play materials developed in recent years, ranging from ones that provide minimal child direction using brief sounds and "talk" to ones that exhibit complex robotic quality that simulate human behaviors. These toys may have the potential for furthering the children's cognitive schema development, specific skill learning, creative inquiry, and socially mediated behaviors. However, present research on their effects is very limited. In *New Technologies in Early Childhood: Partners in Play?* Doris Bergen discusses this research, focusing on the play of infants and toddlers, preschoolers, early elementary students, and children with special needs. A number of evaluation criteria (transparency, challenge, and accessibility) are proposed, based on the affordance possibilities of each type of technology-enhanced toy, as well as on their potential for promoting a wide variety of play experiences (practice, pretense, and games). As technologically-enhanced toys continue to develop, they may extend the play possibilities in ways that foster young children's play and development, or they may stifle some aspects of play that are valuable. It is important that systematic longitudinal research begins to examine their effects, especially as electronically-enhanced technology toys become pervasive in the early childhood years.

In the next chapter, *Engineers and Storytellers: Using Robotic Manipulatives to Develop Technological Fluency in Early Childhood*, Marina Bers suggests exploring young children's capacity as both little storytellers and little engineers to help them develop technological literacy. In the spirit of early childhood manipulatives, robotic manipulatives can engage children in learning abstract ideas by building and programming personally meaningful robotic projects. In this process, they are likely to establish personal

connections with complex ideas, while respecting their own epistemological styles or ways of knowing the world. Marina Bers also suggests that, in
order to support young children's development of technological fluency,
those using educational technologies in early childhood have much to
learn about the importance of involving parents from the family literacy
movement.

Computer technology has the potential to make multiple contributions
to early childhood education, particularly in such core areas as language, literacy, and mathematics. Whether this potential is realized depends on
which technology is used and how the technology is used. In their chapter,
Mathematics and Technology, Douglas H. Clements and Julie Sarama review
the research addressing: (a) recent criticisms of computers in childhood,
(b) the use of technology to support the mathematics learning of young
children, and (c) the professional development for teachers that helps
them use technology to good advantage in their classrooms. Research like
the one they reviewed offers substantial guidance in teaching effectively
with technology. Computers can contribute significantly, but that contribution may be maximized when they are used as a tool by knowledgeable, supported educators working with a research-based curriculum and software.

In the chapter that follows, *Vocabulary Learning by Computer in Kindergarten: The Possibilities of Interactive Vocabulary Books*, Eliane Segers and Anne
Vermeer present an overview of the research on the use of books on computers in kindergarten, with a special focus on their effects on vocabulary
learning. Most research on the use of books with computers elaborate the
already known positive effects of storybook reading on vocabulary. For second language learners, more effort is needed to allow them to catch up
with their peers. Eliane Segers and Anne Vermeer use the term "interactive
vocabulary books" in their chapter. They assume that interactive vocabulary books offer more opportunities to enhance vocabulary for kindergartners. These are books that combine a story with interactive vocabulary
games. In these books, attention is paid to the four basic principles of
vocabulary learning: preparation, semantization, consolidation, and evaluation, and the interactive and adaptive possibilities of the computer are
elaborated. Eliane Segers and Anne Vermeer also present two Dutch examples in their chapter, and research on this type of software is described.
Results are promising; the vocabulary of young children is enhanced with
this type of software. Future research should also address the role of the
teacher, the combination of adaptive software with classroom activities, and
design aspects of the software.

Technology is a prevailing resource. Its software offers available information and resources for classroom management, planning, and development of materials. Children can learn through telecommunications and
the Internet, while teachers can acquire information and innovative ideas

from around the world and communicate with remote experts and peers. They can share curriculum ideas, resources, and promising practices; exchange advice; and collaborate on classroom and professional development projects with peers from another school, city, or country. They can also learn new skills from their distant peers. Learning how to access available services via on-line networks and the Internet can provide early childhood teachers with additional knowledge and classroom resources. A responsive on-line system can provide technological support to help novices become technologically literate and to professionally take advantage of technology. Competent educators using technology can serve as role models for young children on the appropriate use of technology (National Association for the Education of Young Children, 1996).

CONCLUSION

Science and technology are an integral part of our society. Young children informally and intuitively develop knowledge in these disciplines through their interactions with people and objects. Young children observe physical phenomena, use technologically equipment (e.g., telephones, televisions), and generate hypotheses about cause and effect. Traditional and contemporary research provides evidence that very young children can understand the world from a scientific perspective. Knowledge in science and technology can facilitate young children's success in society. They need to become literate in science and technology to be better prepared for the future (American Association for the Advancement of Science, 1999). In the final chapter, *A Future Research Agenda in Early Childhood Science and Technology*, Olivia N. Saracho and Bernard Spodek provide support on the importance of acquiring knowledge in scientific and technological literacy. They also share the views of several professional organizations in relation to scientific and technological literacy including the National Association for the Education of Young Children, the National Science Teachers Association, and the American Association for the Advancement of Science, the National Research Council, and the International Technology Education Association. Saracho and Spodek also provide a research agenda for future research and recommendations for those individuals who work directly or indirectly with young children.

Early childhood educators do not consider science and technology to be a curriculum priority for young children. Science and technology are usually not the focus of preschool or kindergarten education. Insufficient consideration has been given to the importance of what and how young children acquire their knowledge of science and technology. Early childhood educators view the source of knowledge for science and technology as formal, orderly, abstract, and based in a strict reality; whereas young children's learning is informal, relational, concrete, and usually saturated with fantasy (Bowman, 1999). According to Benenson (2001), technology and science differ in their goals, but in several situations, they share ways of thinking (e.g., improving existing designs). Students are able to work with existing artifacts and determine their weaknesses; to improve them; and to learn a subject matter (e.g., science, mathematics, technology, language). The National Science Education Standards (National Research Council, 1996) distinguishes between science and technology by stating that:

> The goal of science is to understand the natural world, and the goal of technology is to make modifications in the world to meet human needs. Technology as design is included in the standards as parallel to science as inquiry. (p. 24)

This goal seems to be a counterpart of the technology education standards. The introduction to the Standards for technological Literacy: Content for the study of technology (International Technology Education Association, 2000) justifies that:

> Design is regarded by many as the core problem-solving process of technological development. It is as fundamental to technology as inquiry is to science and reading is to language arts. (International Technology Education Association, 2000, p. 90)

A national consensus has surfaced on what determines effective science teaching and learning for young children. They have agreed that science can be an active learning vehicle for preschool and primary school children. Science is considered to be a system of discovering, organizing, and reporting discoveries. It is perceived as a mode of thinking and seeking to understand the world rather than memorizing facts (Lind, 1999). This consensus is reflected in documents such as the *National Science Education Standards* (National Research Council, 1996), *Benchmarks for Science Literacy* (American Association for the Advancement of Science, 1993), and *Science for All Americans* (American Association for the Advancement of Science, 1990).

The *National Science Education Standards* (NSES) (National Research Council, 1996) and *Benchmarks for Science Literacy* (American Association for the Advancement of Science, 1993) advocated that all children are able to learn science and need to be provided with opportunities to become scientifically literate at an early age. Both the *National Science Education Standards* (National Research Council, 1996) and *Benchmarks for Science Literacy* (American Association for the Advancement of Science, 1993) corresponded with the guidelines from the National Association for the Education of Young Children (Bredekamp, 1987; Bredekamp & Copple, 1997; Bredekamp & Rosegrant, 1992). All of these documents overlap in their content, especially on the important knowledge and skills in science, mathematics, and technology. For example, *Benchmarks for Science Literacy* (American Association for the Advancement of Science, 1993) states the knowledge and competencies that students should have in science, mathematics, and technology for all grade levels including young children from kindergarten to second grade. The *National Science Education Standards* (National Research Council, 1996) considers that science as inquiry parallels technology in design.

The relationship between science and technology in contemporary times is unavoidable, although school subjects, science, and technology have existed independent of each other. Benchmarks for Science Literacy attribute technology to be science content, but it devotes separate chapters to "the nature of technology" and "the designed world" (American Association for the Advancement of Science, 1993). The National Science Education Standards (National Research Council, 1996), requires that scientific literacy be technologically informed. The science standards considers technology to be more than computers, which correspond to the standards in technology (Dugger, 2001; International Technology Education Association, 2000) and those guidelines provided in the position statement that was developed by the National Association for the Education of Young Children (1996). One might assume that technology education be separated from the content approach and be viewed as a process approach.

REFERENCES

American Association for the Advancement of Science. (1990). *Science for All Americans: Project 2061.* New York. Oxford University Press.

American Association for the Advancement of Science. (1993). *Benchmarks for science literacy.* New York: Oxford University Press

American Association for the Advancement of Science, Project 2061. (1999). *Dialogue on early childhood science, mathematics, and technology education.* Cary, NC: Oxford University Press.

Benenson, G. (2001). The unrealized potential of everyday technology as a context for learning. *Journal of Research in Science Teaching, 38*(7), 730–745.

Bowman, B. T. (1999). Policy implications for math, science, and technology in early childhood education: A context for learning. In American Association for the Advancement of Science, Project 2061. *Dialogue on early childhood science, mathematics, and technology education.* Cary, NC: Oxford University Press.

Bransford, J., Brown, A. L., & Cocking, R. R. (2000). *How people learn: Brain, mind, experience and school.* Washington, DC: National Academy Press.

Bredekamp, S., (Ed.). (1987). *Developmentally appropriate practice in early childhood programs serving children from birth through age eight.* Washington, DC: National Association for the Education of Young Children.

Bredekamp, S., & Copple, C. (Eds.). (1997). *Developmentally appropriate practice in early childhood programs: Revised.* Washington, DC: National Association for the Education of Young Children.

Bredekamp, S., & Rosegrant, T. (1992). *Reaching potentials: Appropriate curriculum and assessment for young children* (Vol. 1). Washington, DC: National Association for the Education of Young Children.

Chinn, C. A., & Brewer, W. F. (1998). Theories of knowledge acquisition. In B. J. Fraser & K. G. Tobin (Eds.), *International handbook of science education* (Part 1, pp. 97–113). Dordrecht, The Netherlands: Kluwer.

Crismond, D. (2001). Learning and using science ideas when doing investigate-and-redesign tasks: A study of naïve, novice, and expert designers doing constrained and scaffolded design work. *Journal of Research in Science Teaching, 38,* 791–820.

Dugger, W. E. (2001). Standards for technological literacy. *Phi Delta Kappan, 82,* 513–517.

International Technology Education Association. (2000). *Standards for technological Literacy: Content for the study of technology.* Reston, VA: Author.

Kolodner, J. L. (2002). Facilitating the learning of design practices: Lessons from an inquiry into science education. *Journal of Industrial Teacher Education, 39,* 9–40.

Lewis, T. (2006). Design and inquiry: Bases for an accommodation between science and technology education in the curriculum? *Journal of Research in Science Teaching, 43*(3), 255–281.

Lind, K. K. (1999). Science in early childhood: Developing and acquiring fundamental concepts and skills. In American Association for the Advancement of Science, Project 2061. *Dialogue on early childhood science, mathematics, and technology education.* Cary, NC: Oxford University Press.

National Association for the Education of Young Children. (1996). Position statement: Technology and young children: Ages three through eight. *Young Children, 51*(6),11–16.

National Research Council. (1996). *National science education standards.* Washington, DC: National Academy Press.

National Research Council (2000). *Inquiry and the national science education standards: A guide for teaching and learning.* Washington, DC: National Academy Press.

New, R. S. (1999). Playing fair and square: Issues of equity in preschool mathematics, science, and technology. In American Association for the Advancement of Science, Project 2061. *Dialogue on early childhood science, mathematics, and technology education.* Cary, NC: Oxford University Press.

Scherz, Z., & Oren, M. (2006). How to change students' images of science and technology, *Science Education, 90*(6), 965–985.

Spodek, B. (1991). What should we teach kindergarten children? In B. Spodek (Ed.), *Educationally appropriate kindergarten practices.* Washington, DC: National Education Association.

CHAPTER 1

SCIENTIFIC AND TECHNOLOGICAL LITERACY RESEARCH

Principles and Practices

Olivia N. Saracho and Bernard Spodek

The terms and circumstances of human existence can be expected to change radically during the next human life span. Science, mathematics, and technology will be at the center of that change—causing it, shaping it, responding to it. Therefore, they will be essential to the education of today's children for tomorrow's world.

—American Association for the Advancement of Science (1993)

INTRODUCTION

Knowledge about science and technology is an important requirement in contemporary society. An increasing number of professions require the use of scientific concepts and technological skills and society as a whole depends on scientific knowledge (Lee & Luykx, 2007). The idea of including scientific and technological knowledge in general education emerged early in the twentieth century. It was reasoned that science education

Contemporary Perspectives on Science and Technology in Early Childhood Education, pages 1–16
Copyright © 2008 by Information Age Publishing
All rights of reproduction in any form reserved.

1

should be for both (a) students who will continue with subjects related to science and technology as a career and (b) for students who need to learn science as part of their general education that makes them literate citizens of the twenty first century (Scherz & Oren, 2006).

Historical changes have influenced the need for scientific and technological knowledge for all. The change from rural to industrial economies also changed the contexts in which students learn have. Rural oriented science underlies both the high technological needs of agricultural manufacturers and those who want to protect the environment. Scherz and Oren (2006) suggested that science and technology be related to authentic scientific research and technological development practice, where students explore real questions.

Two current terms that have surfaced in the literature are *scientific literacy* and *technological literacy*. This chapter defines and provides a rationale for these terms. It also presents recommendations on what knowledge about the nature of science and technology is required for scientific literacy and emphasizes ways of thinking about science and technology that can provide an understanding on how to use this knowledge wisely.

SCIENTIFIC LITERACY

Scientific literacy derived from research and theory relating to the social and cultural facets of *scientific literacy*. In the 1950s *scientific literacy* was concerned with understanding and applying science to society (Conant, 1952; Hurd, 1958; McCurdy, 1958). More recently, many researchers (e.g., Bybee, 1997; Laugksch, 2000; Shamos, 1995) elaborated on the definition of *scientific literacy*. For example, Shamos (1995) used the term to describe the individual's capacity to attain reliable and competent guidance about scientific issues. Specifically, Shamos (1995) suggested that individuals become scientifically literate when they (a) understand the way the science/technology enterprise functions, (b) are comfortable with knowing what science is about, (c) know what they can expect from science, and (d) are aware of the best dissemination techniques to inform the public. DeBoer (2000) linked *scientific literacy* to science education and stimulated educators to develop educational initiatives that would foster *scientific literacy*. In DeBoer's (2000) review of the history of science education, he identified nine goals of science education. The eighth goal consists of "preparing citizens who are sympathetic to science," which can pertain to the development of positive scientific attitudes and students' scientific expertise (Scherz & Oren, 2006).

Scientific literacy has become an international educational slogan and contemporary educational goal (Laugksch, 2000). It "stands for what the general public ought to know about science" (Durant, 1993, p. 129), and "commonly implies an appreciation of the nature, aims, and general limitations of science, coupled with some understanding of the more important scientific ideas" (Jenkins, 1994, p. 5345). Scientific literacy is synonymous with "public understanding of science." The United States uses the term "scientific literacy," whereas France uses the phrase "la culture scientifique" (Durant, 1993). Nevertheless, some researchers (e.g., Champagne & Lovitts, 1989) state that the simple conceptualization of scientific literacy disguises separate meanings and interpretations related to the concept of scientific literacy. It identifies the public who needs to be informed and presents diverse perspectives on what the public needs to know about science.

Scholars who proposed the scientific literacy concept usually failed to clearly define it. However, interest in the concept of scientific literacy (i.e., the notion that the public needs to acquire some science knowledge) surfaced at the beginning of the twentieth century (Shamos, 1995). According to Waterman (1960), "progress in science depends to a considerable extent on public understanding and support of a sustained program of science education and research" (p. 1349). During this time many researchers (e.g., DeBoer, 1991; Roberts, 1983; Waterman, 1960) became interested and provided support for science and science education, which fostered several elements of scientific literacy. Roberts (1983) referred to the period between 1957 and 1963 as the "period of legitimation" (p. 25) of the concept, while the next period he called it a "period of serious interpretation" (p. 26), because many different meanings of scientific literacy became clear. Several scientists (e.g., Agin, 1974; Pella, 1976) have tried to combine the various definitions of scientific literacy to create a comprehensible concept. Thus, scientific literacy "has had so many interpretations that it now means virtually everything to do with science education" (Roberts, 1983, p. 22) and its interpretations as a concept had "come to be an umbrella concept to signify comprehensiveness in the purposes of science teaching in the schools" (p. 29).

The lack of agreement has minimized the value of the concept of scientific literacy. During the last two decades, the United States published various educational reports such as *Science for all Americans: Project 2061* (American Association for the Advancement of Science, 1990) and *Benchmarks for Science Literacy* (American Association for the Advancement of Science, 1993; National Research Council, 1996). The United Kingdom also published several reports such as *Beyond 2000: Science Education for the Future* (Millar & Osborne, 1998), which focused on *scientific literacy.* These publications piqued the interest of science educators, researchers, and policy makers allowing schools to establish *scientific literacy* as a major goal in science education (Scherz & Oren, 2006).

SCIENCE IN EARLY CHILDHOOD EDUCATION

A study and the continuous debate among scientists, mathematicians, engineers, and educators on the specific literacy goals in science, mathematics, and technology for all Americans prompted the American Association for the Advancement of Science to establish literacy goals and to generate a set of guidelines to assist educators in designing curricula that focused on the content standards of Project 2061's *Science for All Americans* (American Association for the Advancement of Science, 1990), which included students at the different grades ranging from kindergarten to the twelfth grade. Initially, it was assumed that curriculum models would be developed to serve as examples of alternative ways to launch experiences for kindergarten to twelfth grade students to help them attain the expected science-literacy outcomes. As a result, the American Association for the Advancement of Science (1993) established the *Benchmarks for science literacy,* which describes (a) the way students need to make progress toward science literacy, (b) the knowledge they need to learn, and (c) the abilities that should be achieved at each grade level. Both publications, *Science for All Americans: Project 2061* (American Association for the Advancement of Science, 1990) and *Benchmarks for science literacy* (American Association for the Advancement of Science, 1993) provide guidelines for the reform in science, mathematics, and technology education.

In relation to young children, the *Benchmarks for science literacy* (American Association for the Advancement of Science, 1993) suggested that, from the first day in school, young children must be actively involved in learning about the world scientifically. Young children need to be motivated to raise questions about nature and to search answers, collect things, count and measure things, make qualitative observations, organize collections and observations, discuss findings, among other activities. These experiences can prompt them to experience the emotional state of science and enjoy learning about science. Later, young children can become more aware of the scientific world. Their early science experiences need to focus on the belief in the unity of nature and its consistency. Young children need to duplicate observations and investigations in the classroom, in the school yard, and at home. For example, young children can compare their results in these different settings such as:

- The results of cooking an egg in each setting.
- Their observations related to pushing and pulling moving objects.
- Recording the growth of a seed.

Such experiences can stimulate the young children's curiosity and motivate them to become interested in their environment and in the mechanisms of nature (American Association for the Advancement of Science,

1993). Thus, *Benchmarks for science literacy* (American Association for the Advancement of Science, 1993) established that all children need to know about the Scientific World View, Scientific Inquiry, and Scientific Enterprise. The *Benchmarks* established the knowledge that each age group needed to gain in these areas. The following goals relate to the information that young children need to know in the Scientific World View, Scientific Inquiry, and Scientific Enterprise by the end of the second grade.

The Scientific World View. A scientific world view refers to the scientist's work and beliefs in science. Beliefs consist of (a) how young children can work together to discover how the world works, (b) the universe as a unified system and results obtained from studying one section can be generalized to other sections, and (c) knowledge that can be consistent but may change. In relation to the scientific world view, young children need to know by the end of the second grade that:

- When a science investigation is done the way it was done before, we expect to get a very similar result.
- Science investigations generally work the same way in different places.

Scientific Inquiry. Scientific inquiry is concerned with more complex concepts. Young children need to actively explore phenomena both in and out of class that is of interest to them. They need to enjoy and be excited about their investigations. Young children also need to share with others what they see, what they think, and what it makes them wonder about. They need to be provided with opportunities to discuss their observations and compare these observations with those of their peers. Young children need to carefully describe their observations, but they should not be required to provide scientifically accurate explanations.

In relation to scientific inquiry young children need to know by the end of the second grade that:

- People can often learn about things around them by just observing those things carefully, but sometimes they can learn more by doing something to the things and noting what happens.
- Tools such as thermometers, magnifiers, rulers, or balances often give more information about things than can be obtained by just observing things without their help.
- Describing things as accurately as possible is important in science because it enables people to compare their observations with those of others.
- When people give different descriptions of the same thing, it is usually a good idea to make some fresh observations instead of just arguing about who is right.

Scientific Enterprise. Scientific activity differentiates between the primary elements of the contemporary world and earlier periods such as those elements required to function in society. Young children need to know the organization of science to obtain public support for basic and applied science. They need to be introduced to four other facets of the scientific enterprise: (1) social structure, (2) discipline and institutional identification, (3) ethics, and (4) scientists' role in public affairs. Young children need to be provided with experiences on these facets rather than be provided with explicit instructions. For example, they can work in small groups to raise and respond to questions about their environment and also share their findings with their peers. In relation to the scientific enterprise, young children need to know by the end of the second grade that:

- Everybody can do science and invent things and ideas.
- In doing science, it is often helpful to work with a team and to share findings with others. All team members should reach their own individual conclusions, however, about what the findings mean.
- A lot can be learned about plants and animals by observing them closely, but care must be taken to know the needs of living things and how to provide for them in the classroom.

Young children can observe live animals (e.g., goldfish, rabbits) in their classroom. They need to be provided with opportunities, in the context of science, to interact and respect their classroom animals. Teachers need to know the National Science Teachers Association's (2005) guidelines for responsible use of animals in the classroom.

For more than three decades, researchers have examined the children's understanding of the nature of science, scientific enterprise, and science goals and methods. Recently, studies have focused on children's understanding of experimentation, progress in experimentation skills, and concepts on the nature of knowledge. A few of the studies examine the students' learning about the composition of technology and its relationship to science and society. Many of these studies were conducted outside the United States. They assess the high-school students' knowledge concerning the role of science and technology and these students' attitudes toward the decision making of scientists and engineers on public issues (American Association for the Advancement of Science, 1993).

SCIENCE AND TECHNOLOGY

Science and technology have been perceived as the indispensable foundation for economic advancement (e.g., Lewis, 2006). The National Science Education Standards (National Research Council, 1996, 2000) on scientific literacy include both science content knowledge (declarative facts and conceptual knowledge) and reasoning knowledge (e.g., analyzing data, building explanations from evidence, engaging with scientific questions). The National Science Education Standards (National Research Council, 1996, 2000) include a major feature for scientific literacy, which is the appropriate use of technology to support learning (Bransford, Brown, & Cocking, 2000; National Research Council, 1996, 2000). In addition, technology and its relationship to science became part of the *Benchmarks for science literacy* (American Association for the Advancement of Science, 1993).

The social and cultural implications of science in a technological society have increased the interest in the concept of scientific literacy. Scherz and Oren (2006) relate technology to "scientific literacy." Many have become concerned about whether children were receiving the education they needed to function in a society that had scientific and technological sophistication (Hurd, 1958). The National Science Foundation has been actively promoting technology education to compliment science by funding significant projects that focus on the Standards for Technological Literacy (International Technology Education Association, 2000 and the National Center for Engineering and Technology Education, www.NCETE.org).

Researchers within the science education community perceive technology as an entrance to children's understanding of scientific concepts (e.g., Benenson, 2001; Crismond, 2001; Kolodner, 2002). They relate science and technology through studies that include pedagogic approaches that enhance both scientific and technological literacy in children. Benenson (2001) maintains that systemic reforms in science were the result of technological demands in society. He demonstrates the way "everyday technology" can serve as the context to promote both scientific and technological literacy in children. Crismond (2001) used novice and expert designers to examine and redesign tasks. The results indicated that expert designers were better at linking tasks with scientific principles. Kolodner (2002) used a "Learning by Design" technique to teach scientific concepts. Her design tasks were used to prompt students in learning scientific principles. These researchers studied the prospects of design in science pedagogy, which recognized the importance of cooperation with technology education.

Scientists employed technology to learn both science content and scientific reasoning skills. Similarly, the children's experiences with technology in science classrooms teach them the productive use of technology for both content and reasoning in the form of modeling, data analysis, and data representation (Gobert & Pallant, 2004). Science education offers a research-based means of technologies that can be used to guide scientific reasoning among all students from kindergarten through twelfth grade. Technology can develop scientific reasoning skills through (a) an organized dialogue with peers to share understandings (O'Neill, 2004; O'Neill

& Gomez, 1998), (b) scaffolded guidance to develop scientific rationales (Reiser, 2004), or (c) reflective guidance in completed and future open-ended studies (Linn & Slotta, 2002; Songer, 2007).

TECHNOLOGICAL LITERACY

Presently many major industries need computers and telecommunication systems for their everyday operations. As a human enterprise, technology possesses its own history and identity independent of science and other disciplines. Historically, it predates science and slowly evolved from knowledge about the way the natural world works to how to control the events in the world. Today, technology is seen to be mutual beneficial with science and other subject areas.

In the United States technology has been omitted from the high school graduation requirements and has been displaced in the elementary school. This position is presently under reform. Many are aware that technology is integrated into everyday life. Elementary schools are using technology projects and providing technology education (American Association for the Advancement of Science, 1993).

The growing importance of technology in our society has made it essential for students to become technologically literate. While *technological literacy* is difficult to define, the United States Department of Education (1996) characterizes it as "computer skills and the ability to use computers and other technology to improve learning, productivity, and performance." Four of its goals to guarantee that both students and teachers have the opportunity to effectively use technology have been identified:

- All teachers in the nation will have the training and support they need to help students learn using computers and the information superhighway.
- All teachers and students will have modern multimedia computers in their classrooms.
- Every classroom will be connected to the information superhighway.
- Effective software and on-line learning resources will be an integral part of every school's curriculum.

Children have to develop computer skills, which are now important to learning reading, writing, and mathematics skills. The International Technology Education Association (2000) simplified the definition of technological literacy as follows:

> Technological literacy is the ability to use, manage, assess, and understand technological products and systems. This ability, in turn, demands certain

mental tools, such as problem solving, visual imaging, critical thinking, *and reasoning*. (p. 123)

The International Technology Education Association (2000) published the book on Standards *for technological literacy: Content for the study of technology* to present a vision on what students should do to become technologically literate. These standards will ensure that the students receive the appropriate instruction in technology by focusing on all grade levels ranging from kindergarten to the twelfth grade. They made the following statement about technological literacy.

Technological literacy is the ability to use, manage, assess, and understand technology. A technological literate person understands an increasingly different ways that evolve over time, what technology is, how it is created, and how it shapes society and in turn is shaped by society. He or she will be able to hear a story about technology on television or read in the newspaper and evaluate the information in the story intelligently, put the information in context, and form an opinion based on the information. A technologically literate person will be comfortable with and objective about technology, neither scared of it or infatuated with it. (International Technology Education Association, 2000, pp. 9–10)

Technology in Early Childhood Education

Technology assumes an important role in our society, one which will expand even more in the future. In the past, technology was concerned with studying or applying the practical arts. It also related to innovations (e.g., pencils, television, aspirin, microscopes) that were used for specific purposes, individual activities (e.g., agriculture, manufacturing), and processes (e.g., animal breeding, voting, war that modified the world). Further, technology has been tied to the industrial and military institutions that produce and use inventions. For all of these reasons, technology influences the economic, social, ethical, and aesthetic developments (American Association for the Advancement of Science, 1993).

Young children often have experience using technology before they attend school. They travel in automobiles, use household utilities, ride in wagons and on bicycles, utilize garden tools, assist with cooking, control the television set, and so on. Young children like to explore, invent, and create things. They need to be provided with opportunities to investigate the properties of materials, to use tools, and to design and construct things. Their experiences need to focus on problems in and around the school that are both of interest to children, possible, and safe.

The use of technology has an important value in the young children's lives, development, and learning. The continuous development of technology has facilitated its use and increased its impact on early childhood education, which has expanded young children's use of technology. It is important that early childhood educators assume responsibility to critically examine the effect of technology on young children and learn to use it wisely with them (National Association for the Education of Young Children, 1996).

We need to allow technology to keep all students well informed about its nature, powers, and limitations. The American Association for the Advancement of Science developed *Benchmarks for science literacy* (American Association for the Advancement of Science, 1993) for what all children need to learn about technology and science, design and systems, and issues in technology. The Benchmarks proposed knowledge that each age group needed to know in these areas. The goals that young children need to achieve by the end of the second grade are discussed here.

Design and technology. Young children should be involved in design and technology activities. Initially, they need to use a variety of tools and solve practical problems. Young children's design and technology projects can help them in solving problems in relation to a broad range of real-world contexts. Their design projects can lead them to deal with technology issues even if they do not know the meaning of the term technology. They need to focus on the use of tools and instruments as well as the use of practical knowledge to solve problems before understanding the underlying concepts (American Association for the Advancement of Science, 1993).

Technology for young children needs to be initiated with their inventive energy and followed by using the tools with a purpose, which will expand their understanding about tools (e.g., container, paper and pencil, camera, magnifier). Design and technology activities can introduce young children to measurement tools and techniques in a natural and meaningful way. For instance, five-year-olds can design and build things for their stuffed animals with tools that are constructed on an appropriate scale. Measurements need to focus on dimensions that are developmentally appropriate for the age of the children. In relation to design and technology, young children need to know by the end of the second grade that:

- Tools are used to do things better or more easily and to do some things that could not otherwise be done at all. In technology, tools are used to observe, measure, and make things.
- When trying to build something or to get something to work better, it usually helps to follow directions if there are any or to ask someone who has done it before for suggestions.

Design and Systems. Engineering is the professional field that has a close relationship to technology. Engineers apply scientific principles to solve practical problems. Children can learn about design and systems by engaging in developmentally appropriate activities in a variety of contexts where they analyze situations and collect pertinent information, describe problems, generate and assess creative ideas, apply their ideas to concrete solutions, and evaluate and improve their solutions. Gradually, children will engage in more sophisticated projects and learn to use feedback with technological systems when they engage in games, conversation, and use tools and machines. Young children can be presented with simple ideas, while slowly being introduced to more complex.

Children under the age of eight years can design and create things with simple tools and a variety of materials. They determine a need that is of interest to them and within their abilities. Then with appropriate assistance, young children plan, design, make, evaluate, and modify their design with appropriate help. Once they experience success with one problem, they may find that their next design project is easier and gain confidence. In relation to design and systems, young children need to know by the end of the second grade that:

- People may not be able to actually make or do everything that they can design.

Issues in Technology. It is important to use technology wisely. Children need to learn how to think critically about technology. Usually technological effects are complex, can be difficult to make an accurate assessment, and may have different values for different individuals.

Young children (kindergarten to second grade) can find that design projects provide them with opportunities to solve problems, utilize tools well, measure things carefully, make reasonable assessments, calculate correctly, and communicate clearly. These projects also allow children to reflect on the effects of their inventions. For example, young children may decide to construct a large shallow tank to make an ocean habitat. They discuss the results of a leaking tank, any interference of other projects or classroom activities, and different ways to learn about ocean habitats. Young children need to learn how individuals affect their environment. Children at this age are able to understand that solving some problems can lead to other problems. It is important that young children have the freedom to solve problems and enjoy working on simple projects that do not require a complex analysis. In relation to technological issues, young children need to know by the end of the second grade that:

- People, alone or in groups, are always inventing new ways to solve problems and get work done. The tools and ways of doing things that people have invented affect all aspects of life.
- When a group of people wants to build something or try something new, they should try to figure out ahead of time how it might affect other people.

Technology broadens the young children's abilities to modify the world. Young children cut, shape, or put together materials; move things from one place to another, reach farther with their hands, voices, and senses. Young children can learn to use technology to attempt to make a better world, although the results of their attempts may become complicated and unpredictable. Establishing realistic expectations on the effects of technology is as important as its capacity for progress (American Association for the Advancement of Science, 1990).

Developmentally Appropriate Technology

The National Association for the Education of Young Children (NAEYC) developed a position statement on developmentally appropriate use of technology with young children from three to eight. In this position statement, NAEYC (1996) uses the term technology in reference to computer technology, although it can be applied to related technologies (e.g., telecommunications and multimedia) that are incorporated in computer technology. In addition, the position statement discusses various areas related to the young children's use of technology: (1) the teachers' role in assessing the appropriate uses of technology; (2) the possible values in appropriately using technology in early childhood programs; (3) the consolidation of technology in a typical learning environment; (4) the opportunities for all children to have access to technology, including children with special needs; (5) the avoidance of stereotyping and violence in software; (6) the teachers and parents' roles as advocates; and (7) the implementation of technology for professional development. This position statement addresses the following principles of child development to make sure that the use of technology is developmentally appropriate.

1. In evaluating the appropriate use of technology, the National Association for the Education of Young Children believes that in any given situation, a professional judgment by the teacher is required to determine if a specific use of technology is age appropriate, individually appropriate, and culturally appropriate.
2. Used appropriately, technology can enhance children's cognitive and social abilities.

3. Appropriate technology is integrated into the regular learning environment and used as one of many options to support children's learning.

4. Early childhood educators should promote equitable access to technology for all children and their families. Children with special needs should have increased access when this is helpful.

5. The power of technology to influence children's learning and development requires that attention be paid to eliminating stereotyping of any group and eliminating exposure to violence, especially as a problem-solving strategy.

6. Teachers, in collaboration with parents, should advocate for more appropriate technology applications for all children.

7. The appropriate use of technology has many implications for early childhood professional development.

Experts in child development, science, and technology have also recommended that the use of technology should be developmentally appropriate. Cooper (2005) suggested that developmentally appropriate environments need to:

- support the child as a unique individual;
- be child controlled;
- be open-ended rather than close-ended;
- be active rather than passive;
- involve many senses;
- encourage exploration, experimentation, and risk taking;
- encourage critical thinking, decision making, and problem solving;
- offer quick feedback, be interruptible, and keep records;
- balance familiarity with novelty;
- be user friendly;
- be progressively leveled, offering new challenges;
- be responsive to child input;
- build on previous learning;
- encourage reflection and metacognition;
- support social interaction (Cooper, 2005, p. 298).

In general, these criteria resemble those used in the selection of all developmentally appropriate materials for young children. It is important to consider that technology is a tool rather than a solution. Technology does not replace human interaction, which also focuses on the children's individual needs. Bilal (2003) recommended that children be used as designers of Web interfaces, while Large et al. (2003) suggested that children be used as designers of Web portals. Design needs to be developmentally appropriate and needs to support the collaboration of children and teachers in creating the design (Bilal, 2003; Large et al., 2003). Using children as design partners shows children a respect for their intelligence and creativity. It also increases the children's interest. Technology needs to use responsible, well-considered design, and high quality content choices to meet the children's developmental needs in their environments (Cooper, 2005).

REFERENCES

Agin, M. L. (1974). Education for scientific literacy: A conceptual frame of reference and some applications. *Science Education, 58*, 403–415.

American Association for the Advancement of Science. (1990). *Science for All Americans: Project 2061*. New York: Oxford University Press.

American Association for the Advancement of Science. (1993). *Benchmarks for science literacy*. New York: Oxford University Press

American Association for the Advancement of Science, Project 2061. (1999). *Dialogue on early childhood science, mathematics, and technology education*. Cary, NC: Oxford University Press.

Benenson, G. (2001). The unrealized potential of everyday technology as a context for learning. *Journal of Research in Science Teaching, 38*, 730–745.

Bilal, D. (2003). Draw and tell: Children as designers of Web interfaces. In M. J. Bates & R. J. Todd (Eds.), *ASIST 2003: Humanizing information technology: From ideas to bits and back: Proceedings of the 66th ASIST Annual Meeting, October 19–22, 2003, Long Beach, CA* (pp. 135–141). Medford, NJ: Information Today.

Bowman, B. T. (1999). Policy implications for math, science, and technology in early childhood education A context for learning. In American Association for the Advancement of Science, Project 2061. *Dialogue on early childhood science, mathematics, and technology education*. Cary, NC: Oxford University Press.

Bransford, J., Brown, A. L., & Cocking, R. R. (2000). *How people learn: Brain, mind, experience and school*. Washington, DC: National Academy Press.

Bybee, R. W. (1997). *Achieving scientific literacy: From purposes to practices*. Portsmouth NH: Heinemann.

Bybee, R.W. (2000). Achieving technological literacy: A national imperative. *The Technology Teacher, 60*, 23–28.

Central Advisory Council for Education (England). (1967). *Children and their primary schools (the Plowden Report)*. London: Her Majesty's Stationary Office.

Champagne, A. B., & Lovitts, B. E. (1989). Scientific literacy: A concept in search of definition. In A. B. Champagne, B. E. Lovitts & B. J. Callinger (Eds.), *This year in school science. Scientific literacy* (pp. 1–14). Washington, DC: American Association for the Advancement of Science.

Conant, J. B. (1952). *Modern science and modern man*. New York: Columbia University Press.

Cooper, L. Z. (2005). Developmentally appropriate digital environments for young children, *Library Trends, 54*(2), 286–302.

Crismond, D. (2001). Learning and using science ideas when doing investigate-and-redesign tasks: A study of naïve, novice, and expert designers doing constrained and scaffolded design work. *Journal of Research in Science Teaching, 38,* 791–820.

DeBoer, G. E. (1991). *A history of ideas in science education: Implications for practice.* New York: Teachers College Press.

DeBoer, G. E. (2000). Scientific literacy: Another look at its historical and contemporary meanings and its relationship to science education reform. *Journal of Research in Science Teaching, 37,* 582–601.

Durant, J. R. (1993). What is scientific literacy? In J. R. Durant & J. Gregory (Eds.), *Science and culture in Europe* (pp. 129–137). London: Science Museum.

Gobert, J. D., & Pallant, A. (2004). Fostering students' epistemologies of models via authentic model-based tasks. *Journal of Science Education and Technology, 13*(1), 7–22.

Hurd, D. P. (1958). Science literacy: Its meaning for American schools. *Educational Leadership, 16,* 13–16.

International Technology Education Association. (2000). *Standards for technological Literacy: Content for the study of technology.* Reston, VA: Author.

Jenkins, E. W. (1994). Scientific literacy. In T. Husen & T. N. Postlethwaite, (Eds.), *The international encyclopedia of education* (Volume 9, 2nd ed., pp. 5345–5350). Oxford: Pergamon Press.

Kolodner, J. L. (2002). Facilitating the learning of design practices: Lessons from an inquiry into science education. *Journal of Industrial Teacher Education, 39,* 9–40.

Large, A., Beheshti, J., Nesset, V., & Bowler, L. (2003). Children as designers of Web portals. In M. J. Bates & R.J. Todd (Eds.), *ASIST 2003: Humanizing information technology: From ideas to bits and back: Proceedings of the 66th ASIST Annual Meeting, October 19–22, 2003, Long Beach, CA* (pp. 142–149). Medford, NJ: Information Today.

Laugksch, R. L. (2000). Scientific literacy: A conceptual overview. *Science Education, 84*(1), 71–94.

Lee, O., & Luykx, A. (2007). Science education and student diversity: Race/ethnicity, language, culture, and socioeconomic status. In S. K. Abell & N. G. Norman G. Lederman (Eds.), *Handbook of research on science education* (pp. 171–197). Mahwah, NJ: Erlbaum.

Lewis, T. (2006). Design and inquiry: Bases for an accommodation between science and technology education in the curriculum? *Journal of Research in Science Teaching, 43,* 255–281.

Linn, M. C., & Slotta, J. D. (2002). WISE science. *Educational Leadership, x*(x), p. 29–32.

McCurdy, R. C. (1958). Toward a population literate in science. *The Science Teacher, 25,* 366–368.

Millar, R., & Osborne, J. F. (Eds.). (1998). *Beyond 2000: Science education for the future.* London: King's College.

National Association for the Education of Young Children. (1996). Position statement: Technology and young children: Ages three through eight. *Young Children, 51*(6),11–16.

National Research Council. (1996). *National science education standards.* Washington, DC: National Academy Press.

National Research Council (2000). *Inquiry and the national science education standards: A guide for teaching and learning.* Washington, DC: National Academy Press.

National Science Teachers Association. (2005). *NSTA position statement: Responsible use of live animals and dissection in the science classroom.* Retrieved on January 28, 2007, from http://www.nsta.org/positionstatement&psid=44

O'Neill, K. D. (2004). Building social capital in a knowledge-building community: Telementoring as a catalyst. *Interactive Learning Environments, 12,* 179–208.

O'Neill, K., & Gomez, L. (1998). *Sustaining mentoring relationships on-line.* Proceedings of Computer Support for Collaborative Work 1998 (pp. 325–334), Seattle, WA.

Osborne, J. F., Black, P. J., Meadows, J., & Smith, M. (1993). Young children's (7–11) ideas about light and their development. *International Journal for Science Education, 15*(1), 83–93.

Pella, M. O. (1976). The place or function of science for a literate citizenry. *Science Education, 60*(1), 97–101.

Reiser, B. J. (2004). Scaffolding complex learning: The mechanisms of structuring and problematizing student work. *The Journal of the Learning Sciences, 13,* 273–304.

Roberts, D. A. (1983). *Scientific literacy. Towards a balance for setting goals for school science programs.* Ottawa, ON, Canada: Minister of Supply and Services.

Scherz, Z., & Oren, M. (2006). How to change students' images of science and technology. *Science Education, 90,* 965–985.

Shamos, M. H. (1995). *The myth of scientific literacy.* New Brunswick, NJ: Rutgers University Press.

Songer, S. (2007). Digital resources versus cognitive tools: A discussion of learning science with technology. In S. K. Abell & N. G. Norman G. Lederman (Eds.) *Handbook of research on science education* (pp. 471–492). Mahwah, NJ: Erlbaum.

United States Department of Education. (1996, June). *Getting America's students ready for the 21st century: Meeting the technology literacy challenge* [Online]. Available: http://www.ed.gov/Technology/Plan/NatTechPlan/

Waterman, A. T. (1960). National Science Foundation: A ten-year résumé. *Science, 131*(3410), 1341–1354.

CHAPTER 2

EARLY CHILDHOOD SCIENCE PROCESS SKILLS

Social and Developmental Considerations

Ithel Jones, Vickie E. Lake, and Miranda Lin

In this chapter, drawing on a constructivist perspective, we consider children's cognitive development in examining the science process skills that should be taught and developed in the early childhood years. By early childhood, we mean the years from birth to age eight. First, we describe the nature of the process skills and discuss the implications of developmental considerations for practice. We then examine the role of the teacher, and specifically, the role of teacher–child relationships in early childhood science education. In this chapter the importance of one specific aspect of the social context in which science conceptual understanding develops is explored. We propose that close teacher–child relationships may be an especially important social configuration in early school-based science. The theoretical model presented is centered on Vygotskian theory (1978), which suggests that children can achieve much more when they are engaged in collective activities. The chapter also explores the ways in which teacher–child contexts, and teacher–child relationships stimulate cognitive and linguistic processes constitutive of early school-based learning. The chapter highlights the need for further research in order to examine the

Contemporary Perspectives on Science and Technology in Early Childhood Education, pages 17–39
Copyright © 2008 by Information Age Publishing

theoretical and practical implications of close teacher–child relationships for young children's scientific understanding.

For many years science educators, and others, have sought to understand how young children acquire knowledge. Under the rubric of "constructivism," educators and researchers have recommended many strategies for teaching science in the early grades. As a well recognized theoretical perspective on "knowing" and "learning," constructivism highlights the significance of the individual learner's prior knowledge in subsequent learning (Ausubel, 1968; Driver & Bell, 1986, Good, Wandersee, & St. Julien, 1993). That is, constructivism emphasizes the importance of each child's active construction of knowledge through the interplay of prior learning and newer learning (Yager, 1995). This view of learning maintains that young learners construct and reconstruct their own meaning for ideas about how the world works (Good et al., 1993; Marin, Benarroch, & Gomez, 2000; Newman, Griffin, et al., 1989). Moreover, as social learners, children actively construct meaning (Rushton & Larkin, 2001), and their learning is embedded within social contexts (Tudge & Rogoff, 1989).

The major elements of Developmentally Appropriate Practice (Bredekamp & Copple 1997) are also derived from constructivist principles. "*Constructivist theory focuses on the mental processes children use in thinking and remembering. It views learning as the self-regulated changes in thinking that occur from the acquisition of knowledge through which learners seek solutions to cognitive challenges*" (Jalongo & Isenberg, 2000). In developmentally appropriate classrooms children learn by actively interacting with materials, peers, and adults. Using this approach, educational decisions are guided by questions related to the age, individual, social, and cultural appropriateness of key experiences (Jones & Gullo, 1999). Though no specific curriculum is implied by the adoption of developmentally appropriate practices, activities that are meaningful to children are emphasized. It is hardly surprising, therefore, that there is increasing recognition that science education is an ideal content area to support young children's learning (Bowman, 1999; French, 2004; Gelman & Brenneman, 2004).

Successful implementation of a constructivist approach to the teaching of science curricula ultimately depend on whether teachers have developed a solid understanding of the subject matter, and an understanding of science inquiry. There is some evidence that teachers hold diverse views of science and mathematics as inquiry such as "*doing hands on*," or "*using kits*" (Bybee, Ferrini-Mundy, & Loucks-Horsley, 1997). Such limited understanding can lead to inappropriate classroom practices. For example, providing "fun" activities or "hands on" does not necessarily guarantee that students are engaging in meaningful scientific inquiry. More important, simply interacting with materials and peers does not guarantee conceptual understanding (Miller & Driver, 1987). It follows that one of the major responsibilities of early childhood teachers is to teach at children's level of understanding. Equally important is an understanding of young children's unique developmental needs in the context of early childhood science teaching.

SCIENCE TEACHING IN EARLY CHILDHOOD

Traditionally, science has been given minimal attention in early childhood programs (Bowman, 1999; De Boer, 1991). This was to a certain extent because educational research had cast doubt on young children's abilities to understand scientific concepts. In particular, Piagetian theory was used to justify not tackling some topics until students had reached the milestone of "formal operations" (Metz, 2004). Recently, however, research in developmental and cognitive psychology has challenged this view by suggesting that young children are capable of concept-based learning (Gelman, 1998; Gelman & Brenneman, 2004, Kuhn, 2002). Consequently, there is growing awareness that access to engaging experiences in science during the early childhood years can provide benefits to all children (French, 2004).

It is generally recognized by educators that science education is important in the early childhood years because it helps children learn about their world and discover answers through their own mental and physical activity. There is, however, something unique about the way young children view the world. For example, there are qualitative differences in the ways a four-year-old interprets events, or thinks, in comparison to a ten-year-old (Elkind, 1999; Shonkoff & Phillips, 2000). Until about age four, children are not able to evaluate falsifiable claims (Kuhn, 2000; Wellman, Cross, & Watson, 2001; Wimmer & Perner, 1993). That is, until children have reached the "theory of mind" milestone, their scientific thinking will be limited (Kuhn, 2002). There is also something unique about the ways young children learn and discover concepts (Zimmerman, 2005). Exploration and play, for example, are important learning activities for teaching science in the early childhood years. According to Elkind (1999) *"early childhood is a most important period for math, science and technology, but only if we adapt such instruction to the unique needs, interests, and abilities of young children"* (p. 70). Focusing on the processes of science allows teachers to adapt their instruction to meet the needs of young children. At the same time application of the process skills can form the core of inquiry based, or hands-on learning (Funk et al., 1985).

SCIENCE PROCESS SKILLS

It is now recognized that science is a process of inquiry (National Research Council, 1996), and that the role of the teacher is to design learning experiences that help students learn about the nature of scientific inquires. It follows that to be successful with inquiry, children must develop their ability to use process skills, such as observation, classification, and measuring (Harlen, 2000; Miller & Driver, 1987). During the early childhood years, children use these skills as they engage in formal and informal science activities. There are two categories of process skills: basic and integrated (Funk et al., 1985). Because of the unsophisticated nature of young children's thinking, teachers tend to pay less attention to the integrated skills such as formulating hypotheses and controlling variables. Instead, they focus on the basic skills such as observation, classifying, and measuring.

Most early childhood science texts (e.g., Charlesworth, 2007; Harlan & Rivkin, 2004), as well as documents such as the Benchmarks for Science Literacy (AAAS, 1993), address the science skills in fairly broad terms. Such documents also recommend that teachers address the development of these skills using an inquiry approach. That is, the process skills should be used and developed in the context of active investigations. These investigations will, most likely, occur during formal science lessons. We argue, as others have (e.g., French, 2004, Gelman & Brenneman, 2004), that the science process skills can, and should also, be developed during regular early childhood classroom activities. This is because these skills are the same as those that are regularly used by children in quality developmentally appropriate early childhood programs. Thus, an integrated approach weaves the process skills into the total learning process, thereby enabling children to apply the same skills during more formal science investigations.

OBSERVATION

As a practical activity, observation involves more that the use of the five senses. It is also a mental activity (Harlen, 1985, 2000). It follows that there are important developmental considerations in the use of observation. First, because children in the early grades (i.e., pre-K to K) are preoperational thinkers they will tend to center on a single characteristic. Furthermore, because of children's inability to adopt the perspective of others, they will tend to make observations that are based on their own point of view.

To a certain extent a child's ability to accurately observe depends on their linguistic ability (Nelson, 1999). This is because the extent to which children can describe their observations will be tied to their vocabulary development. For example, suppose we show an 18-month-old child a large rock. The child will be able to explore the rock and perhaps feel its surface. Yet, describing these observations will depend, to a large extent, on the child's vocabulary. This child, despite having handled and manipulated the rock, might be limited to saying that the rock is heavy. Another child with more extensive vocabulary might say that the rock has sharp edges, notches, bumps, serrations, etc. Having the appropriate language skills will enable children to look at different aspects and refine their observations. It follows that in early childhood science, teachers should give children the vocabulary, or linguistic tools, so that they can refine and develop their observation skills.

Research findings suggest that young children have fairly well developed observation skills. Infants as young as one month, for example, can imitate gestures by other individuals even when they are no longer in view (Meltzoff & Moore, 1989). Then, by the time they are 12 months old, infants can learn new behaviors simply by watching others (Bauer & Wewerka, 1995). Children as young as eight months can represent numbers by matching the number of objects visually depicted on display with the number of drumbeats (Starkey, Spelke, & Gelman, 1983). Thus, even very young children actively observe and become attuned to the world around them. In fact, young children seem to have an inborn motivation to observe and, in turn, develop competencies.

For the very young, observation will involve using all of the senses (Charlesworth & Lind, 1995; Funk et al., 1985). They will likely want to touch and handle objects, and will even want to examine objects with their lips and tongues. Because of young children's limited language skills, they are less likely to use words to describe their observations. This does not mean that they are not able to reflect, or react, to the meaning of what they have observed. Typically, there will be an emotional reaction tied to their observations. Observations that are pleasing to young children are likely to be repeated over and over again. Further, these observations will often be conducted in the presence of older siblings or adults. As children are interacting, and observing, adults will react by providing words that help children describe their observations. In fact, this is a time of extensive vocabulary development (Anglin, 1993) and therefore an ideal opportunity to expose children to new words and phrases.

By the time children are about eight months old, they will have reached the intellectual milestone of *object permanence*. At this stage, children will tend to repeat an action in order to get the same response from an object or person, such as shaking a rattle to get the same sound. This is defined as a process of *secondary circular response*, meaning that the infant repeats an action to elicit a response from another source. Caregivers should provide opportunities for children to elicit secondary circular responses by providing interesting sights, sounds, and events. The critical component here, however, is interaction with people.

Older children will enjoy searching for hidden objects. Then, at about twelve to eighteen months they will be ready to experiment with objects to solve problems. This is a characteristic of *tertiary circular reactions* when they repeat actions and modify their behaviors to see what will happen. To support this stage, teachers or caregivers should provide an appropriate context or environment. Novel materials, play props, and constructions toys, for example will be useful in supporting and developing children's observation skills.

For two-year-olds, observation takes on a different perspective because they can visualize events internally and maintain mental images of objects and remember. This allows them to try out what they have observed. Providing ample opportunities for children to play best accommodates this trying out of actions they see others do. A play area with props and toys will support children's learning in this area.

Observation for infants and toddlers will center around day-to-day activities in the home or perhaps a day care center. Daily activities such as mealtimes are opportunities for children to use their senses. Caregivers can draw children's attention to the properties of the food such as taste and smell. For example, talk about what the meal looks like; draw attention to the aroma, or perhaps the colors. Similarly, bath time can be a wonderful opportunity to provide children with opportunities to explore and observe. These contexts, and others, can be used to support children's developing observational skills, to the extent that they match their developmental level.

CLASSIFYING

Classifying is a skill that relies heavily on observations. It is usually defined as the ability to organize objects into groups on the basis of specific characteristics (Funk et al., 1985; Sugarman, 1983). Classifying allows children to learn from their experiences and make sense of their world. Moreover, classification is considered a basic ability for logical thinking. Usually, in classifying, objects are grouped for a particular purpose. Typically, the skill of classifying progresses from classifying on the basis of a single characteristic to a hierarchical from of classification (Funk et al., 1985). We know that children's ability to classify gradually develops through various stages in early childhood (Flavell, 1985).

Young children will be able to put objects into groups, but they will be unable to explain how they organized their objects. Then, by the time they are in preschool they will be able to classify objects by single characteristics (Salkind, 1985). It will not be until they are in the upper elementary grades, however, that they will be able to use more complex forms of classifying (Martin, 2003).

By the age of five, children have developed a theory of mind (German & Leslie, 2001), meaning that they can predict others' intention, and recognize that beliefs do not necessarily correspond to reality (Wellman, 2002). Thus, by the time children are in kindergarten they can reason about categories of objects and animals in the real world. However, even though they can place things in categories, they will often change the characteristics on which they base their groupings. Furthermore, they will often fail to classify all of the objects they have been given, usually because they do not appear to fit into their category.

The skill of classification continues to develop, to the extent that first-grade students will be able to classify by a single trait, and the chosen groupings will have become more stable. Gradually, during the elementary grades, children will develop the ability to classify using multiple traits. It will not be until children are in the early concrete operational stage that they are able to consider relationships that are subordinate to a larger group.

Classification activities typically start with collections of objects. For example, two, and three-year-old children will enjoy sorting and ordering collections of their toys such as building blocks, toy cars, or soft toys. Adults can also encourage classifying by providing children with collections of objects as rocks, shells, seeds, leaves, colored shapes, or stickers. Children can then be encouraged to identify common features and sort the items into groups. For example, children might be asked to put all the objects that are alike in one group with the expectation that you will likely get a variety of responses. Classification can also be encouraged during children's daily home activities. Collections of objects will also serve as the basis of classification activities in pre-kindergarten and kindergarten. For example, collections of shells or rocks provide excellent opportunities to look for similarities and differences. Then, children can place their collection into two or more groups on the basis of the similarities or differences. Daily classroom activities are also opportunities for the kindergarten teacher to develop children's ability to classify. For example, during the morning activity children can be grouped according to various criteria such as those with a packed lunch and those who will eat the school lunch. Such activities are important because the ability to classify does not come naturally or spontaneously for young children, and therefore they need opportunities to conduct many sorting activities.

MEASURING

Measuring is a skill involving the quantification of observations. The science activities of observing and classifying often involve describing or comparing in terms of a quantity. In addition, the observations will often involve comparing properties to a standard. For example, we might count items or compare objects based on size or weight. Measuring is therefore a skill that involves assigning numbers or values to objects or events. These objects can also be arranged in a continuum based on a specific set of values. For example, when children have classified objects into groups they can count and compare their groups.

Measuring can involve numbers, distances, time, length, area, weight, volume, and temperature. Typically, in early childhood the focus is on measuring length, volume, weight, time, and temperature. Yet, these concepts can be difficult for young children especially preoperational thinkers who have yet to develop the ability to conserve. According to Piaget (1983), conservation of length, area, and weight is not attained until children are in the elementary grades. Consequently, in early childhood, measurement will involve direct comparisons and the use of nonstandard measurements.

Young children can be provided with many opportunities to develop their measuring skills. Again, daily activities provide the most appropriate contexts for adults to guide children in quantifying their observations. Initially, adults can provide young children with vocabulary so that they can begin to quantify their observations. For example, children will benefit from repeated experiences with adults using terms such as big, small, tall, short, long, wide, heavy, light, etc.

Children can be introduced to nonstandard or informal measurements when they are in pre-kindergarten or kindergarten. Then, they should be encouraged to develop their own systems of measurement. For example, children can use body parts such as fingers, hands, feet, or body lengths to measure distances. Similarly, they can use items such as marbles, paper clips, peas, plastic bears, or nails to weigh objects. As with the skills of observation and classifying, daily classroom activities provide numerous opportunities for kindergarten and primary grade students to develop their measuring skills.

COMMUNICATING

Science activities also involve sharing information in an accurate and clear manner with others (Funk, et al., 1985; Harlen, 2000). Communication, involves the ability to communicate verbally with others by sharing ideas or discussing ideas or findings. Communication also involves written communication skills such as reading about a scientific concept, or perhaps writing about observations and ideas (Funk et al., 1985). It is important to realize, however, that communication involves more than the use of oral and written language. Other forms of communication such as pictures, models, music, movement, and play acting are also very important, and should be made available to young children.

Essentially, communication describes a process whereby individuals let others know their thoughts. When children make observations or discoveries, they share what they have observed with others by communicating. Clearly, as indicated above, there are many different, and important, ways of doing this. Language, however, lies at the heart of the skill of communicating. This is because language provides opportunities for children to clarify and express their ideas about scientific phenomena. Children also use language to think and reason. By talking about their thinking, and by explaining their observations, young children will begin to make sense of their observations, and develop an understanding of scientific phenomena.

During the early childhood years, children's vocabulary grows at a particularly rapid rate (Anglin, 1993). It is therefore an ideal time to introduce children to words that will help them to make sense of their observations. For example, words that are used in measuring, such as small, big, tiny, large, thick, and so forth can be easily introduced during daily classroom activities. Providing children with the appropriate vocabulary will also support the development of their communication skills.

In early childhood science, communication provides an opportunity for children to reflect on what they do. This is because communication involves the expression of ideas and thoughts. This means that communication can help children evaluate their ideas and overcome the difficulty of understanding. An example of this is when a child comes to the teacher with a problem and while explaining it discovers how to resolve the problem. Other times, presenting information in the form of graphs, charts, or pictures can be more effective in promoting understanding.

Parents and caregivers can greatly influence infants and toddlers learning and communication skills by providing various opportunities for them to talk and listen to other children or adults. Young children actively communicate with children and adults. They are predisposed to attend to the language spoken by others around them. They are attracted to human faces, and look especially often at the lips of the person speaking. Adults can be responsive by engaging in conversations with children.

Then, by the time children are in pre-kindergarten and kindergarten they are usually ready to engage in a broader range of communicative tasks. For example, the classroom environment can be arranged to support the communication of ideas using pictures, graphs, and charts. During the morning meeting or circle time teachers can encourage children to explain, discuss, share, describe, and question. Kindergarteners will also enjoy representing their ideas by drawing pictures. For example, after children have completed a "hands-on" science activity they can be encouraged to draw a picture and write about their experience.

Communication in early childhood also involves creating artifacts or models. Creating models and artifacts provides a reason for children to communicate and, in doing so they use the terminology of the science concept they have been studying. As children become more experienced, they will be ready to use more sophisticated forms of communication such as graphs, charts, and tables. For example, bar graphs can be used to record data so that it can be easily shared with others. More complex data will require the use of tables or charts to record information. Whatever approach or strategy a teacher uses, it is important to make oral communication an integral part of the activity. This way, the language will occur in a naturalistic and meaningful context.

ESTIMATING AND PREDICTING

The skill of predicting involves using existing information to determine a future event (Harlen, 2000). A prediction is usually based on prior knowledge, observation, or a combination of both. Estimation is a similar skill, and can be thought of as a special type of prediction. The skill of estimating involves using prior knowledge to approximate and amount. Estimating assumes some prior knowledge of measurement but it does not involve actually measuring objects (Harlen, 2000). Estimating and prediction are similar or related skills because they both involve a type of thinking that require forecasting an event or measure based on available information (Funk et al., 1985).

In many ways, estimating and predicting are natural everyday activities for young children. This is because the natural world is very orderly, and many events can easily be predicted. Furthermore, the daily lives of young children are filled with predictable events. For example, young children learn that there is a predictable order to daily events such as meals, bath time, and bedtime. They also learn about predictable events in their play activities. Pushing the toy car will make it move. Dropping a ball on a hard surface will cause it to bounce back up. Their interactions with parents, caregivers, siblings, and others are also relatively predictable. For example, young babies know that certain behaviors will elicit certain responses from a parent.

The natural world is also very predictable. There are many events that can be accurately predicted such as sunrise and sunset, the ocean's tides, or the four seasons. Other events, however, are more difficult to predict such as forecasting the weather. Yet, despite the difficulty in predicting the weather, even young children can look outside and announce to their parents that it looks like it is going to rain.

Prediction is an important skill to develop in young children because it encourages them to think and respond to external stimuli. Essentially, prediction is a cognitive process that requires children to use what they already know (prior knowledge), and data that is immediately available or observable (existing knowledge) to predict future events (future or new knowledge). By predicting, children are learning to use existing information and this, in turn, helps them to assume control over their lives. The young girl who notices the dark, black clouds outside and predicts that it will probably rain, might then decide to wear a raincoat before going outside to play. Children who are able to use available information appropriately, in various contexts, are more likely to act in more efficient ways.

Prediction not only helps children in their daily lives, but it is also an important skill in science. This is because it helps children to make sense of their observations. The extent to which children can accurately predict will be related to their knowledge base as well as their ability to observe. Thus, the more experiences children have had with a variety of science related phenomena, then the more likely they are to be able to accurately predict events related to the same phenomena. Clearly, therefore, there is a developmental progression in children's ability to use existing information; thus, preoperational thinkers are less likely to be able to accurately predict certain phenomena. The preoperational child will tend to center on specific attributes, which hinders his or her ability to accurately predict.

As with the other skills, many daily activities can be used to support the development of children's ability to estimate and predict. With younger children, adults can easily model estimation and prediction. For example, the caregiver who asks, "*Let's see what happens if...*" helps children learn how to accurately predict. To be successful at predicting the child has to have a wealth of pre-existing experiences. This is because the child draws on his or her prior knowledge to predict future events. It follows that experiences similar to those that are used to support the development of the other skills, such as observation and classification, will also help with prediction and estimation (Funk, et al., 1985). A broad range of hands-on, exploratory activities will provide young children with a good foundation for more formal science activities.

In the pre-kindergarten and kindergarten classrooms, children can be encouraged to make all sorts of predictions and estimations during their daily activities. Prediction activities can also be fairly easily incorporated into play activities. For example, before building a tower of blocks, children can predict how many blocks will be added before the tower collapses. Children will also enjoy "racing" their toy cars by rolling them down a small ramp. Such activities provide valuable opportunities young children to predict events.

INFERRING

Inferring is a skill that involves using logic to make assumptions or draw conclusions based on observations. If a child smells the aroma of baking bread from the kitchen and says "*I can smell something baking*," he or she has made an observation. However, if the child says, "*Mommy must be baking bread in the bread machine*," he or she has made an inference. Clearly, the first comment is more likely to be accurate than the second. The observation is more likely to be accurate because it is based on information obtained through one of the senses. The inference, on the other hand is an explanation for the observation, and is more susceptible to error.

An inference is similar to a prediction in that it is a person's best guess concerning why something happened. In contrast, a prediction concerns what will happen next. Suppose children are predicting whether an object, such as a wooden block, will sink or float. They can test their prediction and record their findings. Then if the teacher asked, "*Why do you think the wooden block floated?*" he or she would be asking the students to make an inference. In this case, it would make sense to ask the inference question after the students have had many opportunities to test whether different objects will sink or float. This is because the ability to make inferences is tied to prior knowledge.

Inferential reasoning is an important skill in science because many times it is not possible to directly observe. For example, suppose a teacher takes a bag containing 10 ice cubes and places it outside in direct sunlight. The teacher then places another bag of ice cubes in a cupboard in the classroom, and another in the refrigerator. Then the children can directly observe as the ice melts into water. They will also be able to observe that the ice cubes that were left outside in the warm sun melted first, then the ice in the cupboard, and finally the ice in the refrigerator. All of these are directly observable events. Yet, if the teacher asks, "*Why did the ice melt?*" she would be asking the students to make an inference. This is because it is not possible for the children to observe "why" the ice melted. Instead, children would have to use available information to infer that the temperature of the air probably had something to do with why the ice melted.

In order to develop children's ability to make inferences, they have to first understand the differences between observations and inferences. Therefore, young children will need ample opportunities to observe and make inferences. Fortunately, daily activities in the home and the early childhood classroom provide many opportunities for young children make inferences.

Parents and caregivers can model inferring for young children from everyday observations. For example, hearing a car door close and saying "*Your Daddy is home*" or noticing that a plant has wilted and saying that it needs some water are inferences based on observations. Through daily activities in the home or child care center, children, from a very young age, can learn to use their observations to make inferences. During mealtimes, for example, adults can make inferences such as drawing a child's attention to the steam rising from the plate of food and stating that it's probably because the food is hot. Similarly, outside play provides opportunities for making inferences, such as inferring that it must have been raining because the grass is wet.

Children's literature offers plenty of opportunities for children to reason inferentially. During joint book reading, adults can share the illustrations on the cover of the book and make inferences about the content of the book. Then when reading the book and looking at the illustrations, adults can encourage children to look for contextual information to help them make inferences.

THE INTEGRATED SCIENCE PROCESS SKILLS

Children can use and develop their basic science skills during most day to day classroom activities. The integrated science process skills, however, tend to be more demanding for young children because they involve higher levels of reasoning and thinking. They are called integrated skills because they involve the use of one or more of the basic skills (Padilla, 1991). The integrated skills include identifying and controlling variables, formulating and testing hypotheses, defining operationally, experimenting, interpreting data, and constructing models. These skills are usually developed by using concrete processes. However, they require deeper levels of thought as well as some abstract thought.

The integrated skills present difficulties for young children because of the unique ways in which they see cause and effect relationships. Preoperational thinkers, for example, will often provide magical explanations for their observations. These young children also think transductively, which means that they see relationships where they do not exist. That is, they join abstract and concrete conceptions as if they are the same. Although young children will be able to conduct investigations, they will have difficulty interpreting their findings and drawing meaningful conclusions. This does not mean that young children are not capable of using and developing these skills in the early grades. What it means is that we should carefully select activities that are appropriate for the child's developmental level. During early childhood, teachers should focus on the most concrete activities, and recognize the limits of young children's learning. By the time they are in the primary grades, most children will begin to make causal explanations. Gradually, given appropriate physical and social experiences, children will develop the integrated science skills and, subsequently, their ability to think logically.

Identifying and controlling variables is a skill that involves being able to identify variables that will affect the outcome of an experiment. Variables are factors that can change and affect the outcome of an experiment. This skill involves manipulating one factor to investigate the outcome of an event, while other factors are held constant. Care should be taken with this skill because young children will often become confused with multiple variables.

Formulating and testing hypotheses involves examining existing information to make an educated guess about the outcome of an experiment. A hypothesis is a tentative prediction concerning the relationship between two variables. When children hypothesize they are, essentially, attempting to explain their observations, or to generalize from their inferences. An example of making a hypothesis would be stating that plants will grow when they are exposed to sunlight.

Defining operationally means using observations as well as prior knowledge to describe or label objects and events. Defining operationally adds precision to children's descriptions because they define variables in terms that everyone can understand. By developing this skill, children are also learning to be accurate and consistent when they engage in scientific investigations. For example, in investigating the effect of sunlight on plant growth, children would need to provide an operational definition of plant growth. In this case, it could be defined as the number of new leaves or perhaps in terms of the number of "paper clip lengths" the plant has grown in five days.

Experimenting requires the use of many of the basic and integrated skills to design and conduct a scientific test. Usually, an experiment begins with observations or a question to be answered. Next, variables are identified and a hypothesis formulated. Designing the experiment involves operationally defining the variables of interest and determining the variable or variables that have to be controlled. The test is then conducted and observations made in order to collect data. The data is interpreted in terms of the original question or hypothesis. Finally, conclusions are made and the findings communicated to others.

Interpreting data is a skill that requires children to collect observations or measurements, organize the data, and draw meaningful conclusions from the data. For example, when investigating the effect of sunlight on plant growth children might count the number of new leaves and organize the data on a bar graph. Organizing the data visually will enable the children to draw meaningful conclusions.

Constructing models is a skill that requires children to create a mental or physical illustration of an object or event. Models are usually constructed to visually represent objects or phenomena that cannot be seen. For example, children might construct a model comparing the size of the earth and the moon. This model would enable children to see the relative size of the earth and moon

The integrated skills, because of their abstract nature, will be difficult for young children. Yet, young children can be introduced to these skills by engaging them in simple science investigations. The emphasis here should be on a simple investigation because young children will have difficulty planning investigations that consist of multiple stages. When young children conduct investigations, they will usually resort to formulating their plan as they are conducting the investigation.

As with the basic skills, the starting point for young children's scientific investigation is exploration. The teacher can help children think about investigations by asking appropriate questions and encouraging children to come up with their own questions. Teachers can also help children to plan and conduct their own investigations. Then, they can encourage children to try to interpret and explain their findings. Ideally, this should be done in the context of concrete experiences.

SOCIAL CONTEXTS OF SCIENCE LEARNING IN EARLY CHILDHOOD

Science activities with young children are both constituted and enriched by relevant conversation (French, 2004). In other words, during children's socialization into science, conversation between children and adults, as well as between peers, become crucial to scientific participation. This is because social interaction is the primary route by which a child reflects on the meaning of his or her experiences, and it is through social exchanges that children develop and refine their science process skills. In short, it is through oral language that children come to understand science concepts.

Oral language and, more specifically, "decontextualized" language is potentially important in early childhood science learning. Decontextualized language (Snow, 1983) is characterized by the verbal encoding of mental and linguistic processes as well as narrative-like language (e.g., temporal and causal conjunctions). This type of oral language share many design features with the language used by teachers during reading and writing lessons, as well as the language used in early reading texts (DeStefano, 1984; Heath, 1983). Decontextualized language has been defined as using language to "monitor and reflect on experience, and reason about, plan and predict experiences" (Westby, 1985). That is, it is a highly decontextualized oral register that relies on the expression of meaning through choice of words. Thus, this oral register includes linguistic features that can enhance children's ability to recontextualize information (Gillam et al., 1999; Van Oers, 1998). It follows that use of decontextualized language could enable young children to reflect on the meaning of their observations, and to recontextualize their science experiences. That is, as children engage in science observations and activities in social groups they use language such as conjunctions, mental and linguistic verbs, and adverbs (Westby et al, 1999) to help the listener to create a mental model of an event or, in this case observations in science (Segal & Duchan, 1997).

Decontextualized language is characterized by metacognitive talk (i.e., talk about mental and linguistic states), and is frequently observed in classrooms where social interaction between peers, and between adults and children is a critical component of the instruction. Researchers have recently begun to recognize the importance of oral language and social interaction in school-based learning. For example, in recent years researchers have been concerned with the social contexts in which school-based skills develop (e.g., Jones, 2002, Pellegrini et al., 2000). Drawing on both Piagetian (1983) and Vygotskian (1978) theory these researchers, and others, have attempted to explain the ways in which various aspects of social relationships facilitate cognitive processes. These theories propose that cognitive development results from the co-construction of knowledge between participants. Drawing on this theoretical framework, research in children's oral language and early literacy learning (e.g., Pellegrini et al., 1998), for example, has emphasized the facilitative role of social context. Recent studies, for example, have described social context in fairly global terms such as children interacting with peers or adults (e.g., Reeder et al., 1996). Other studies have documented the significance of interaction for children's social and cognitive development. While findings from these studies have generated important insights into the ways in which social contexts influence children's cognitive development, there is a need to advance beyond general conceptualizations of adult and peer interaction and its relationship to more specific areas of children's development.

SOCIAL CONTEXTS THAT SUPPORT SCIENCE

The social contexts in which young children develop specific skills such are just beginning to be explored. For example, recent research (e.g., Jones, 1998; Pellegrini et al., 1998) in the area of early literacy learning has examined peer interaction and the role of peer relationships on children's use of literate language. These studies take a Piagetian stance, positing that conflict and resolution cycles, characteristic of complementary relations, promote cognitive development. Specifically, the conflict-resolution cycles characteristic of interactions between closer relationships such as friends, compared to non-friends, is related to children's reflection upon the social, cognitive, and linguistic processes constitutive of their interactions (Pellegrini et al., 1997). This reflection is considered an important component of literate language and school-based literacy because the conflict-resolution cycles place children in contexts where they must reflect on the meaning of their interaction, thus promoting cognitive decentration. Such reflection would most likely also be important in the context of science learning in early childhood.

During classroom science activities children interact with materials and peers and directly observe science phenomena. This interaction and the subsequent understanding of a science concept or skill occur within a social context consisting of familiar peers and adults. Within this context children engage in social exchanges that lead to conflict-resolution cycles and place children in contexts where they must reflect on the meaning of their interaction. In turn, this reflection leads to cognitive decentration and subsequent conceptual understanding.

The sparse data on this topic offers some support to this proposition (e.g., Jones, 2002; Pellegrini et al., 1998, 2000). Extant research suggests that closeness in peer relationships maximize children's expression of literate language and their levels of story re-reading (Pellegrini et al., 2000). Moreover, recent findings suggest that different peer relationships are not as equally facilitative of school-based learning (Atay, 2004; Jones, 2002). One practical implication of this perspective is that young children should be given ample opportunity to interact in peer groups. That is, children should be given opportunities to use their science process skills with other peers. Moreover, early childhood science should not be a solitary activity. Also, the nature of peer relationships within classroom instructional groups will likely influence the way children come to understand the meaning of their science observations, classifications, or measurement, and subsequently their understanding of science phenomena.

TEACHER–CHILD RELATIONSHIPS

Beyond the peer context, the teacher–child context is arguably the most important context in terms of early learning. Teacher–child interaction around classroom events can take on a number of different forms. The nature of this interaction, however, will vary based on the quality of the teacher–child relationship. It is well established that relationships between children and adults influence the development of a range of competencies in the preschool and early school-age years (Birch & Ladd, 1996; Pianta, 1997).

Teacher–child relationships in the early grades can provide children with social support and emotional security (Howes & Smith, 1995). More importantly, children with positive relationships with their teachers seem to be able to exploit the learning opportunities available in their classrooms (Howes, & Smith, 1995). Yet, the nature of the teacher–child relationship can vary in nature and quality. Whereas some teacher–child relationships are close and affectionate, others can be more conflictual and hostile (Pianta, Steinberg, & Rollins, 1995). Pianta and his colleagues (Pianta et al., 1995; Pianta, 1994) have demonstrated that teacher–child relationships can be characterized by the degree of involvement between a child and his or her teacher, and the positive or negative emotional quality of that involvement (Pianta, Nimetz, & Bennett, 1997). This involvement includes various dimensions of conflict, closeness, and overdependency (Pianta et al., 1997). Others have documented teacher–child relationships in terms of the warmth and sensitivity of their interactions (Elicker &Fortner-Wood, 1995). More important, it is claimed that children who have less directive, less harsh, and less detached teachers are more likely to experience positive interactions and will display higher levels of language development (Whitebook, Howes, & Philips, 1990). Of particular interest are the procedures and mechanisms found in positive teacher child interactions that lead to the oral language and social exchanges that promote an understanding of science concepts.

The writings of Vygotsky (1978) on adult-child interaction offer some insight into the processes involved in teacher–child interaction. This sociocultural perspective emphasizes the situatedness of thinking and speaking in the context of activity (Wertsch, Hagstrom, & Kikas, 1995). Indeed, Vygotsky's assertion that cognitive development is embedded in the context of social relationships is well established (Lave & Wenger, 1991, Rogoff, 1990). Vygotsky's theory suggests that children can achieve much more when they are engaged in collective activities. This proposition rests on the assumption that learning creates the "zone of proximal development" (ZPD) and, in the process of learning, internal development processes are awakened "that are able to operate only when the child is interacting with people in his environment and with his peers" (Vygotsky, 1978, p.90). The ZPD includes two essential elements, namely a joint activity that constitutes an integrated cognitive system, and a process of internalization associated with those experiences or joint activity. The language that is exchanged within the interaction facilitates both the joint activity and subsequent internalization.

Through this co-constructive process, the teacher and child interact to create the zone of proximal development. In doing so, they each bring different levels of understanding to any given task and, through a process of interaction, compromise, and shared experiences reach a new level of understanding (Goldstein, 1999). The success of this joint process, however, depends on the quality of the teacher–child relationship. In short, there is an affective, or interrelational (Goldstein, 1999) dimension to children's learning within the ZPD.

CONCLUSION

When children engage in formal and informal science activities they use and develop a number of science process skills. The skills of observing, classifying, measuring, communicating, inferring, estimating, and predicting develop in children during the early childhood years. Yet, because of their unique cognitive abilities, limits are placed on how young children can use these skills. Most classrooms, however, can be organized to provide on going opportunities for children to develop their science process skills. Exemplary early childhood science teaching strategies engage all of the learners and rely on dynamic social interaction.

Young children develop and refine the process skills in the context of social interaction. Children's use of decontextualized language enables them to reflect on the meaning of their science experiences. In addition, the communicative roles of the teacher and students as co-participants in a classroom community shape children's understanding of science concepts. Within this sociocultural perspective the dialectic relationship of interaction and context leads to the social construction of shared understanding. Moreover, the quality of peer relationships and teacher child relationships are related to the types of social exchanges and oral language use that can lead to conceptual understanding. To improve the quality of interaction during science activities, more emphasis needs to be placed on teaching the skills associated with effective interaction and collaborative learning. Such emphasis on collaborative skills would, in turn, foster the use of explanations during problem solving and scientific inquiry.

REFERENCES

American Association for the Advancement of Science. (1993). *Benchmarks for science literacy.* New York: Oxford University Press.

Anglin, J. M. (1993). *Vocabulary development: A morphological analysis.* Monographs of the Society for Research in Child Development, 58 (10, Serial No. 238).

Atay, T. (2004). *The effects of social relationships and temperament on kindergarten students' use of literate language.* Unpublished doctoral dissertation. Florida State University, Tallahassee.

Ausubel, D. (1968). *Educational psychology: A cognitive view.* New York: Holt, Rinehart & Winston.

Bauer, P., & Wewerka, S. (1995). One-to two-year-olds' recall of events: The more expressed, the more impressed. *Journal of Experimental Child Psychology, 59,* 475–496.

Birch, S., & Ladd, G. (1996). Interpersonal relationships in the school environment and children's early school adjustment: The role of teachers and peers. In K. Wentzel & J. Juvonen (Eds.), *Social motivation: Understanding children's school adjustment* (pp. 199–225). New York: Cambridge University Press.

Bowman, B. T. (1999). Policy implications for math, science, and technology in early childhood education. In American Association for the Advancement of Science, *Dialogue on early childhood science, mathematics, and technology education* (pp. 40–49). Washington, DC: AAAS.

Bredekamp, S., & Copple, C. (1997). *Developmentally appropriateness practice in early childhood programs.* Washington DC: NAEYC.

Bybee, R., Ferrini-Mundy, J., Loucks-Horsley, S. (1997). National standards and school science and mathematics. *School Science and Mathematics, 97,* 325–334.

Charlesworth, R. (2007). *Math and science for young children.* Albany, NY: Delmar.

Charlesworth, R., & Lind, K. K. (1995). *Math and science for young children.* Albany, NY: Delmar.

DeBoer, G. E. (1991). *A history of ideas in science: Implications for practice.* New York: Teachers College Press.

DeStefano, J. (1984). Learning to communicate in the classroom. In A.D. Pellegrini & T. D. Yawkwy (Eds.), *The development of oral and written language in social contexts* (pp. 155–165). Norwood, NJ: Ablex.

Driver, R., & Bell, B. (1986). Students' thinking and learning of science: A constructive view. *School Science Review, 67,* 443–456.

Elicker, J., & Fortner-Wood, C. (1995). Research in review. Adult-Child relationship in early childhood settings. *Young Children, 51,* 69–78.

Elkind, D. (1999). Educating young children in math, science, and technology. In American Association for the Advancement of Science, *Dialogue on Early Childhood Science, mathematics, and technology education.* Washington, DC: AAAS.

Elkind, D. (1998, February). *Educating young children in mathematics, science, and technology.* Paper presented at the Forum on Early Childhood Science, Mathematics, and Technology Education. Washington DC.

Flavell, J. H. (1985). *Cognitive development.* Engelwood Cliffs, NJ: Prentice-Hall.

French, L. (2004) Science as the center of a coherent, integrated early childhood curriculum. *Early Childhood Research Quarterly, 19,* 138.149.

Funk, J. H., et al (1985). *Learning science process skills.* Dubuque, IA: Kendal/Hunt.

Gelman, S. A. (1998). Concept development in preschool children. In American Association for the Advancement of Science, *Dialogue on early childhood science, mathematics, and technology education.* Washington, DC: AAAS.

Gelman, R., & Brenneman, K. (2004). Science learning pathways for young children *Early Childhood Research Quarterly, 19,* 150–158.

German, T. P., & Leslie, A. M. (2001). Chlidren's inferences from knowing to pretending and believing. *British Journal of Developmental Psychology, 19*, 59–83.

Gillam, R., Pena, E., & Miller, L. (1999). Dynamic assessment of narrative and expository discourse. *Topics in Language Disorders, 20*, 33–47.

Good, R. G., Wandersee, J. H., & St. Julien, J. (1993). Cautionary notes on the appeal of the new "ism" (constructivism) in science education. In K. Tobin (Ed.), *The practice of constructivism in science education*. Washington, DC: AAAS Press.

Goldstein, L. (1999). The relational zone: The role of caring relationships in the co-construction of mind. *American Educational Research Journal, 36*, 647–673.

Harlan, J. D., & Rivkin, M. S. (2004). *Science experiences for the early childhood years: An integrated affective approach*. Englewood Cliffs, NJ: Merrill.

Harlen, W. (2000). *Teaching of science in primary schools*. London: Fulton.

Harlen, W. (1985). *Teaching and learning primary science*. New York: Teachers College Press.

Heath, S. (1983). *Ways with words*. New York: Cambridge University Press.

Inhelder, B., & Howes, C., & Smith, E. (1995). Children and their child care teachers: Profiles of relationships. *Social Development, 4*, 44–61.

Jalongo, M., & Isenberg, M. R. (2000). *Exploring your role: A practitioner's introduction to early childhood education*. Upper Saddle River, NJ: Prentice-Hall.

Jones, I. (1998). Peer relationships and writing development: A microgenetic analysis. British *Journal of Educational Psychology, 68*, 229–241.

Jones, I. (2002). Social relationships, peer collaboration, and children's oral language. *Educational Psychology, 22*, 63–73.

Jones, I., & Gullo, D. (1999). Differential social and academic effects of developmentally appropriate practices and beliefs. *Journal of Research in Childhood Education, 14*, 26–35.

Kuhn, D. (2002). What is scientific thinking and how does it develop? In U. Goswami (Ed.), *Blackwell handbook of cognitive development*. Malden, MA: Blackwell.

Lave, J., & Wenger, E. (1991). *Situated learning: Legitimate peripheral participation*. Cambridge, UK: Cambridge University Press.

Marin, N., Benarroch, A., & Gomez, E. (2000). What is the relationship between social constructivism and Piagetian constructivism? An analysis of the characteristics of the ideas within both theories. *International Journal of Science Education, 3*, 225–238.

Martin, D. J. (2003). *Elementary science methods: A constructivist approach*. Belmont, CA: Wadsworth.

Meltzoff, A., & Moore, M. K. (1989). Imitation in newborn infants: Exploring the range of gestures imitated and the underlying mechanisms. *Developmental Psychology, 25*, 954–964.

Metz, K. M. (2004). Children's understanding of scientific inquiry: Their conceptualization of uncertainty in investigations of their own design. *Cognition and Instruction, 22*, 219–290.

Miller, R., & Driver, R. (1987). Beyond processes. *Studies in Science Education, 14*, 33–62.

National Research Council. (1996). *National Science Education Standards*. Washington, DC: National Academies Press.

Nelson, K. (1999). *Language in cognitive development: The emergence of the mediated mind.* Cambridge: Cambridge University Press.

Newman, D., Griffin, P., et al. (1989). *The construction zone: Working for cognitive change in school.* New York: Cambridge University Press.

Padilla, M. J. (1991). Science activities, process skills, and thinking. In S. M. Glynn (Ed.), *The psychology of learning science* (pp. 205–217). Hillsdale, NJ: Erlbaum.

Pellegrini, A. D., Melhuish, E., Jones, I., Trojanowska, L., & Gilden, R. (2000). Social contexts of learning literate language: The role of varied, familiar, and close relationships. *Learning and Individual Differences, 12,* 375–389.

Pellegrini, A. D., Galda, L., Bartini, M., & Charak, D. (1998). Oral language and literacy in context: The role of social relationships. *Merrill-Palmer Quarterly, 44,* 38–54.

Piaget, J. (1958). *The growth of logical thinking from childhood to adolescence: An essay on the construction of formal operational structures.* New York: Basic Books.

Piaget, J. (1965). *The child's conception of the world.* Totowa, NJ: Littlefield, Adams, & Co.

Piaget, J. (1983). Piaget's theory. In W. Kessen (Ed.), *Handbook of child psychology* (Vol. 1, pp. 103–128). New York: Wiley.

Pianta, R. (1994). Patterns of relationships between children and kindergarten teachers. *Journal of School Psychology, 32,* 15–31.

Pianta, R. (1997). Adult-child relationship processes and early schooling. *Early Education and Development, 8,* 11–26.

Pianta, R. C., Nimetiz, S. L., & Bennett, E. (1997). Mother–child relationships, teacher–child relationships, and school outcomes in preschool and kindergarten. *Early Childhood Research Quarterly, 12,* 263–280.

Pianta, R., Steinberg, M., & Rollins, K. (1995). The first two years of school: Teacher–child relationships and deflections in children's classroom adjustment. *Development and Psychopathology, 7,* 295–312.

Reeder, K., Shapiro, J., Watson, R., & Goelman, H. (Eds.). (1996). *Literate apprenticeships: The emergence of language and literacy in the preschool years.* Norwood, NJ: Ablex.

Rogoff., B. (1990). *Apprenticeship in thinking.* New York: Oxford.

Rushton, S., & Larkin, E. (2001). Shaping the learning environment: Connecting developmentally appropriate practices to brain research. *Early Childhood Education Journal, 29,* 25–33.

Salkind, N. J. (1985). *Theories of human development.* New York: Wiley.

Shonkoff, J. P., & Phillips, D. A. (2000). *From neurons to neighborhoods: The science of early childhood development.* Washington DC: National Academy of Sciences–National Research Council.

Segal, E., & Duchan, J. (1997). Interclausal connectives as indicators of structuring in narratives. In J. Costermans & M. Fayol (Eds.), *Processing interclausal relationships* (pp. 95–119). Mahwah, NJ: Erlbaum.

Snow, C. (1983). Literacy and language: Relationships during the preschool years. Harvard *Educational Review, 53,* 165–189.

Starkey, P., Spelke, E. S., & Gelman, R. (1983). Detection of intermodal numerical correspondences by human infants. *Science, 222,* 179–181.

Sugarman, S. (1983). *Children's early thought: Development in classification.* Cambridge: Cambridge University Press.

Tudge, J., & Rogoff, B. (1989). Peer influences on cognitive development: Piaget-ian and Vygotskian perspectives in M. H. Bornstein & J. S. Bruner (Eds.), *Interaction in human development: Crosscurrents in contemporary psychology.* Hillsdale, NJ, Erlbaum.

Van Oers, B. (1998). The fallacy of decontextualization. *Mind, Culture, and Activity, 5,* 135–142.

Vygotsky, L. S. (1978). *Mind in society: The development of higher psychological processes.* Cambridge, MA: Harvard University Press.

Wellman, H. M. (2002). Understanding the psychological world: Developing a theory of mind. In U. Goswami (Ed.), *Blackwood handbook of cognitive development.* Malden, MA: Blackwell.

Wellman, H. M., Cross, D., & Watson, J. (2001). Meta-analysis of theory of mind development: The truth about false belief. *Child Development, 72,* 655–684.

Wertsch, J., Hagstrom, F., & Kikas, E. (1995). Voices of thinking and speaking. In L. Martin, K. Nelson, & E. Tobach (Eds.), *Sociocultural psychology: Theory and practice of doing and knowing* (pp. 276–290). New York: Cambridge University Press.

Westby, C. (1985). Learning to talk-talking to learn: Oral-literate language differences. In C. Simon (Ed.), *Communication skills and classroom success: Assessment and therapy methodologies for language and learning disabled students* (pp. 181–218). San Diego, CA: College-Hill.

Westby, C., Dezale, J., Fradd, S., & Lee, O. (1999). Learning to do science: Influence of culture and language. *Communication Disorder Quarterly, 21,* 50–64.

Whitebook, M., Howes, C., & Phillips, D. (1990). *Who cares? Child care teachers and the quality of care in America. Final report of the National Child Care Staffing Study.* Oakland, CA: Child Care Employee Project.

Wimmer, H., & Perner, J. (1983). Beliefs about beliefs: Representation and constraining function of wrong beliefs in young children's understanding of deception. *Cognition, 13,* 103–128.

Yager, R. E. (1995). Constructivism and the learning of science. In S. M. Glynn (Ed.), *Learning science in the schools: Research informing practice* (pp. 35–58). Hillsdale, NJ: Erlbaum.

Yager, R. E. (2000). The constructivist learning model. *Science teacher, 67,* 44–45.

Zimmerman, C. (2005). *The development of scientific reasoning skills: What psychologists contribute to an understanding of elementary science learning.* Paper commissioned by the National Academies of Science. (National Research Council's Board of Science Education, Consensus Study on Learning Science, Kindergarten through Eighth Grade). Final report available at: http://www7.nationalacademies.org/bose/Corinne_Zimmerman_Final_Paper.pdf

CHAPTER 3

KNOWLEDGE ACQUISITION AS CONCEPTUAL CHANGE

The Case of Theory of Biology

Grady J. Venville

At the start of each academic year, I give a short survey to my incoming elementary and middle years pre-service teachers about living things and animals. The survey is based on Bell and Freyberg's (1985) work and asks participants whether a cow, person, whale, spider, and worm are animals and whether a fire, person, and a moving car are living things. My intention with the activity is to introduce the pre-service teachers to the kinds of naïve and unschooled ideas that young children (and sometimes adults) have about the natural world. I develop the activity by having the pre-service teachers share their answers to the survey in groups and then participate in a discussion. It is a truly powerful experience for all participants. Generally we have consensus that a person is living, a car is not living, and a cow is an animal. The other objects/organisms, however, almost always create debate and consternation as individuals in the groups share their conflicting opinions.

I do not document the numbers of pre-service teachers who think that a fire is living or a spider is not an animal for several reasons, but as a rough estimate there is usually at least one person to each group of five or six who is of the opinion that a fire is a living thing or that a spider is not an animal.

Contemporary Perspectives on Science and Technology in Early Childhood Education, pages 41–63
Copyright © 2008 by Information Age Publishing

"A spider is an arachnid," or, "A fire needs oxygen," they might correctly claim. The pre-service teachers sometimes appeal that they need a definition of "living," or "animal," and complain that the questions are ambiguous. To know that a definition would be helpful is a good sign, but I can't escape the concern I feel thinking that these are the ideas of some of the people who will be responsible for the science education of the young children in my society. I finalize the introductory session with a photograph of a sign on the entrance to the local freeway that says that animals are not permitted. This is followed by a discussion about the everyday way we use words and how that differs from the scientific meanings or concepts that are associated with the same words.

Why is it that a considerable number of people can successfully negotiate their way through a minimum of 10 years of science education and not know suitable criteria to use to make the fundamental classification that defines the field of biology, the distinction between living and non-living things? The purpose of this chapter is to explore this question by examining what we know, and what we don't know, about how young children learn to make this distinction. To do this, I have taken the perspective that understanding the scientific concept of life is a fundamental aspect of developing a *theory of biology* and the process by which this takes place is *conceptual change*. I will begin the chapter with an exploration of what the terms *theory* and *conceptual change* mean in terms of student learning. The body of the chapter is then developed by examining the literature in order to answer a series of questions posed by Chinn and Brewer (1998) as a framework for understanding and evaluating theories of knowledge acquisition. The chapter then concludes with a discussion about the implications for research and education.

THEORY AND CONCEPTUAL CHANGE

In terms of learning and understanding, theories can be considered as cognitive, explanatory structures that "help us find the deeper reality underlying surface chaos" (Carey, 1985, p. 194). Theories organize knowledge in people's minds and are used as a framework for understanding the world around them. Vosniadou (1999) argued that knowledge acquisition starts early in infancy and is guided by general principles organized into "framework theories" (p. 2). While some researchers have argued that early cognitive explanatory structures cannot be considered authentic theories (Caravita & Halldén, 1994), others have revealed the consistent use of these representations, suggesting implicit, authentic theories (Pozo & Gomez Crespo, 2005). Inagaki and Hatano (2002) took a median line arguing that naïve theories involve deep explanatory principles that children use to predict, construe, and explain phenomena, but they are clearly different from scientific theories. Children's theories are generally considered few in number and offer deep explanations of broad reaching ideas that might correspond to the disciplines in a university: psychology, mechanics, economics, religion, government, biology, and history (Carey, 1985). Research suggests that children start with only a few of these theories, for example, a naïve theory of mechanics (Vosniadou, 1994), and a naïve theory of psychology (Carey, 1985). Conceptual development can be considered as the emergence and elaboration of new theoretical domains.

Describing the structure of knowledge as theories is by no means universal. An alternative that has considerable support in the literature is that children's knowledge is in the form of isolated pieces of information called phenomenological primitives (p-prims) (di Sessa, 1993). P-prims are considered as fundamental pieces of knowledge that need no explanation themselves, but are used to explain situations in an implicit and spontaneous way. For example, Southerland, Abrams, Cummins, and Anzelmo (2001) proposed 'need as a rationale for change' as a p-prim used by students from second to twelfth-grade to explain biological phenomena such as birds flying south for the winter (i.e., the birds 'need' to stay warm) and plant growth (i.e., the plant 'needs' sunlight, so grows that way). They found the idea of p-prims useful to understand students' tentative, shifting explanations in biology, but suggested they coexist with conceptual frameworks or theories. While various cognitive structures may coexist, Welman and Gelman (1998) argued that foundational domains, or major concepts, such as naïve theory of biology, are much more influential than other pieces of knowledge. Other commentators agree that the difference between theories and other conceptual structures can be considered as one of degree (Carey, 1985, Vosniadou, 1999). Concepts, for example, are generally considered as embedded within the more comprehensive framework theories.

The process of learning and development within a child's theory of biology will be viewed in this chapter as a process of conceptual change (Duit & Treagust, 2003). While there are obvious and well documented differences between scientists and children (Duit, 1999; Halldén, 1999; Vosniadou, 1999), scientific change and conceptual change in children "are both the product of human minds trying to understand the world around them" (Gopnik & Wellman, 1994, p. 258). Conceptual change has been used extensively as a theoretical construct for analysing learning, particularly in science and mathematics education (Duit & Treagust, 2003; Tsai & Wen, 2005) but also in other fields (Guzzetti & Hynd, 1998). Excellent reviews of the various theoretical positions about conceptual change are provided by Havu-Nuutinen (2005) and Tyson, Venville, Harrison and Treagust (1997). The basic premise of conceptual change is that learning is not necessarily a regular, incremental process where new knowledge is simply added to the knowledge already stored in the learner's mind. From a conceptual change perspective, learning involves some kind of interaction between the new knowledge being learned and the existing knowledge structures of the learner. This interaction means that the existing knowledge is either enriched in a limited process or it is revised in a major way (Vosniadou, 1994).

Research about conceptual change has been situated from both epistemological and ontological perspectives (Duit & Treagust, 2003). Researchers taking an epistemological view of conceptual change have investigated the cognitive structures of knowledge and how these are impacted by learning. For example, Vosniadou (1994) investigated mental models and the role of presuppositions in conceptual change. Another line of epistemological research examined the way new concepts are considered by the learner (Hewson & Thorley, 1989; Hewson, 1996). According to these researchers, the learner must first be dissatisfied with their existing understanding of a concept and the new ideas must become intelligible, or understandable, to the learner. The learner then must participate in learning activities that make the new knowledge plausible and ultimately fruitful before true conceptual change has taken place. Research from an ontological perspective of conceptual change has focused on the changes in the nature of the actual knowledge under consideration (Chi, Slotta & deLeeuw, 1994). For example, Lautrey and Mazens (2004) investigated students' understanding of heat and sound and to what degree these concepts were considered to have the properties of matter, or the properties of physical processes. Also from an ontological perspective, Venville and Treagust (1998) found that for students to have a more sophisticated understanding they had to change the way they viewed genes from being a particle that is passed from parents to offspring, to being a process involving protein production.

Other researchers have argued for a more holistic or multidimensional vision (Tyson, et al., 1997) to include the investigation of how motivation (Palmer, 2005; Pintrich, Marx & Boyle, 1993), emotions (Zembylas, 2004) and classroom social and contextual factors impact on the process of conceptual change (Havu-Nuutinen, 2005; Ravanis, 2004; Southerland, Kittleson, Settlage & Lanier, 2005; Venville, 2004; Venville, Gribble & Donovan; 2005). More recently 'intentional' conceptual change has been advocated where the intentions of the learner are taken into consideration in the learning process (Sinatra & Pintrich, 2003).

A FRAMEWORK FOR ANALYSIS OF THEORY OF BIOLOGY

Springer (1999) said that two of the most important questions we can ask about theory change are: What happens? and, What makes it happen?

Questions about what happens in theory change are relatively easy (Springer, 1999). Hence, there is considerable literature within the domain of biology about what happens when children begin to develop a theory of biology. In contrast, "the explanatory question is more difficult, [and as a consequence] there have been relatively few detailed suggestions as to what drives changes in an early theory of biology, and about how such a theory emerges in the fist place" (Springer, 1999, p. 45). Chinn and Brewer (1998) presented similar questions in a more elaborate framework for understanding and evaluating theories of knowledge acquisition. The framework consists of eight questions they suggested any theory of knowledge acquisition should address. The framework is useful for researchers and teachers because it can reveal where the current theory of knowledge is incomplete and provides a guide for developing instruction.

I have borrowed from Chinn and Brewer's (1998) framework to structure the discussion in the next section of this chapter to understand and evaluate young children's knowledge acquisition about a theory of biology. The questions considered in this chapter include: What is the nature of the knowledge change? Are there intermediate stages in knowledge change? What initiates knowledge change? What factors influence knowledge change? What is the fate of the old knowledge and the new information after knowledge change occurs? And, What is the relationship between belief and knowledge? The science domain of biology and the early years of education provide boundaries to focus the literature review. In order to enrich the discussion, however, relevant literature outside these boundaries have been drawn upon. Based on the findings of the studies reviewed under each of the questions, I make general assertions about knowledge acquisition within the domain of theory of biology. These assertions may be used to make comparisons with knowledge acquisition in other domains.

WHAT IS THE NATURE OF THE KNOWLEDGE CHANGE?

There is a substantial body of literature about the nature of the conceptual changes in children's theory of biology from cognitive developmentalists, in particular from the research programs of Piaget (1929), Carey (1985), Keil (1989, 1992, 1994), their colleagues and critics. The concepts of living and non-living are considered as basic ontological concepts that underpin a theory of biology. Carey provided a lucid description of 'ontologically basic categories' and the entwined nature of ontological commitments and intuitive theories and argued that ontological development cannot be separated from theory development.

Ontology is the study of what exists... Our conceptual system includes hundreds of thousands of concepts. Intuitively, it is easy to see that there are not hundreds of thousands of *fundamentally* different kinds of things. A car is the same kind of thing as a truck, and even the same kind of thing as a house, at least as compared to a thunderstorm, a war, or a baseball game. The first group is made up of human artifacts and the second of events, both of which are ontologically basic categories. (Carey, 1985, pp. 162–163)

In her detailed monograph, Carey (1985) attempted to trace the development of several concepts related to theory of biology through early childhood; living thing, animal, person, plant, the concept of a particular species, such as raccoon, and concepts of various internal body parts and bodily processes. She found that young children at four years of age have a naïve psychological theory that is based on their knowledge of human activities and society. This naïve psychology is an intuitive theory that explains behavior in terms of wants and beliefs. It concerns both human and animal behavior because animals are seen as behaving beings. Carey said that five-year-old children have no understanding of biological essence because they have not differentiated the domain of biology from the domain of psychology. Therefore, young children understand concepts such as fruit, plant and animal in terms of their behavior and properties as they affect people (e.g., the smell of a skunk, the taste of a lemon).

Carey (1985) provided evidence to support her idea that between the ages of four and 10, biology emerges as a separate domain of intuitive theorizing from naïve psychology. She claimed that knowledge of animals and living things is restructured over this period in a child's life. "The kind of restructuring involved is at least of the weaker sort needed to characterize novice-expert shifts that do not involve theory change and most probably is of the stronger sort needed to characterize theory changes that involve conceptual change" (Carey, 1985, pp. 189–190).

Keil (1994) concurred with Carey's (1985) assertion that more powerful theories that are better able to explain the world continually emerge from previous theories. Keil's thesis differentiated from Carey's because his research did not show any evidence that supports the idea that a theory of biology gradually emerges from a naïve psychology. Keil argued that while younger and younger children have fewer biological beliefs about living things, they seem to have a set of abstract principles that result in intuitions about a large set of biological phenomena. In this sense, he directly refuted the idea that a theory of biology originates from loosely associated biological ideas, but he did not provide an explicit alternative explanation of the origin of biological thought. Springer (1999) and Inagaki and Hatano (2002) also argued that a theory of biology does not emerge from other framework theories. According to Spinger, a theory of biology appears by about age four or five and that it develops and exists as an independent and self-regulating theory that can be informed by other theories such as a naïve psychology or naïve mechanics.

The notion of 'life theorizer' was first used by Jaakkola (1997) to describe children who mentioned the goal of maintaining life, or avoiding death, for more than one body organ such as the heart, the blood or the brain. Only a third of four-year-old children in Jaakkola's study and more than ninety percent of six-year-olds were classified as life theorizers demonstrating a dramatic change in the children's ways of thinking about organs between these ages. More importantly, the children interviewed by Jaakkola began to use the abstract concept of life to predict and explain aspects of the human body. Life theorizers associated specific functions with organs such as, 'the brain is for thinking.' Whereas non-theorizers gave global and non-specific explanations such as, 'the brain is for keeping the body good,' or no explanation at all. Further work based on this notion of life theorizer was conducted by Slaughter, Jaakkola and Carey (1999) who investigated children's changing understanding of the concept death and any correlation with them being life theorizers. Their research demonstrated that the children's concept of life transformed from focusing on movement, activity, or usefulness, to a theory of biology based on biological goals of all living things. At the same time, the children's concept of death transformed from the idea that death is living on in altered circumstances (e.g., death is like a sleep that you can't wake up from; or death is to live on in anther place like heaven or under the ground) to death as the cessation of life or of biological functioning.

Assertion 1: *An independent, self-regulating, intuitive theory of biology emerges around the age of four or five years and constitutes a coherent network of concepts such as life, death, plant, animal, person, heart, brain, grow, and move.*

ARE THERE INTERMEDIATE STAGES IN KNOWLEDGE CHANGE?

Piaget (1929) investigated several concepts that are closely associated with a theory of biology including consciousness and animism. He described stages of development for many science related concepts. For the concept of life, Piaget claimed four stages, the first in children less than six years of age who tend to identify objects as living when they are observed as active (like a ticking clock) or useful (like a spoon to eat with). The second of Piaget's stages occurs between the ages of about seven and eight years of age when children's conception of living things is narrowed to apply only to objects that show some kind of movement. This is followed by a stage between eight and 12 years, when things that can spontaneously move by themselves are considered alive. The final stage is when life is restricted to animals and plants (Piaget, 1929).

Since Piaget conducted his experiments, there have been a number of researchers who extended and critiqued his work on stages. Laurendeau and Pinard (1962), for example, noted Piaget's lack of acknowledgement that children can use more than one criterion for life at one time. Carey (1985) criticized Piaget's presupposition that children's understandings of this concept developed in stages and the fact that he did not tabulate all his data but selected parts of interviews to exemplify his stages. Based on detailed investigations of several criteria children use to make judgments, Carey suggested one reason for children's incorrect classification of objects and organisms is inadequate biological knowledge. Carey acknowledged that while Piaget was more concerned with children's development of domain general causal notions, she had shifted the focus to more domain specific conceptual knowledge. Despite the criticisms of Piaget, both Carey and Laurendeau and Pinnard represented their findings in stages, akin to Piaget's, that showed the children's understanding of life progressed steadily from the age of four. By the age of 10, more than 50% of children had an adult concept that only animals and plants are alive.

In contrast with the studies by Laurendeau and Pinnard (1962) and Carey (1985), Bell and Freyberg (1985) reported an interesting phenomenon called a 'U-shaped curve'. Unlike previous studies that focused on stages in development, Bell and Freyberg simply tabulated the number of children who correctly identified a number of organisms and objects as living or non-living. The results showed a drop in the number of students who correctly identified objects, such as fire and a moving car, as non-living between the ages of about nine and 12. Moreover, a different experiment showed a similar, but reverse, bell shaped curve with older children (about nine years of age) less likely to identify a whale, spider and worm as animals than younger children (of about seven years of age). Bell and Freyberg thought that the U-shaped curve coincided with a deepening or broadening view of the world that can temporarily confound earlier understandings. As children grow older, for example, they might learn that a spider belongs to a group called arachnids, a fly to insects or that a whale belongs to a group called mammals. If the child does not understand hierarchical classification, they may then decide that the fly and the whale are not animals. These results indicated that learning may not necessarily occur in discrete stages as documented by previous researchers, that conceptual development may be less orderly and predictable and include reversals in thinking.

In my own work in a naturalistic classroom setting with five- and six-year-old children, I grouped children into two groups, those with non-scientific framework theories and those with scientific framework theories (Venville,

2004). Students were considered to have a non-scientific framework theory if they used non-scientific criteria more frequently that scientific criteria to classify things as either living or not living. For example, some of these children classified things as being alive because they are useful or could be associated with people in some way. Others said things were not living if they were broken. Children who used scientifically acceptable criteria more often than non-scientific criteria were considered to have a scientific framework theory. These children tended to use criteria such as movement (i.e., that things move, walk, scratch, or fly), nutrition (that things need food or water), and growth and reproduction (things have babies or seeds or grow). I came to the conclusion that when students' biological framework theory is in transition from non-scientific to scientific, students begin to use criteria including movement, death, the presence of body parts and use analogies with people when thinking and talking about other living and non-living things (Venville, 2004). These transitional criteria are not used consistently, however, and students considered in transition continue to use both non-scientific and scientific criteria.

Ravinis (2004) also found that preschool children constructed "precursor models" (p. 999) of friction that are compatible with scientific models and that the construction of these models requires systematic guidance in an educational context. Liu and Lesniak (2006) investigated the progression in students' understanding of matter from Grade 1 to 10 and described a sequence of five interrelated and 'overlapping waves' representing spurts in knowledge development. In each of these content areas, including the development of children's theory of biology, the learning does not seem to be linear, rather the learning described is "multifaceted, contextual and dynamic" (Liu & Lesniak, 2006, p. 340).

Assertion 2: *Transition to a theory of biology is not characterized by a linear staircase of ideas or hierarchical stages but may be indicated by a number of dynamic features.*

WHAT INITIATES KNOWLEDGE CHANGE?

Springer (1999) claimed that the critical factor driving the acquisition of a theory of biology is the accumulation of factual knowledge and some key inferences generated from this knowledge. Springer's focus was on children's theoretical beliefs about kinship, or familial relationships. He argued that the critical development leading to children's first theoretical reasoning about kinship occurs when they learn that babies grow inside their mothers. This knowledge allows the children to link certain kin relations to birth, and to make theoretically based (though sometimes incorrect) predications about the characteristics of family members (e.g., that a parent with curly hair is more likely to have a child with curly hair). Springer argued that children's first theory of kinship is biological but not genetic, that it does not develop from a theory of psychology, and that it is strongly data driven.

Other researchers have postulated the role of the accumulation of facts in theory development within the domain of biology. Keil (1992) and Pauen (1999) hypothesized that there may be innate knowledge acquisition devices for highly abstract, domain-specific knowledge. Children are predisposed to learn certain facts about the biological world that help them distinguish people, animals and plants from non-living kinds. The facts include that biological things reproduce, have complex internal structure, grow, and undergo irreversible changes, regulate resources such as food and water, can move without the help of external forces, are less predictable than non-biological things, and have parts that work together to support each other in a complementary manner (Keil, 1994; Pauen, 1999).

The role of accumulation of facts in theory change also is addressed by the work of Slaughter, Jaakkola and Carey (1999). These researchers paint a very plausible picture of young children accumulating facts, for example, that you would die if something goes seriously wrong with your heart, that only plants and animals die, that the body rots after death, and that dead things don't need food or air. They suggest that such mutually reinforcing factual knowledge builds up in the children's cognitive structures until it reaches a point where the biological concepts of life and death become differentiated. This is the point where the child becomes a life theorizer with a variety of concepts embedded in a vitalistic biology. At this point, the authors suggest, the new vitalistic theory of biology directs further learning. The child has reached a kind of conceptual threshold where further learning will accrue relatively easily and quickly because the addition of any more facts and information can now be used to further develop and embellish the theory rather than support the emergence of the theory.

Assertion 3: *A theory of biology is initiated by the accumulation of facts and this results in conceptual change over time.*

Aside from the accumulation of facts, some researchers have recognised the use of the process of analogy and models for initiating knowledge change. While Carey (1985) and Piaget (1929) said that children find it difficult to recognise plants as living things until they are about 10 years of age, Inagaki and Hatano (2002) demonstrated that much younger children, about four and five years of age, recognize commonalities between plants and animals for processes such as growth and the need for water and/or food. Moreover, they suggested that words such as grow, die, and wither are often used for plants as well as animals and may be a way of enabling children to grasp the commonalities. Children do have a relatively rich knowledge about humans, because they are humans. Children as young as three years know that humans have body parts, move (e.g., walk and throw a ball), reproduce (have babies), eat, drink, and grow. Inagaki and Hatano suggested that children can draw analogies between humans and other living things and make inferences that are very useful in everyday biological problem solving. Inagaki and Hatano propose that children's use of such personal analogies may reflect their adaptive and reflective mind.

Models, which are considered a form of analogical reasoning (Justi & Gilbert, 2006), also have been used to enrich young students' theories of biology with abstract concepts such as gene and DNA (Venville & Donovan, 2007). In a Year 2 class (six- and seven-year-olds), a simple wool model to represent DNA was used to explain why babies look like their parents. Findings indicated that meaningful learning occurred as a result of the DNA model for many of the students in the class because networks of knowledge were developed between their understandings of living and non-living things, and concepts of inheritance, gene, and DNA. The model created a concrete image for the students to associate with the concepts of gene and DNA, things that they were told are too small to see.

Assertion 4: *Analogies and models can play a positive role in initiating and sustaining conceptual change within a theory of biology.*

WHAT FACTORS INFLUENCE KNOWLEDGE CHANGE?

Metz (1998) suggested that the rich interaction of collaboration, cognition, and domain specific knowledge that is required for conceptual change for scientists may be a force that we can tap into for the science education of young children. Investigating learning in the complex and chaotic environment of the classroom, however, is enormously difficult. There are many challenges when attempting to document what is happening to individual children's conceptions when they are involved in multiple social interactions with their teacher, their peers, and also with people outside school. Social interaction in the classroom, however, generally has been considered to be an important aspect of children learning science (Cobern, 1998; Moje & Shepardson, 1998).

The kind of social interactions that seem to be of critical importance are conceptually focused interactions between the teacher and student because they are more likely to foster conceptual change than procedurally focused interactions (Fleer, 1995). Havu-Nuutinen (2005) examined the role of small group social discourse for 10 Finnish, six-year-old kindergarten children's learning about floating and sinking. Like Fleer, they found that for conceptual change to occur, conceptually oriented teacher-child interactions were important. While the peer interactions tended to be descriptive, the teacher-child interactions entered a higher stage of reasoning by drawing cause and effect relationships and synthesizing, comparing, and summarizing views. Through the guidance and conceptualization of the teacher during instruction, new properties and concepts of floating and sinking entered discussions, unsuitable concepts were challenged, and better ones defined.

Southerland et al. (2005), investigated third graders' understanding of condensation in an inquiry-based urban classroom. While they found the teachers' explicit assessments of students' ideas were supportive of conceptual change in small groups, the strongest force that shaped meaning making was persuasive power. They concluded that in conjunction with instruction that focuses on the role of evidence in sense making in science, young students require explicit instruction that is persuasive and compelling.

Research on the social aspects of learning with five- and six-year-old students in 10 inner London primary schools was designed to investigate how 'good thinking' that is likely to support cognitive development could be differentiated from 'common' practice (Venville, Adey, Larkin & Robertson, 2003). The research was conducted while the students participated in science and mathematics activities such as classification (including the classification of living and non-living things) and ordering in small groups. The findings indicated that habits of good thinking can be fostered in regular science lessons if difficulty is an accepted part of the learning process. The challenge should be at a level just beyond that which the children have already achieved so that it is possible for them to use new ideas to find solutions (Venville et al., 2003). Moreover, the researchers suggested that children should talk about, act on and put effort into thinking about problems and teachers should encourage children to explain problems, ideas, questions and possible solutions that they have about science. Through these actions, thinking becomes a discernible part of the classroom environment (Venville et al., 2003).

Another study specifically about six- and seven-year-old students' theory of biology targeted the problem of students using only one criterion to make judgments about whether something is alive (Venville & Donovan, 2007). Planned instruction in small groups explicitly encouraged the children to use several criteria and argue and justify their classification of living and non-living things. Two weeks after the intervention, the majority of students in the class were better able to distinguish living from non-living things and were more familiar with and used more scientific criteria. Understandings of the concept were developed in a way that enabled these students to apply the idea that living things have several common characteristics (Venville & Donovan, 2007).

Assertion 5: *Conceptually focused discussion that is strongly mediated by persuasive arguments from the teacher or students has the potential to support and sustain conceptual change about a theory of biology.*

An important issue to raise about small group discussion is the question of who benefits and who does not benefit from this kind of social interaction? The social aspects of the classroom learning environment in one Year 1 class (five- and six-year-olds) I investigated were of benefit to those children who already had a scientific theory of biology (Venville, 2004). That is, children who generally understood the concept of life in terms of growth, nutrition, movement, and reproduction, could use the scientific ideas expressed in the classroom discussion to strengthen their theory of biology. For example, students who had a basic theory of biology were able to participate in a meaningful way and benefit from classroom discussions about whether the moon has babies or not. Children who did not think in a scientific way about living things, however, were least likely to benefit from such social interaction in the classroom. For children who understood that a living thing is something that has a home, or something that is not broken, classroom discussion about whether the moon has babies or whether plants breathe is completely irrelevant.

My work in this same classroom also showed that even if there was conceptually focused discussion, naïve, non-scientific theories were unlikely to be clearly expressed, communicated or elaborated in a meaningful way (Venville, 2004). For example, Sally, was able to express her opinion during classroom discussion that a tree is not alive when its leaves are ripped off and that a car is dead if the lights break. But there was never an opportunity for her to explain that she thought everything is living when it is functional and not living when it is broken or transformed in some way.

Assertion 6: *Students with a scientific theory of biology are more likely to benefit from classroom discussion than students without a scientific theory of biology.*

Vygotsky (1986) argued that social interaction plays a fundamental role in the development of cognition and language is a critical component of this social interaction. Introducing a new concept cannot be initiated without the support of language. The difficulty with scientific concepts is that the scientific definition is often confused with the everyday way the word is used. According to Vygotsky, conceptual development involves the move from 'everyday' to 'schooled', or 'scientific' concepts (Wertsch, 1990). Everyday concepts are closely tied with the word or name of the object or condition under consideration. Conversely, scientific concepts are systematic, considered independently from the immediate image created by the word and can be manipulated in the mind (Gallimore & Tharp, 1990).

Language is a powerful potential mediator in the process of conceptual change with regard to a theory of biology (Venville, 2004). The English words living and alive are used in a variety of ways that are not consistent with their scientific definitions. For example, the use of the word living to indicate the place of residence, such as, 'I'm living in a flat,' or the use of the words alive and dead to indicate some kind of electrical or vital power, such as 'The electric wire is alive (or dead),' are common phrases that are likely to cause confusion for young children grappling with early science language.

Research on Brunei primary school students' understandings of biology when instruction is in the second language of English reinforced the importance of language for learning (Salleh, Venville & Treagust, 2007). The transition from Malay to English as the language of instruction in Primary 4 (when students are eight or nine years old) restricted students' ability to express their understandings in biology, to discuss biological concepts, and to interpret and analyze biological questions. Students were confused between three language factors; 1. the meaning of everyday concepts in Malay, 2. the meaning of everyday concepts in English, and 3. the meaning of scientific concepts. For example, the Malay word 'hidup' is used to mean 'start up' as in 'start up the car'. When hidup is directly translated into English, however, it means something akin to 'bring alive'. The everyday use of this word in Malay and its meaning in English, further confuses young children who seem to have a natural tendency to think that moving cars are living things.

Assertion 7:   *Language difficulties can create barriers to the process of conceptual change about a theory of biology.*

WHAT IS THE FATE OF THE OLD KNOWLEDGE AND THE NEW INFORMATION AFTER KNOWLEDGE CHANGE OCCURS?

Pozo, Gómez and Sanz (1999) investigated the issue of whether conceptual change should involve the replacement of old concepts in the context of chemistry. They advocated that after learning science, students' old and new representations (of atoms, for example) can coexist and that students need to learn how to select and use these contrasting representations in different ways according to the context. Therefore, learning chemistry may not require the replacement of previous ideas but a change in their function. The naïve ideas should be integrated into new theories or conceptual models, which provide the old ideas with a different, more theoretical meaning. In this sense, science teaching should not aim to replace misconceptions by scientific concepts but to make students reflect on the differences between the two apparently overlapping systems (Pozo, Gómez & Sanz, 1999).

In the context of a theory of biology, Caravita and Falchetti (2005) investigated seven to 12-year-old students' ideas about whether bones are alive and found that scientific ideas do not necessarily displace the intuitive ideas but they may "overshadow" or "supplement" them (p. 168). For example, when students learn from experience that broken bones repair, or that bones grow, they may keep this knowledge separate from their science knowledge. Many young children in this study knew that living things grow and repair themselves, but they frequently stated that bones are not alive. Caravita and Falchetti hypothesized this was because students' perception of bones as inert objects is highly constraining when they formulate a claim about the living status of bones. Some of the older children were able to recognize that their intuitive ideas were inappropriate and overshadowed them with their science knowledge that bones are indeed alive, or at least a living part of a living organism.

One student I found to demonstrate conceptual change during instruction gives further insight into the fate of old knowledge after knowledge change occurs (Venville, 2004). After instruction, six-year-old Ayan used scientific criteria almost exclusively to justify whether various objects and organisms were living or not living. With a couple of the objects discussed in the interview, however, she was confused and instead of relying on her new, scientific criteria, she returned to her pre-instructional idea that something was living if it had a home. Post-instruction, she said that a car and house were not living because they are outside and not in a home. These examples were in stark contrast with other objects such as the table, which she said was not living because it doesn't eat, talk or move. From this example, it seems that the old ideas don't necessarily disappear completely and immediately. It would be interesting to have interviewed Ayan another six and/or 12 months later to see if the old theory gradually did disappear. My experience with undergraduate university level students alluded to in the opening paragraphs of this chapter, however, indicate that non-scientific theories about living and non-living things may persist well into adult life for some people. All people, to some extent must have dual knowledge structures so that they can function in appropriate ways in everyday life. Even though most of us understand, from a scientific view, that human beings are animals, we continue to drive on freeways and enter restaurants regardless of the signage that says no entry to animals.

Assertion 8:   *Naïve, non-scientific understandings may coexist even when a scientific theory of biology is adopted as the primary explanatory framework.*

WHAT IS THE RELATIONSHIP BETWEEN BELIEF AND KNOWLEDGE? AND, WHAT FACTORS INFLUENCE BELIEF CHANGE?

Distinguishing knowledge from belief and opinion raises "knotty problems for thinkers" (Kalekin-Fishman, 1999, p. 92) because the terms refer to different ways of categorizing concepts and predict different levels of difficulty in effecting conceptual change. Kaelekin-Fishman claimed that knowledge is established through scientific inquiry and, as such, is distinct from opinion or belief. Learners have beliefs and opinions that they think are knowledge and the goal of education is to change mistaken opinions or beliefs into concepts that represent knowledge.

I presented evidence to support the idea that beliefs (including correct and incorrect scientific facts) about living things are more fluid and susceptible to change than the underlying knowledge based on theoretical frameworks (Venville, 2004). By observing and documenting detailed classroom interactions of Year 1 (five- and six-year-old) children learning about living things, I found several examples of reversals in students' ideas related to living things and the persistence of incorrect beliefs despite direct instruction to the contrary. The reversals and the persistence of incorrect beliefs seemed to be most commonly associated with particular objects and organisms that are difficult for children to classify as living or non-living such as the sun, clouds, and grass. Once a child generally understood living things as a scientist, that is, that living things grow, need food, move, and breathe, there was no evidence that such a scientific theory could be reversed. Children were observed to have correct and incorrect beliefs embedded within a theory of biology and these beliefs were fluid and malleable, but the theory tended to be stable.

One particular example documented was a child, Anna, who had a relatively good scientific theory about living things (Venville, 2004). She was deeply confused, however, about whether the sun is a living thing and changed her mind several times through the five-week course of instruction. She knew that the sun is a special kind of star and recalled stories about stars dying. In Anna's mind the sun went to the other side of the world to make it daylight, so it moved. Moreover, she thought the sun didn't grow because it is already big enough to do its job of making London sunny! These incorrect ideas about the sun, along with other, more scientific ideas, meant that Anna changed her belief that the sun is living, to the belief that it is not living, back to the idea that it is living by the end of instruction. Her basic underlying theory that living things move, have babies, and have a heart, however, remained consistent and was reinforced through instruction.

Assertion 9: *Beliefs are more easily influenced than framework theories by evidence and arguments presented in the social milieu of the classroom.*

IMPLICATIONS FOR PRACTICE AND RESEARCH

It is important to consider the implications of this body of research for researchers and practitioners. It is very clear from the literature that there is a considerable conceptual change between the ages of four and 10 when children initially do not understand the biological domain in the same way that adults and scientists do (Assertion 1). The average age at which this change occurs is of little relevance to teachers. As any experienced educators knows, they are likely to have in their class, children with a broad spectrum of ideas. What is far more important is the process of determining the nature of each child's naïve theory and the best approaches to use to help the child move forward. An immediate research question that comes to mind is about how teachers and early childhood educators can help students to explain, in an elaborate way, their naïve theories of biology and what effect this approach has on conceptual change.

The research reviewed in this chapter also suggests that the transition to a theory of biology may be characterized by a number of dynamic features (Assertion 2). For example, recognizing that living things are like humans in some way or associating functions such as movement, growth, and death with living things may be indicators of a transitional stage between a non-scientific theory and a scientific theory. These transitional ideas might not be used correctly, but the associated thinking seems to indicate a positive shift in biological thought processes. The implications for practitioners and researchers are that these transitional ideas might give insight into useful teaching strategies for conceptual change. Elaborating analogies between humans and animals and plants, for example, that they all grow and die and they all require water might be an appropriate initial step to take (Assertion 4). Taking advantage of these transitional phases may benefit those children who do not have a scientific theory of biology, that is, those children who are unlikely to be cognitively engaged in typical classroom discussion (Assertion 6).

Almost all researchers strongly advocate the role of factual knowledge in the initial development of a theory of biology and the elaboration of that theory once it has been established in the child's mind (Assertion 3). Rich, educational experiences of living things, and life processes, and systematic observation of objects and organisms are likely to be beneficial in this process. Metz (1998) pointed to a lack of coherent themes in science curricula that precludes systematic knowledge building. While this may or may not be the case with particular documented curricula, it is the translation of the curriculum into classroom practice that is at issue. While young children might study units about whales, dinosaurs, plants, and minibeasts (a popular word to describe invertebrates in early childhood education) links back to the big idea of a theory of biology are rarely made. Wandersee and Fisher (2000) concur that focusing on too many details can obscure the big picture and that biology students of today are so steeped in detail that they often miss the big picture. While acknowledging the importance of factual information, particularly for initial theory building, Wandersee and Fisher advocate an approach where learners need to organize their biology knowledge "into coherent patterns, and they need to polish and refine their knowledge structures" (pp. 46–47). Teaching strategies that enable young learners to organize the knowledge they accumulate into coherent patterns that build their theory of biology need to be developed, trialed, and evaluated.

The literature suggested that naïve, non-scientific beliefs may coexist with new, scientific understandings (Assertion 8) and that while framework theories are difficult to change, more superficial ideas about a theory of biology may ebb and flow (Assertion 9). These factors indicate a dynamic, multilayered cognitive milieu in learning contexts. The implication of this is that the teachers can embrace fluid and multidimensional metaphors to guide the learning contexts they create in their classrooms and to describe, predict, and understand student learning.

There has been considerable research on the cognitive aspects of development but less on the 'hot' (Pintrich, Marx & Boyle, 1993) aspects of conceptual change in the area of children's early understanding of biology. Sinatra (2005) does, however, acknowledge a 'warming trend', as is evident in this chapter. Pintrich, Marx and Boyle outlined the hot aspects of conceptual change as the social and motivational aspects most readily observed in the classroom situation. In this chapter I have documented research that indicates that conceptually focused discussion, explicit instruction as well as the processes of argumentation and justification all have the potential to support and sustain conceptual change (Assertion 5). Implications of this research for teachers is that they must find ways that enable and encourage their students to talk specifically about science concepts related to a theory of biology, to explain their ideas in full, to listen to each other, to embrace difficulty as an opportunity to learn, to point out inconsistencies and problems with ideas and explore alternative solutions to problems (Venville et al., 2003).

As a consequence of the potential benefits social interaction has on young children's learning of science, the finding that language difficulties can create barriers to the process of conceptual change is not surprising (Assertion 7). Unfortunately, the social milieu in the classroom is more likely to be beneficial for children who already use a scientific way of thinking about plants and animals but fails to include those students whose thinking is not consistent with scientifically accepted ways of viewing the biological world (Assertion 6).

An implication of these findings is that there is a need for more research about the ways that teachers can maximize the benefits of social interaction and other, more affective, aspects of conceptual change. Motivation, for example, has long been documented as a significant force in supporting learning, but this is an area where comparatively little research has been conducted with young children, perhaps because they are generally considered to be more inquisitive and motivated than middle school, or high school students. Fisher (2000) outlines several factors that are known to increase motivation including; giving each student a voice in the class, encouraging students to work in groups to discuss their ideas among themselves, and creating opportunities for students to create and test their own explanatory models. Sinatra and Pintrich's (2003) book on intentional conceptual change explores a number of ways that the affective aspects of learning can be used to enhance conceptual change including motivation, persuasive messages, metacognition, interest, achievement goals, and personal epistemologies.

In conclusion, it is evident that the review presented in this chapter revealed an extraordinary amount of information that we have developed about knowledge acquisition and conceptual change within the domain of theory of biology. In particular, the research is beginning to provide lucid answers to the question of what happens when children acquire a theory of biology. While there has been much research that investigated what makes conceptual change happen, there is considerable room to develop classroom-based research to uncover the best approaches to pedagogy to enhance learning.

REFERENCES

Bell, B. F. & Freyberg, P. (1985). Language in the science classroom. In R. Osborne & P. Freyberg (Eds.), *Learning in science: The implications of children's science* (pp. 29–40). Auckland, New Zealand: Heinemann.

Caravita, S. & Falchetti, (2005). Are bones alive? *Journal of Biological Education, 39*(4), 163–170.

Caravita, S. & Halldén, O. (1994). Re-framing the problem of conceptual change. *Learning and Instruction, 4*(special issue), 89–111.

Carey, S. (1985). *Conceptual change in childhood.* Cambridge, UK: The MIT Press.

Chi, M. T. H., Slotta, J. D., & deLeeuw, N. (1994). From things to process: A theory of conceptual change for learning science concepts. *Learning and Instruction, 4,* 27–43.

Chinn, C. A. & Brewer , W. F. (1998). Theories of knowledge acquisition. In B. J. Fraser & K. G. Tobin (Eds.), *International handbook of science education* (part 1, pp. 97–113). Dordrecht, The Netherlands: Kluwer.

Cobern, W. W. (Ed.). (1998). *Socio-cultural perspectives on science education.* Dordrechet, The Netherlands: Kluwer.

diSessa, A. (1993). Toward an epistemology of physics. *Cognition and Instruction, 10,* 105–225.

Duit, R. & Treagust, D. F. (2003). Conceptual change: A powerful framework for improving science teaching and learning. *International Journal of Science Education, 25*(6), 671–688.

Duit, R. (1999). Conceptual change approaches in science education. In W. Schnotz, S. Vosniadou & M. Carretero (Eds.), *New perspectives on conceptual change* (pp. 263–282). Oxford, UK: Elsevier Science.

Fisher, K. M. (2000). Meaningful and mindful learning. In K. M. Fisher, J. H. Wandersee & D. E. Moody (Eds.), *Mapping biology knowledge* (pp. 77–94). Dordretch, The Netherlands: Kluwer.

Fleer, M. (1995). The importance of conceptually focused teacher-child interaction in early childhood science learning. *International Journal of Science Education, 17*(3), 325–342.

Gallimore, R., & Tharp, R. (1990). Teaching mind in society: Teaching, schooling and literate discourse. In L. C. Moll (Ed.), *Vygotsky and education* (pp. 175–205). Cambridge, UK: Cambridge University Press.

Gopnik, A. & Wellman, H. M. (1994). The theory theory. In L. A. Hirschfeld & S. A. Gelman (Eds.), *Mapping the mind: Domain specificity in cognition and culture* (pp. 257–293). Cambridge, UK: Cambridge University Press.

Guzzetti, B. & Hynd, C. (1998). *Perspectives on conceptual change: Multiple ways to understand knowing and learning in a complex world.* Mahwah, NJ: Lawrence Erlbaum.

Halldén, O. (1999). Conceptual change and contextualization. In W. Schnotz, S. Vosniadou & M. Carretero (Eds.), *New perspectives on conceptual change* (pp. 53–66). Oxford, UK: Elsevier Science.

Havu-Nuutinen, S. (2005). Examining young children's change process in floating and sinking from a social constructivist perspective. *International Journal of Science Education, 27*(3), 259–279.

Hewson, P. W. & Thorley, N. R. (1989). The conditions of conceptual change in the classroom. *International Journal of Science Education, 11*(special issue), 541–553.

Hewson, P. W. (1996). Teaching for conceptual change. In D. F. Treagust, R. Duit & B. J. Fraser (Eds.), *Improving teaching and learning in science and mathematics* (pp. 131–140). New York: Teachers College Press.

Inagaki, K. & Hatano, G. (2002). *Young children's naïve thinking about the biological world.* New York: Psychology Press.

Jaakkola, R. (1997). The development of scientific understandings: Children's construction of their fist biological theory. Unpublished Ph.D. thesis. Massachusetts Institute of Technology, Cambridge, MA.

Justi, R. & Gilbert, J. (2006). The role of analog models in understanding of the nature of models in chemistry. In P. J. Aubusson, A. G. Harrison & S. M. Ritchie (Eds.), *Metaphor and analogy in science education*. Dordrecht, The Netherlands: Springer.

Kalekin-Fishman, D. (1999). Knowledge, belief, and opinion: A sociologist's view of conceptual change. In W. Schnotz, S. Vosniadou & M. Carretero (Eds.), *New perspectives on conceptual change* (pp. 91–110). Oxford, UK: Elsevier Science.

Keil, F. (1989). *Concepts, kinds, and cognitive development.* Cambridge, MA: The MIT Press.

Keil, F. (1992). The origins of an autonomous biology. In M. Gunnar & M. Maratsos (Eds.), *Minnesota Symposium on Child Psychology* (pp. 103–137). Mahwah, NJ: Erlbaum.

Keil, F. (1994). The birth and nurturance of concepts by domains: The origins of concepts of living things. In L. A. Hirschfeld & S. A. Gelman (Eds.), *Mapping the mind: Domain specificity in cognition and culture.* Cambridge, UK: Cambridge University Press.

Laurendeau, M. & Pinard, A. (1962). *Causal thinking in the child: A genetic and experimental approach.* New York: International Universities Press.

Lautrey, J. & Mazens, K. (2004). Is children's naïve knowledge consistent? A comparison of the concepts of sound and heat. *Learning and Instruction, 14*(4), 399–424.

Liu, X. & Lesniak, K. (2006). Progression in children's understanding of the matter concept from elementary to high school. *Journal of Research in Science Teaching, 43*(3), 320–347.

Metz, K. E. (1998). Scientific inquiry within reach of young children. In B. J. Fraser & K. G. Tobin (Eds.), *International handbook of science education* (pp. 81–96). London, UK: Kluwer.

Moje, E. B. & Shepardson, D. P. (1998). Social interactions and children's changing understanding of electric circuits: Exploring unequal power relations in 'peer'-learning groups. In B. Guzzetti & C. Hynd (Eds.), *Perspectives on conceptual change: Multiple ways to understand knowing and learning in a complex world* (pp. 225–234). Mahwah, NJ: Lawrence Erlbaum.

Palmer, D. (2005). A motivational view of constructivist-informed teaching. *International Journal of Science Education, 27*(15), 1853–1881.

Pauen, S. (1999). The development of ontological categories: Stable dimensions and changing concepts. In W. Schnotz, S. Vosniadou & M. Carretero (Eds.), *New perspectives on conceptual change* (pp. 15–31). Oxford, UK: Elsevier Science.

Piaget, J. (1929). *The child's conception of the world.* London, UK: Routledge and Kegan Paul.

Pintrich, P. R., Marx, R. W., & Boyle, R. A. (1993). Beyond cold conceptual change: The role of motivational beliefs and classroom contextual factors in the process of conceptual change. *Review of Educational Research, 63*, 167–199.

Pozo, J. I., Gómez Crespo, M. A. (2005). The embodied nature of implicit theories: The consistency of ideas about the nature of matter. *Cognition and Instruction, 23*(3), 351–388.

Pozo, J. I., Gómez, M. A., & Sanz, A. (1999). When change does not mean replacement: Different representations for different contexts. In W. Schnotz, S. Vosniadou & M. Carretero (Eds.), *New perspectives on conceptual change* (pp. 161–174). Oxford, UK: Elsevier Science.

Ravanis, K. (2004). What factors does friction depend on? A socio-cognitive teaching intervention with young children. *International Journal of Science Education, 26*(8), 997–1007.

Salleh, R., Venville, G., & Treagust, D. T. (2007). When a bilingual child describes living things: An analysis of conceptual understanding of science from a language perspective. *Research in Science Education, 37*(3), 291–312.

Sinatra, G. M. & Pintrich, P. R. (Eds.). (2003). *Intentional conceptual change.* Mahwah, NJ: Lawrence Erlbaum.

Sinatra, G. M. (2005). The 'warming trend' in conceptual change research: The legacy of Paul R. Pintrich. *Educational Psychologist, 40*(2), 107–116.

Slaughter, V., Jaakkola, R., & Carey (1999). Constructing a coherent theory: Children's biological understanding of life and death. In M. Siegal & C. C. Peterson (Eds.), *Children's understanding of biology and health* (pp. 71–96). Cambridge, UK: Cambridge University press.

Southerland, S. A., Abrams, E., Cummins, C. L., & Anzelmo, J. (2001). Understanding students' explanations of biological phenomena: Conceptual frameworks or p–prims? *Science Education, 85*, 328–348.

Southerland, S. A., Kittleson, J., Settlage, J., & Lanier, K. (2005). Individual and group meaning-making in an urban third grade classroom: Red fog, cold cans, and seeping vapor. *Journal of Research in Science Teaching, 42*(9), 1032–1061.

Springer, K. (1999). How a naïve theory of biology is acquired. In M. Siegal & C. C. Peterson (Eds.), *Children's understanding of biology and health* (pp. 45–70). Cambridge, UK: Cambridge University press.

Tsai, C-C. & Wen, M. L. (2005). Research and trends in social science education from 1998 to 2002: A content analysis of publication in selected journals. *International Journal of Science Education, 27*(1), 3–14.

Tyson, L. M., Venville, G., Harrison, A. G., & Treagust, D. F. (1997). A multidimensional framework for interpreting conceptual change events in the classroom. *Science Education, 81*, 387–404.

Venville, G. & Treagust, D. F. (1998). Exploring conceptual change in genetics using a multidimensional interpretive framework. *Journal of Research in Science Teaching, 35*(9), 1031–1055.

Venville, G. J. & Donovan, J. (2007). Developing Year 2 students' theory of biology with the concepts of gene and DNA. *International Journal of Science Education, 29*(9), 1111–1131.

Venville, G. J. (2004). Young children learning about living things: A case study of conceptual change from ontological and social perspectives. *Journal of Research in Science Teaching, 41*(5), 449–480.

Venville, G., Adey, P., Larkin, S., & Robertson, A. (2003). Fostering thinking through science in the early years of schooling. *International Journal of Science Education, 25*(11), 1313–1331.

Venville, G., Gribble, S. J., & Donovan, J. (2005). An exploration of young children's understandings of genetics concepts from ontological and epistemological perspectives. *Science Education, 89*(4), 614–633.

Vosniadou, S. (1994). Capturing and modelling the process of conceptual change. *Learning and Instruction, 4*, 45–69.

Vosniadou, S. (1999). Conceptual change research: State of art and future directions. In W. Schnotz, S. Vosniadou & M. Carretero (Eds.), *New perspectives on conceptual change* (pp. 3–13). Oxford, UK: Elsevier Science.

Vygotsky, L. (1986). *Thought and language*. London, UK: The MIT Press.

Wandersee, J. H. & Fisher, K. M. (2000). Knowing biology. In K. M. Fisher, J. H. Wandersee & D. E. Moody (Eds.), *Mapping biology knowledge* (pp. 39–54). Dordretch, The Netherlands: Kluwer.

Welman, H. M. & Gelman, S. A. (1998). Knowledge acquisition in fundamental domains. In D. Kuhn & R. S. Siegler (Eds.), *Handbook of child psychology, Vol 2: Cognition, perception, and language* (5th ed, pp. 523–573). New York: Wiley.

Wertsch, J. V. (1990). The voice of rationality in a sociocultural approach to mind. In L. C. Moll (Ed.), *Vygotsky and education* (pp. 111–126). Cambridge, UK: Cambridge University Press.

Zembylas, M. (2004). Young children's emotional practices while engaged in long-term science investigation. *Journal of Research in Science Teaching, 41*(7), 693–719.

CHAPTER 4

AFFECT AND EARLY CHILDHOOD SCIENCE EDUCATION

Michalinos Zembylas

Early childhood educators would undoubtedly agree that the early years of schooling are crucial in the development of children's social, emotional, and cognitive development. Over the last few decades, science education has made substantial progress in research and theory development about young children's cognitive development (Chaille & Britain, 1997; Harlan, 1988; Holt, 1993; Howe, 1993; Kamii & DeVries, 1993; Landry & Foreman, 1999). Science educators have analyzed children's alternative conceptions of various natural phenomena and suggested teaching interventions that can help young children change their prior conceptions and adopt accepted scientific ideas (e.g., see, Inagaki, 1992; Ravanis, 1994; Sharp, 1995; Solomonidou & Kakana, 2000; Vosniadou & Brewer, 1992).

Many views of learning science in early childhood education emphasize the worthy goal of creating "developmentally appropriate" (Bredekamp & Copple, 1997) activities that provide young children with opportunities to develop their cognitive understanding in science (Hadjigeorgiou, 2001). However, as Spodek (1986, 1992) has suggested, in addition to the developmental perspective, the cultural and social context should also be considered in early childhood education programs. Although research and theory on children's cognitive development and science learning has been

Contemporary Perspectives on Science and Technology in Early Childhood Education, pages 65–85
Copyright © 2008 by Information Age Publishing

largely inspired by the works of Piaget and Vygotsky—who fully recognized the interrelatedness of cognitive and social/affective processes (Dai & Sternberg, 2004)—most research in science education has clearly favored cognitive aspects of learning, e.g., cognitive processes of thinking or measurable cognitive outcomes. As a result, little attention has been given to integrating cognitive, social, and affective development into (early childhood) science education (Zembylas, 2005b).

In particular, *affective* factors have been largely neglected in science education research which has been dominated by a "conceptual change" view of learning (Alsop & Watts, 2003).[1] Studies that deal with the role of affect in science teaching and learning for children under 7 or 8 years of age are relatively difficult to find. This is an important oversight because work aimed at understanding science teaching and learning in early childhood education may have significant implications for curriculum programs designed to address children's needs by failing to consider affective factors along with cognitive ones. What has often been less understood, as Siraj-Blatchford and Siraj-Blatchford (2002) write, is the fact that "children's constructions are determined by their interests, attitudes and their motivations *as well as* by their prior knowledge and experience" (p. 209, emphasis added). Howe (1993) has gone as far as arguing that research which ignores affective factors, among other issues, and sees cognitive level as the only relevant variable in early childhood science education, is "simplistic, if not misguided" (p. 228).

There is, of course, much more in early childhood science education than cognition. Emotions such as intellectual curiosity, pleasure, and joy as well as disappointment and disaffection shape attitudes, moods and motivations for science teaching and learning (Alsop, 2005). The National Research Council (1996) and the forum on Early Childhood Science, Mathematics, and Technology Education, convened by Project 2061 of the American Association for the Advancement of Science (Chittenden & Jones, 1998; Elkind, 1998) emphasize the importance of "habits of mind," values and attitudes in children's ways of thinking and acting. As Hadjigeorgiou (2001) points out: "It should be recognized that attitudes towards science might very well be not just as important as a strong conceptual base, but *more important*, since they are the prerequisites or the motivators for children's engagement in science activities" (p. 64, emphasis added). Once developed at an early age, these attitudes may facilitate or hinder young children's long-term relationship to science (Chittenden & Jones, 1998; Elkind, 1998).

Concerns about attitudes toward science, are not new as Osborne, Simon, and Collins (2003) indicate in their recent review of the literature and its implications. The investigation of children's attitudes to science has a long tradition for the last three to four decades and a substantial body of literature has accumulated concerning the relationship between science learning and the affective domain. However, there has been little exploration of attitudes in early childhood science (Pell & Jarvis, 2001) but most important, perhaps the focus of the research line on attitudes has been generally *narrow* and *decontextualized*. Attitudes have been primarily investigated on a psychological basis and in isolation from the analysis of the socio-historical context of learning (Zembylas, 2005a). As Matthews (2004) explains, the instruments that measure children's attitudes in science "try to separate what pupils feel about science as an activity from how they feel about science in lessons" (p. 282).

Furthermore, there has been relatively little work that has explicitly addressed affect, feelings, or the emotions compared to the large literature on attitudes to school science. Recently several researchers have called for a rethinking of research on affect in science education so that it can account for the variety of affective aspects involved and their complexities, as well as the impact of contextual factors on affect in science education. Nowadays, there is a growing interest in affective issues in relation to science teaching and learning and an increasing body of empirical data is gradually accumulating (Alsop, 2001; Alsop & Watts, 2003; Laukenmann et al., 2003; Santos & Mortimer, 2003; Watts & Alsop, 1997; Watts & Walsh, 1997; Zembylas, 2004a).

The purpose of this chapter is to review recent research on affective issues in early childhood science education published in journals and books, focusing on the theoretical and practical accomplishments of this work. The first part discusses the factors that have contributed to the neglect of research interest in young children's emotional development in science education, and the limited number of studies conducted on the role of early childhood teachers' emotions in the context of science teaching. The second part reviews and critiques empirical and theoretical studies of affective issues in early childhood science education published within the last ten years (1996-present). The last part examines the consequences of this research for science teaching and learning in early childhood education, and sketches some directions for future research.

HISTORICAL PERSPECTIVES ON RESEARCHING AFFECT IN EARLY CHILDHOOD SCIENCE EDUCATION

Although empirical evidence documents that young children's attention and interest are captured by science (French, 2004), there has been considerable neglect in investigating affective issues in science education (Zembylas, 2005a). The lack of research purporting to such issues in early childhood science education may be unrelated to the overall difficulties researchers encounter when they attempt to study young children. The challenge of researching affect, however, becomes even more complicated because the affective domain has not been given the same status as the intellect or this lack of research may be because affects are considered as difficult "objects" of study (Simon, 1982; Woods, 1996).[2] In fact, as Wieder and Greenspan (1993) indicate, "research on emotional development evolved quite separately from the work on the impact of the social world on cognitive development" (p. 78).

In addition, "the archetypical image of science itself [with its] long-standing Cartesian tradition of separation, prizing apart the mind and body, divorcing and polarizing reason from feeling" (Alsop & Watts, 2003, p. 1044) is an aspect that further complicates any effort to appreciate the affective factors associated with studying science. Consequently, relative to the overall development of young children and the contribution of science education in it, greater emphasis has been paid to children's cognitive development, as a result of the long-standing cognitive tradition in science education research. It is worthwhile to mention here that Landry and Forman (1999) make a distinction between research on early science education and research on early cognitive development, and thus emphasize that research on early science education is relatively limited.

Another reason for the neglect of the affective domain in early science education is that although the emotional basis of learning in early childhood has been widely documented over the last few decades (Hyson, 2004; Raver, 2002; Shonkoff & Phillips, 2000; Wieder & Greenspan, 1993), the contributions of children's early emotional experiences to their capacity to learn science are only recently being recognized. So far, two major tendencies seem to have occurred with respect to affective issues in early science education. The first tendency has been to consider affects as "either incidental or assumed" (Wieder & Greenspan, 1993, p. 77), such as when children enjoy playing with materials. Many guides to early science education emphasize the importance of engaging young children emotionally with science (e.g., see, Chaille & Britain, 1997; Seefeldt & Galper, 2002). Yet, very few of those works have been based on actual empirical research investigating how young children's emotions, feelings, and attitudes are developed in particular social and cultural contexts of learning science. More often than not, affects have been assumed to be there, however, their influence has not been studied systematically. Or, affects may have been considered incidental, given that the overwhelming focus of interest has always been on cognitive development. However, science educators have realized in recent years that the absence of affective components (such as interest and motivation) are likely to play central roles in children's growing disengagement from science learning (Alsop, 2005; Osborne et al., 2003), thus a compelling case has been provided for paying more attention to affective issues sooner rather than later in children's educative experiences.

The second tendency with respect to affective issues in science education—not only in early childhood but also more generally—has been the inclination to isolate cognitive from emotional aspects in investigations of science learning and teaching, that is, to address one "category" only in the absence of the other (Zembylas, 2005b). Again, recent work has emphasized that affective factors may indeed support or impede children's cognitive development (Dole & Sinatra, 1998; Duit, 1999; Pintrich, 1999; Sinatra & Pintrich, 2003), thus the importance of integrating knowledge about the role of affective factors in science teaching and learning within contexts of children's cognitive development seems to become more prominent. Although the links between affective aspects and children's cognition are fairly well documented, the links to actual "conceptual change—a major focus of research interest in early childhood science education during the last few years—have not been documented. Research on conceptual change has tended to ignore affective aspects such as, the role of processing strategies in mediating emotional influences on beliefs, the role of emotion in the maintenance and change of beliefs, conceptions, and attitudes, and the role of emotions and the social goals they serve in distributed cognition (Zembylas, 2005b). The recommendation for further research that explores the interrelations between emotion and cognition is also highlighted by Duit and Treagust (2003) who acknowledge that, "the number of studies on the interaction of cognitive and affective factors in the learning process is limited" (p. 679). A similar neglect of the affective domain has also been documented in relation to teaching and the teacher's role in science education. This area of research has been reviewed elsewhere (see, Zembylas, 2005a), thus the discussion here will be limited to issues of affect in children's development.

To sum up, this brief historical perspective on previous research in early childhood science education highlights the need for a critical consideration of the affective and social reality in the classroom. That is, there has to be a critical discourse developed that aims to make visible, and subject to examination, the affective aspects of science teaching and learning. The predominance of cognitive perspectives seems to extend the widely held cultural perception that emotion is an obstacle to rational thinking in science. This assumption, however, is no longer valid, especially after recent work indicates that the complexity of classroom discourses requires research to consider the influence of factors such as, beliefs, emotion, motivation, goals, modes of knowing science, peers, gender, social class, and ethnicity (Lemke, 2001). It has only recently become apparent in early childhood science education that the neglect of affective aspects is limiting our understanding of early science education. Consequently, it is highlighted that *understanding* young children's emotional development and early childhood teachers' emotions needs to consider the particular social and cultural context in which science education takes place.

REVIEW OF RESEARCH

This review draws attention to recent research that examines affective issues in early childhood science education. A search has been conducted to find studies that explore the role of affect and the implications of considering this role for science teaching and learning in early childhood education. The inclusion criteria that were used for this review were as follows: empirical or theoretical studies published in journals or books between 1996–present, focusing on affect and early science education. The relevant literature was located by electronic searches of the Educational Resources Information Center (ERIC) and the psychological literature database (PsychINFO) and keyword searches via internet search engines. To facilitate the analysis of the studies located, I used the following guiding questions:

- Who conducted the research and what is its theoretical framework?
- What was the research focus and what methods were used?
- What were the findings?
- What do these studies contribute to our knowledge about affect and early childhood science education?

Affect and Science Learning

In a series of publications, Osborne and Brady (Osborne, 2000; Osborne & Brady, 2001, 2002) analyze their attempts to illuminate the qualities of affect found in the acts of teaching and learning science for young children. The emotional, aesthetic, and spiritual states are driving forces in doing science from and early age, as Osborne and Brady argue in their work. The theoretical framework of this work is built on a critique of binary assumptions between art and science, intellectual and emotional, spiritual, and sensual. It is also set against contemporary calls for a utilitarian science that is fixed on testing thus ignoring the role of "whimsy, playfulness, passion, spirituality, beauty, and many other words rarely applied to science education" (Osborne & Brady, 2001, p. 36). This research is focused on providing descriptions of stories from working with small children in which "doing science" is shown to involve affective qualities that help these young children see things not seen before, see things as something other than "normal," and see things that aren't at all (Osborne & Brady, 2001).

Furthermore, Osborne and Brady argue that the affective qualities of doing science enrich the problem solving processes in which young children are engaged. As they write: "There is the quality of this 'immediate union of the knowing subject and the object known' in all the stories we tell" (p. 55). The affective qualities include "feelings of joy, sensuality, [and] beauty" (Osborne, 2000, p. 119) and they are associated with problem solving. Thus, any effort to separate subject and object is artificial.

The implications of this view on science learning and teaching are immense, of course. As Osborne and Brady (2002) explain:

> When asking children to "do" science we also ask them to explore the nature of science, thinking on a meta-level about acts of design and personal agency in science. We provided many different materials for making the stepping-stones and we asked questions about the qualities of the materials and the relationships between those and their resulting designs. The activities were shaped by the children's desires, aesthetic, and their past histories, which were in turn altered by their experiences in this class. (p. 38)

Such an understanding of science learning in early childhood education blurs the boundaries between aesthetics and science, and reason and emotion, and redefines what it means to do science with young children. A sense of wonder, connectedness and reenchantment are central components of Osborne and Brady's approach. Their research provides illustrative examples of how such a perspective enables young children to see new things, enlarging the creative possibilities of doing science. This revisioning of early childhood science education fundamentally involves a radical political dimension, as Osborne and Brady admit. "We would like to argue," they point out, "that rather than increased test scores or vague concepts such as scientific literacy, the outcomes of education should be more ambiguous. [...] We would argue that instead of increased test scores, science education should concern itself with the transformation of both the teacher's and learner's roles and this entails a transformation of subject matter" (2002, pp. 330–331).

In a three-year ethnographic case study of a teacher in an early childhood classroom, Zembylas (2004a) analyzes young children's emotional practices engaged in long-term science investigations. The focus of this study is on classroom organization and the teacher's rationale for this kind of investigation, as well as the nature of the emotional tone in the classroom. The theoretical framework of the study is based on the idea of emotion as *performative* (Zembylas, 2005a), and builds on poststructuralist views of emotions as performative acts, thus emphasizing the significance of social and cultural context and norms in the constitution, expression, and communication of emotion.³ The methodology of this study is qualitative and ethnographic, and the data sources are classroom observations, in-depth interviews with the teacher, and collection of documents of all kinds (e.g., lesson plans, a diary, philosophy statements, children's worksheets, and school records).

The analysis in this study indicates that talking about and doing science, and expressing emotions about science and its learning are often intertwined and difficult to separate. In particular, Zembylas shows how young children's emotional practices contribute to the classroom *emotional tone*, that is, the general emotional culture in the classroom. He describes various episodes which indicate how the classroom emotional tone may often be a contributor to the motivation of young children and their teacher in taking or avoiding certain actions. The findings of this study suggest that:

> young children's emotional practices in science learning are interpersonally and socially complex: how, for example, to understand such practices we also have to understand the sociological and interpersonal relations of children and their teachers, and how understanding those relations involves understanding children's emotional practices; and how, at a still greater level of complexity, children's emotional practices can be understood only if we understand the world of their learning in science with those emotional practices and that understanding this world involves understanding those emotional practices. (Zembylas, 2004a, p. 715)

This research shows how important the social and emotional context of early childhood science education is, and challenges perspectives which attempt to overgeneralize and oversimplify children's learning in science by leaving out the complexity and importance of emotions.

The importance of affective issues such as the role of wonder, attitudes, aesthetics, and dispositions is also reiterated in four other studies published between 2001 and 2002. Hadjigeorgiou (2001) presents arguments and evidence from a pilot study with young children in which the role of wonder is emphasized. It is maintained that activities which may not appear to be "developmentally appropriate" should not necessarily be excluded from early childhood programs in science education. Although this study is not strictly empirical but mostly argumentative, it contributes to the body of work that attempts to bring cognitive and affective components together. Young children can be engaged in science, as Hadjigeorgiou says, through using stories to attract them and enrich their reasoning and problem solving.

The use of literature and especially poetry is also highlighted in Watts (2001, 2005). Although this piece does not refer explicitly to early childhood science education, but it is rather "general," it shows the power of poetry—a favorite component of any early childhood curriculum—to stimulate observation, imagination and emotion in early childhood science. Watts builds on his previous work on affective issues in science education (e.g., Watts & Alsop, 1997; Watts & Walsh, 1997),[4] and provides examples in which poems—published poems or poems written by children and teachers—are used to enrich science learning. It is worthwhile to mention that in their published work, both Osborne and Zembylas refer to similar examples in which the affective dimension of writing poems has a powerful effect on the science learning of young children.

Siraj-Blatchford and Siraj-Blatchford (2002) refer to the work of Piaget and Vygotsky to emphasize the interconnectedness between the cognitive and the affective development of young children. Although the role of affect in early childhood science education is not the primary focus of this research, Siraj-Blatchford and Siraj-Blatchford analyze the importance of children's *dispositions*—understood as "habits of mind"—to sustain an interest in problem-solving and exploration. The researchers follow a qualitative methodology of data collection and they conduct interviews with 54 five-year-olds in London. The goal of this study is to explore children's technological constructs in relation to positive learning dispositions in science and technology. A good deal of the researchers' efforts is focused on analyzing both the cognitive and the affective components of children's metacognitive strategies. It is argued that, "Instructive activities need to be matched to the child's current understandings, capabilities and interests so that the teacher's knowledge of their developing understandings, capabilities and interests may also be considered crucial" (p. 212). The researchers of this study argue that young children should be encouraged to enrich their learning dispositions toward science.

Pell and Jarvis (2001) develop the first attitude to science scales for use with children of early age. Their investigation is part of a project to improve children's achievement in science. The contribution of this study is the development of an attitudinal instrumental to assess young children's attitude to science in the context of their attitudes to school and other subjects; this is the first time that such an instrument is developed for this age level. The attitudinal scales developed are: "liking school," "independent investigator," "science enthusiasm," "social context," and "difficult subject." Pell and Jarvis point out that "there is clear evidence that quite young pupils can provide worthwhile indicators of how they view science" (p. 859). Their findings confirm other studies that young pupils are enthusiastic about science, despite that it is perceived as a difficult subject. As the children grow older, however, there is a decline in their enthusiasm for science. This study indicates that the development of attitudinal measures for young children can enrich science educators' knowledge about the decline of enthusiasm for science in the primary school and thus it has implications for teacher professional development and educational policies.

Affect and Science Teaching

It is encouraging that in the last few years science educators also investigate the relationship between science teaching and emotion at the early childhood education level. Zembylas' (2002, 2004b, 2004c) reports on a three-year ethnographic case study of an experienced early childhood teacher provide details about the ways in which teacher emotion can contribute both to the educational experiences of children and to the professional experiences of the teacher herself. He argues that positive and negative emotions play a significant role in a teacher's construction of her science pedagogy, curriculum planning and relationships with young children and colleagues. Zembylas emphasizes how the emotional aspects of the science teacher-self in becoming or being a science teacher and the development of positive social and emotional relationships with children are inextricably linked. As he suggests, "If we want progress in science education, we need to look more carefully at the emotions of science teaching, both negative and positive emotions, and use this knowledge to improve the working environment of science teachers" (2002, p. 98), as well as the emotional development of young children.

Zembylas' work develops a conceptual and methodological framework that is based on an interdisciplinary approach in researching emotions. Theoretically, his analysis draws upon poststructuralist tools such as Foucauldian genealogy. For this reason, Zembylas terms this work as *genealogies of emotions in science teaching*. The aim of genealogy is to explore the conditions under which early childhood teachers' emotions in science teaching are shaped and performed, to discover how these emotions are "disciplined," to destabilize and denaturalize the regime that demands the expression of certain emotions and the disciplining of others, and to elucidate the *emotional rules* that are imposed and the boundaries entailed by those rules. This kind of research also demonstrates how the performance of emotional labor is an important aspect of reality in science teaching (Zembylas, 2004b). The teacher in Zembylas' study is willing to do the emotional labor that involves some suffering because the emotional rewards are gratifying (e.g., relationships with her students). Thus, it is suggested that a perspective on emotion in early childhood science education may focus, at least in part, on the functions of emotion in creating inspiring emotional cultures in the classroom that enrich children's socio-emotional development. Also, recognizing that teachers and young children are agents in constructing such cultures, educators, teachers, and administrators are more likely to grasp the complexities and possibilities of (positive and negative) emotional labor in early childhood science education.

Finally, Zembylas' (2004c) account on some emotional issues in early childhood science teaching illustrates the role of emotion in establishing and maintaining a teacher's self-esteem. This is particularly significant given the existing documentation that early childhood teachers often lack confidence in their science knowledge and skills and thus avoid teaching science. These findings may offer a promising route for early childhood teachers' efforts to construct way the empower themselves and overcome the feeling of personal inadequacy and powerlessness. Thus, to investigate early childhood teachers' self-confidence in science teaching is to describe how teachers struggle to reject normative discourses and find their own voice. This finding has significant implications because many early childhood teachers of science have limited confidence toward science and their ability to teach science (Brickhouse & Bodner, 1992; Watters et al., 2000). Zembylas' entire work suggests that a teacher's emotions impact children at the early childhood level by influencing the development of a supportive or discouraging emotional culture in the classroom for learning science.

Two other recent studies are focused on early-years educators' attitudes toward science and/or science teaching as well as the implications of those attitudes. Kallery (2001) develops a questionnaire to find Greek early-years educators' attitudes to astrology and astronomy. The results indicate that a large fraction (59%) of the one hundred and three educators who participated in this study cannot distinguish between science and pseudoscience. This research confirms other studies that the content knowledge and understanding of early childhood educators in science is limited. The implications are important, because as Kallery argues, it is possible that the educators' attitudes may also influence not only what is presented to young children, but also how it is presented to them. Therefore, limited knowledge or negative attitudes of early childhood teachers of science may have a negative impact on children's affective domain (Coulson, 1992). This implication is something which highlights the need for further investigation of early childhood teachers' attitudes toward science.

A study by Cho, Kim, and Choi (2003) explores early childhood teachers' attitudes toward science teaching. This study is built on the same assumptions as the previous one by Kallery, that is, early childhood teachers are often hesitant about teaching science, because they lack confidence in their conceptual knowledge and understanding of teaching science. The goal of this research is to develop a scale that can measure early childhood teachers' attitudes toward science teaching. Although the reliability is high, the construct validity of the scale is not fully supported by the factor analyses. The participants in this study were 100 early childhood teachers from New York City. According to the findings, early childhood teachers express concerns or fear regarding teaching science to young children, something that is associated with an emotional and affective domain of teaching science. Also, it is shown that these teachers may not have clear scientific concepts although they are familiar with concrete activities to teaching science to young children. This finding demonstrates that early childhood teachers' concerns are focused on managing hands-on activities rather than acquiring a solid content knowledge of science. Both the Cho et al. and Kallery studies are important because there is little information about the prevailing attitudes of early childhood educators in science education and the implications for teaching science.

Finally, two other articles focus on how best early years teachers can be inducted into the teaching and learning of science, and what some didactic strategies may be used for the (social, cognitive, and emotional) initiation of preschool children to science. Watts and Walsh (1997) report on the value of diaries and narratives in exploring teachers' reflections and feelings about science—such as despair, fear, strangeness, joy, excitement, and powerlessness. They provide several examples from their studies on early childhood teachers who teach science and draw attention to the inner emotional world of teachers' thoughts and imaginations. Watts and Walsh suggest that looking at teachers' diaries, autobiographies, and narratives can reveal breaks in patterns and irregularities and enable both personal reflection and reorientation of meaning and understanding. The researchers also emphasize that the induction of early childhood teachers into the teaching of science is not an easy or straightforward task. Similar to Zembylas' writings, Watts and Walsh's work indicates how the conceptual and emotional struggles of teachers may impact their own learning in science as well as the learning and emotional well-being of their students.

Ravanis and Bagakis (1998) discuss the sociocognitive perspective of different didactic strategies for science education at the kindergarten level. Although affect is not explicitly addressed in this framework, there is reference to the significance of constructing pedagogical activities that promote social, emotional, and cognitive aims. The authors describe their theoretical framework—neo-Piagetian, socioconstructive, and Vygotskian—and provide examples of teaching interventions from their research with young children. In these examples, they show how the understanding of a scientific phenomenon involves the development of children's social, cognitive, and emotional abilities. Although this type of work is in its beginning stages, it is valuable in linking specific teaching interventions with young children's development at various levels—something that is missing from most early years pedagogical accounts; in such accounts, the suggested interventions for the affective development of children in science are not usually grounded in specific research findings.

Critical Commentary

The studies reviewed here range from descriptive, to quantitative measures, to ethnographic and qualitative methodologies. These studies make a valuable contribution to the exploration of affect in early childhood science education, highlighting the advantages of taking into consideration affective issues as well as the challenges of exploring such issues theoretically or methodologically. Most of the studies cited in this review—especially those which use qualitative methodologies—report the multilevel role of affect in science teaching and learning. Central to these studies is how affects enrich or often impede learning and teaching. These findings include claims that an affective engagement with science is inevitable and thus further exploration of the role of affects helps young children and teachers gain a deeper understanding and appreciation of the intensity, commitment, passion, and self-esteem that are often associated with science. Yet, policy makers increasingly focus their attention on high-stakes standardized tests as measures of success in science learning. As a result, according to some of these studies, children's affective engagement with science is gradually diminishing as they grow older. Other studies—especially those by Osborne and Brady, Zembylas, and Siraj-Batchford and Siraj-Blatchford—emphasize the importance of studying and theorizing early childhood science education on the basis of the interrelatedness of emotion and cognition. This view acknowledges the social and cultural dimensions of learning and teaching experiences in science, and does not neglect that these experiences are felt and embodied. The advantages of this perspective are twofold: (a) It draws attention to the importance of studying early childhood science education in cultural and political contexts where learning and teaching experiences are constantly at stake; (b) an integrated notion of emotion and cognition—rather than a dichotomy between them—provides a useful approach that refuses the singularity of each "component" separately.

Clearly, the theoretical assumptions grounding the studies reviewed here are different. These assumptions shift dramatically, for example, when one moves from studies that examine "attitudes" to those that explore "emotion" or "affect," more generally. Undoubtedly, each perspective has a lot to offer, if one considers that the research output in this area has not yet flourished. It is important for early childhood science educators to discuss and analyze the advantages and disadvantages of each perspective. For instance, employing more holistic and/or poststructuralist perspectives in understanding affect in early childhood science education forces science educators to constantly revisit their assumptions with respect to what constitutes "significant" learning and teaching science.

Clearly, an area that needs more work in the future—given the prevalence of cognitive perspectives—is theorizing the interrelatedness between emotion and cognition. It is certainly encouraging that scholarship in other fields provides useful groundwork, i.e., that the mind is actually a seamless blend of thinking and feeling (e.g., see, Damasio, 1994, 1999, 2003; LeDoux, 1998, 2002). The issue here is not so much to delineate the clear "boundaries" between emotion and cognition, but to problematize these boundaries and to show how they can be constructed differently in more holistic, meaningful, and productive ways (Dai & Sternberg, 2004).

In general, it seems that the role of affect in early childhood science education deserves further attention. The relatively few studies conducted so far within the last ten years emphasize that early childhood educators should consider the implications of the affects aspects of learning and teaching science in planning effective instruction for young children. It is surprising, for example, that despite the emphasis of the National Research Council (with the discussion on the personal and social perspective of science) and the American Association for the Advancement of Science (with the value put on the notion of "habits of mind"), there hasn't been much research output investigating the link between affect and science at the early childhood level. However, according to these organizations, as well as the findings of the studies reviewed here, systematic attention to the role of affect in science education needs to be paid early on when children are young (see also Eshach & Fried, 2005), if we are to accomplish and sustain positive attitudes toward science.

IMPLICATIONS AND FUTURE DIRECTIONS

Early childhood science educators have approached research on the role of affect with a lot of skepticism. They have instead focused most of their efforts to explore young children's cognitive development as something separate from their social and emotional development. Although in the last few years the research on affect in early childhood science education has made some progress toward understanding the role of emotion in early childhood science, much work is needed. One thing that is clear so far is that both teaching and learning science are necessarily affective. Apart from the notion that affective issues have important implications on curricular decisions and classroom culture, one can argue that a number of fundamental problems remain unresolved in the area of research on affect in early childhood science education. These problems are constitutive aspects of possible directions for research.

For early childhood teachers, the emotions of discomfort, lack of self-esteem, and anxiety they experience when they deal with science can arguably lead to many negative implications from refusal to teach science to stress and burnout in the worse case. Given these findings, the study of teacher emotion becomes an important area of research in early childhood science education. Future studies can focus on different ideas such as the influence of affective issues on a teacher's self-concept, perception, and judgment, how young children are influences by their teachers' emotions, and how teacher emotions influence curricular decisions and curriculum reform, all in the context of early childhood science education.

For young children, one of the research questions that need to be explored is *how* affect influences successes and failures in science learning and what the "appropriate" science instruction for young children is. Central to this issue is the need to develop teaching practices that promote passion, empowerment and self-development. Most work so far has been descriptive in terms of identifying factors relevant to affects and how these influence curriculum, teaching, and learning in early childhood science. Effective teaching strategies that promote conceptual understanding of science are those that also support the development of young children's self-esteem and their capacity for accepting ambiguity and analyzing their choices and actions early on in their lives. The well-known notion of "scaffolding" (Collins, Brown, & Newman, 1989; Vygotsky, 1997), for instance, has important emotional aspects that need to be considered, both in theory and in practice. Scaffolding is not only related to strengthening children's intellectual capability, but also to helping children cope with the emotional demands of making mistakes, undertake tasks with ambiguity and avoid confrontation with others—what has been called "emotional scaffolding" (Rosiek, 2003). This tool, as well as others, can be used to promote emotional literacy, equity, and interest in early childhood science education, and provide learning environments that encourage exploration and choices (cf. Matthews, 2004).

Missing from current research in this area is also an exploration of affect as embedded in school culture, ideology, discourse, and power relations. Very few studies pay attention to political and cultural issues—e.g., how different pedagogical practices establish and regulate emotional rules and require emotion management in the context of early childhood science education. While Osborne and Brady, as well as Zembylas' studies appear to be an exception, there needs to be further evidence of their claims since their work is based on an examination of a few case studies.

Finally, both new methodological and theoretical issues need to be considered in future research in this area. The further development of appropriate research methods and instruments that allow researchers to analyze the different affective aspects of children's learning activities and teachers' pedagogical practices is crucial. For example, it will be useful to employ multiple methods such as the combination of quantitative and qualitative methods or the use of longitudinal studies. Similarly, theoretical ideas beyond constructivism (e.g., poststructuralist views) offer important directions away from a decontextualized analysis of affect.

SUMMARY

Some important accomplishments have been made in the last few years in the area of early childhood science education. Early childhood science educators have begun to acknowledge the importance of affect and its implications for teaching and learning science to young children. Acknowledging that affect is the very site of transforming early childhood science teaching and learning, educators can explore alternative ideas and new tools for initiating and sustaining self-development in young children. Only then science educators will be able to document in rich and reliable ways the emotional experiences of young children and teachers in the classroom and advance the development of multidimensional theories of affect in early childhood science education.

NOTES

1. "Conceptual change" is broadly defined as learning that changes some existing conceptions. The conceptual change perspective of learning has been described by Posner and his colleagues (Posner et al., 1982; Strike & Posner, 1985, 1992). This perspective has been widely influential and generative within the field of science education during the past three decades (Duit & Treagust, 2003). Science educators have proposed theories that build on Posner et al.'s model and attempt to explain how students change their conceptions when they learn certain scientific concepts (Chinn & Brewer, 1993; Chi et al., 1994; Duit, 1999; Thagard, 1992; Vosniadou & Brewer, 1987, 1994).

2. One of the difficulties in discussing research on affect is the confusion over terminology (McLeod, 1992). Thus, it is useful to make here some clarifications about various terms that are being used in the literature on affect because they can have different meanings. Attitude is generally defined as a predisposition to respond in a favorable or unfavorable way with respect to a person, and objects, or an idea. This definition has three components: (a) the emotional response to the object, (b) the behavior toward the object, and (c) beliefs about the object. In other words, this definition suggests that emotions contribute to attitude formation; they are not attitudes (Rajecki, 1982, as cited in Hart, 1989). Attitudes refer to a total situation that involves emotions, beliefs, and behaviors whereas emotions are considered as acts or practices that are not only biologically based (i.e., feelings), but also constructed based on social rules and codes. Further, another distinction between attitudes and emotions is that the latter are relatively short in duration whereas the former are often long term (McLeod, 1992).

3. Poststructural analysis questions structural interpretations of knowledge and values. The shift from structural to poststructural analysis began literally in literary criticism and linguistics and then spread to many other disciplines. In simple terms, structuralists form models and develop systematic inventories of elements that would account for the form and meaning of texts, while poststructuralists investigate the way in which this project is subverted by the workings of the texts themselves.

4. See also the special issues on "Science education and affect" of the *International Journal of Science Education*, Vol. 25, issue 9, edited by Alsop and Watts (2003). Despite the immense contribution of this special issue, there is no article that explicitly addresses early childhood science education.

REFERENCES

Alsop, S. (2001). Seeking emotional involvement in science education: Food-chains and webs. *School Science Review, 83*(302), 63–68.

Alsop, S. (Ed.). (2005). *Beyond Cartesian dualism: Encountering affect in the teaching and learning of science.* Dordrecht: Springer.

Alsop, S., & Watts, M. (2003). Science education and affect. *International Journal of Science Education, 25,* 1043–1047.

Bredekamp, S., & Copple, S. (1997). *Developmentally appropriate practice in early childhood problems.* Washington, DC: National Association for the Education of Young Children.

Brickhouse, N., & Bodner, G. (1992). The beginning science teacher: Classroom narratives of convictions and constraints. *Journal of Research in Science Teaching, 29,* 471–485.

Chaille, C., & Britain, L. (1997). *The young child as scientist: A constructivist approach to early childhood science education.* New York: Longman.

Chi, M. T. H., Slotta, J. D., & deLeeuw, N. (1994). From things to processes: A theory of conceptual change for learning science concepts. *Learning & Instruction, 4,* 27–43.

Chinn, C. A., & Brewer, W. F. (1993). The role of anomalous data in knowledge acquisition: A theoretical framework and implications for science instruction. *Review of Educational Research, 63,* 1–49.

Chittenden, E., & Jones, J. (1998). Science assessment in early childhood programs. *Dialogue on early childhood science, mathematics, and technology education.* Washington, DC: Project 2061, American Association for the Advancement of Science.

Cho, H-S., Kim, J., & Choi, D. H. (2003). Early childhood teachers' attitudes toward science teaching: A scale validation study. *Educational Research Quarterly, 27*(2), 33–42.

Collins, A., Brown, J. S., & Newman, S. E. (1989). Cognitive apprenticeship: Teaching the craft of reading, writing and mathematics. In L. B. Resnick (Ed.), *Knowing, learning, and instruction: Essays in honor of Robert Glaser* (pp. 453–494). Hillsdale, NJ: Erlbaum.

Coulson, R. (1992). Development of an instrument for measuring attitudes of early childhood educators towards science. *Research in Science Education, 22,* 101–105.

Dai, D. Y., & Sternberg, R. J. (Eds.). (2004). *Motivation, emotion, and cognition: Integrative perspectives on intellectual functioning and development.* Mawah, NJ: Lawrence Erlbaum Associates.

Damasio, A. R. (1994). *Descartes' error: Emotion, reason, and the human brain.* New York: Avon Books.

Damasio, A. R. (1999). *The feeling of what happens: Body and emotion in the making of consciousness.* New York: Harcourt Brace & Co.

Damasio, A. R. (2003). *Looking for Spinoza: Joy, sorrow and the feeling brain.* New York: Harcourt Brace & Co.

Dole, J. A., & Sinatra, G. M. (1998). Reconceptualizing changes in the cognitive construction of knowledge. *Educational Psychologist, 33*(2/3), 109–128.

Duit, R. (1999), Conceptual change approaches in science education. In W. Schnotz, S. Vosniadou, & M. Carretero (Eds.), *New perspectives in conceptual change* (pp. 263–282). Kidlington, Oxford: Elsevier Science.

Duit, R., & Treagust, D. (2003). Conceptual change: A powerful framework for improving science teaching and learning. *International Journal of Science Education, 25,* 671–688.

Elkind, D. (1998). Educating young children in math, science, and technology. *Dialogue on early childhood science, mathematics, and technology education.* Washington, DC: Project 2061, American Association for the Advancement of Science.

Eshach, H., & Fried, M. (2005). Should science by taught in early childhood? *Journal of Science Education & Technology, 14,* 315–336.

French, L. (2004). Science as the center of a coherent, integrated early childhood curriculum. *Early Childhood Research Quarterly, 19,* 138–149.

Hadjigeorgiu, Y. (2001). The role of wonder and 'romance' in early childhood science education. *International Journal of Early Years Education, 9,* 63–69.

Harlan, J. (1988). *Science experiences for the early childhood years.* Columbus, OH: Merrill.

Hart, L. (1989). Describing the affective domain: Saying what we mean. In D. McLeod & V. Adams (Eds.), *Affect and mathematical problem solving* (pp. 37–45). New York: Spring-Verlag.

Holt, B. (1993). *Science with young children.* Washington, DC: National Association for the Education of Young Children.

Howe, A. C. (1993). Science in early childhood education. In B. Spodek (Ed.), *Handbook of research on the education of young children* (pp. 225–235). New York: Macmillan.

Hyson, M. (2004). *The emotional development of young children: Building an emotion-centered curriculum.* New York: Teachers College Press.

Inagaki, K. (1992). Piagentian and post-piagentian conceptions of development and their implications for science education in early childhood. *Early Childhood Research Quarterly, 7,* 115–133.

Kallery, M. (2001). Early-years educators' attitudes to science and pseudo-science: The case of astronomy and astrology. *European Journal of Teacher Education, 24,* 329–342.

Kamii, C., & DeVries, R. (1993). *Physical knowledge in preschool education: Implications of Piaget's theory.* New York: Teachers College Press.

Landry, C., Foreman, G. (1999). Research on early science education. In C. Seefeldt (Ed.), *The early childhood curriculum* (pp. 133–158). New York: Teachers College Press.

Laukenmann, M., Bleicher, M., Fuß, S., Gläser-Zikuda, M., Mayring, P., & von Phöneck, C. (2003). An investigation of the influence of emotions factors on learning in physics instruction. *International Journal of Science Education, 25,* 489–507.

LeDoux, J. (1998). *The emotional brain: The mysterious underpinnings of emotional life.* New York: Touchstone Books.

LeDoux, J. (2002). *The synaptic self: How our brains become who we are.* New York: Viking Press.

Lemke, J. L. (2001). Articulating communities: Sociocultural perspectives on science education. *Journal of Research on Science Teaching, 38,* 296–316.

Matthews, B. (2004). Promoting emotional literacy, equity and interest in science lessons for 11–14 year olds: The 'Improving Science and Emotional Development' project. *International Journal of Science Education, 26,* 281–308.

McLeod, D. B. (1992). Research on affect in mathematics education: A reconceptualization. In D. A. Grouws (Ed.), *Handbook of research on mathematics learning and teaching* (pp. 575–596). New York: Macmillan.

National Research Council. (1996). *National science education standards.* Washington, DC: National Academy Press.

Osborne, M. D. (2000). A rose in a mirror. *Research in Science Education, 30,* 107–122.

Osborne, M. D., & Brady, D. J. (2001). The magical and the real in science and in teaching: Joy and paradox control. In A. C. Barton & M. D. Osborne (Eds.), *Marginalized discourses and science education: Reframing science for all* (pp. 35–57). New York: Peter Lang.

Osborne, M. D., & Brady, D. J. (2002). Imagining the new: Constructing a space for creativity in science. In E. Mirochnik & D. Sherman (Eds.), *Passion and pedagogy: Relation, creation, and transformation in teaching* (pp. 317–332). New York: Peter Lang.

Osborne, J., Simon, S., & Collins, S. (2003). Attitudes towards science: A review of the literature and its implications. *International Journal of Science Education, 25,* 1049–1079.

Pell, T., & Jarvis, T. (2001). Developing attitude to science scales for use with children of ages from five to eleven years. *International Journal of Science Education, 23,* 847–862.

Pintrich, P. (1999). Motivational beliefs as resources for an constraints on conceptual change. In W. Schnotz, S. Vosniadou, & M. Carretero (Eds.), *New perspectives on conceptual change* (pp. 33–50). Kidlington, Oxford: Elsevier Science.

Posner, G., Strike, K., Hewson, P., & Gertzog, W. (1982). Accommodation of a scientific conception: Toward a theory of conceptual change. *Science Education, 66,* 211–227.

Ravanis, K. (1994). The discovery of elementary magnetic properties in pre-school age: A qualitative and quantitative research within a Piagetian framework. *European Early Childhood Education Research Journal, 2*(2), 79–91.

Ravanis, K., & Bagakis, G. (1998). Science education in kindergarten: Socio-cognitive perspective. *International Journal of Early Years Education, 6,* 315–327.

Raver, C. (2002). Emotions matter: Making the case for the role of young children's emotional development for early school readiness. *Social Policy Report/Society for Research in Child Development, 16*(3). Available online: http://www.srcd.org/spr.html

Rosiek, J. (2003). Emotional scaffolding: An exploration of the teacher knowledge at the intersection of student emotion and the subject matter. *Journal of Teacher Education, 54,* 399–412.

Santos, F., & Mortimer, E. (2003). How emotions shape the relationship between a chemistry teacher and her high school students. *International Journal of Science Education, 25,* 1095–1110.

Seedfeldt, C., & Galper, A. (2002). *Active experiences for active children: Science.* Saddle River, NJ: Merrill/Prentice-Hall.

Sharp, J. (1995). Children's astronomy: Implications for curriculum development at key stage 1 and the future of infant science in England and Wales. *International Journal of Early Years Education, 3*(3), 17–49.

Shonkoff, J., & Phillips, D. (Eds.). (2000). *From neurons to neighborhoods: The sciences of early childhood development.* Washington, DC: National Academy Press.

Simon, H. A. (1982). Comments. In M. S. Clark & S. T. Fiske (Eds.), *Affect and cognition: The seventeenth annual Carnegie symposium on cognition* (pp. 333–342). Hillsdale, NJ: Erlbaum.

Sinatra, G. M., & Pintrich, P. R. (Eds.). (2003). *International conceptual change.* Mahwah, NJ: Erlbaum.

Siraj-Blatchford, J., & Siraj-Blatchford, I. (2002). Discriminating between schemes and schema in young children's emergent learning of science and technology. *International Journal of Early Years Education, 10*(3), 205–214.

Solomonidou, C., & Kakana, D. (2000). Preschool children's conceptions about the electric current and the functioning of electric appliances. *European Early Childhood Education Research Journal, 8*(1), 95–111.

Spodek, B. (1986). Development, values and knowledge in the kindergarten curriculum. In B. Spodek (Ed.), *Today's kindergarten: Exploring the knowledge base, expanding the curriculum* (pp. 32–47). New York: Teachers College Press.

Spodek, B. (1992). Early childhood curriculum and cultural definitions of knowledge. In B. Spodek & O. Saracho (Eds.), *Issues in early childhood curriculum* (pp. 1–20). New York: Teachers College Press.

Strike, K., & Posner, G. (1985). A conceptual change view of learning and understanding. In L. T. West & A. L. Pines (Eds.), *Cognitive structure and coual change* (pp. 211–331). Orlando, FL: Academic Press.

Strike, K., & Posner, G. (1992). A revisionist theory of conceptual change. In R. Duschi & R. Hamilton (Eds.), *Philosophy of science, cognitive psychology, and educational theory and practice* (pp. 147–176). Albany: State University of New York Press.

Thagard, P. (1992). *Conceptual revolutions.* Princeton, NJ: Princeton University Press.

Vosniadou, S., & Brewer, W. (1994). Mental models of the day/night cycle. *Cognitive Science, 18,* 123–183.

Vosniadou, S., & Brewer, W. (1992). Mental models of the earth: A study of conceptual change in childhood. *Cognitive Psychology, 24,* 535–585.

Vosniadou, S., & Brewer, W. (1987). Theories of knowledge restructuring in development. *Review of Educational Research, 57*, 51–67.

Vygotsky, L. S. (1997). *Educational psychology.* New York: Saint Lucie Press.

Watters, J. J., Diezmann, C. M., Grieshaber, S. J., & Davis, J. M. (2000). Enhancing science education for young children: A contemporary initiative. *Australian Journal of Early Childhood Education, 26*(2), 1–7.

Watts, M. (2005). Orchestrating the confluence: A discussion of science, passion, and poetry. In S. Alsop (Ed.), *Beyond Cartesian dualism: Encountering affect in the teaching and learning of science* (pp. 149–159). Dordrecht: Springer.

Watts, M. (2001). Science and poetry: Passion vs. prescription in school science? *International Journal of Science Education, 23*, 197–208.

Watts, M., & Alsop, S. (1997). A feeling for learning: Modeling affective learning in school science. *The Curriculum Journal, 8*, 351–365.

Watts, M., & Walsh, A. (1997). Affecting primary science: A case from the early years. *Early Childhood and Care, 129*, 51–61.

Wieder, S., & Greenspan, S. (1993). The emotional basis of learning. In B. Spodek (Ed.), *Handbook of research on the education of young children* (pp. 77–87). New York: Macmillan.

Woods, P. (1996). *Researching the art of teaching: Ethnography for educational use.* London: Routlege.

Zembylas, M. (2002). Constructing genealogies of teachers' emotions in science teaching. *Journal of Research in Science Teaching, 39*, 79–103.

Zembylas, M. (2004a). Young children's emotional practices while engaged in long-term science investigations. *Journal of Research in Science Teaching, 41*, 693–719.

Zembylas, M. (2004b). Emotion metaphors and emotional labor in science teaching. *Science Education, 55*, 301–324.

Zembylas, M. (2004c). Emotional issues in science teaching: A case study of a teacher's views. *Research in Science Education, 34*, 343–364.

Zembylas, M. (2005a). *Teaching with emotion: A postmodern enactment.* Greenwich, CT: Information Age Publishing.

Zembylas, M. (2005b). Three perspectives on linking the cognitive and the emotional in science learning: Conceptual change, socio-constructivism and poststructuralism. *Studies in Science Education, 41*, 91–116.

CHAPTER 5

NEW TECHNOLOGIES IN EARLY CHILDHOOD

Partners in Play?

Doris Bergen

One of the major characteristics of young children's play is that whatever is in their environment can be used as play materials. For example, the magazine left lying on the floor, the last bites of cereal on the high chair tray, the mud in the yard, the car keys, or the television remote control can all become play facilitators. The essence of play (at any age) is in its ability to enable players to transform their world through their active engagement, flexible thought, and creative control, using whatever materials are available to them. Every object in the environment provides "affordances" that elicit actions; that is, that suggest ways it can be used in work or in play (Carr, 2000; Gibson, E. J., 1969; Gibson, J. J., 1979; Norman, 1993). For young children play affordances suggest that the magazine can be shaken and the pages ripped; the cereal bits rolled or piled; the mud squeezed, pressed and spread; the car keys shaken and banged against furniture; and the remote control pressed on and off (or thrown across the room). Of course, because these actions can then be used symbolically, all of these afforded objects can be used in a pretend script (e.g., going shopping) or a social game (e.g., hide and find). Some objects have a wide range of affordances while others suggest only one or two ways to act upon them. When

Contemporary Perspectives on Science and Technology in Early Childhood Education, pages 87–104
Copyright © 2008 by Information Age Publishing

87

toys are designed for play, the affordances of the toys may be very specific or very general. For example, dolls or blocks suggest a wide range of affordances while puzzles are designed with a particular affordance in mind. This may be why dolls and blocks can hold attention for a very long age period, while puzzles often have a short age period of interest, just until mastery is achieved. (Puzzle pieces, of course, can also be used in symbolic ways or in games that can extend their play possibilities.)

Although in present parlance, the term "technology" is usually used to mean electronically-enhanced objects, many objects have been designed over the centuries that have been used for "the change and manipulation of the human environment" which is a major purpose for which technology is created (see, Encyclopedia Britannica; www.britannica.com). Objects such as wheels, tools, forks, combs, and steps, as well as toasters, automobiles, sewing machines, and typewriters are all examples of technology. Technology involves design that meets a need, it is multidimensional, it involves values, and it is both socially shaping and shaped (see, http://atschool.eduweb.co.uk/trinity/watitec.html for further discussion of the nature of technology).

While children in earlier times had a few specially designed toys (a type of technology), today their environment is filled with toy technology of both the electronic and non-electronic kind. The recent pervasive electronic technological invasion of the toy industry includes toys ranging from simple plush toys that say or sing a few phrases when a button is pushed or a string is activated to sophisticated robotic animals or childlike characters that simulate many of the actions of real animals or children. The toy industry is producing about 20 new "interactive character products" each year (Newman, 1999). Even familiar pretend-enhancing toy figures now come with computer-chips that enable them to talk. Many of the latest interactive character products purport to teach young children various skills, such as reading, writing, and learning letter names and numbers. For elementary age children, there is a plethora of computer-chip-enhanced game playing devices, and these have left many of the old-style toys that used to appeal to children this age in the dust. In recent years, the top selling toys have all contained electronically-enhanced features. Although all of these toys are considered interactive, they range from ones that allow much child initiative and control to ones that make the toy the "actor" and the child the "reactor" (see, Bergen, 2001).

The question that is often raised by early childhood educators and parents is what the effect on play these toy technologies are having, and subsequently what that means for young children's developmental progress. Most present research involves observing how children initially interact with the toys but there is as yet little research on the effects of these toys on children's brain organization, learning, behavior, animistic thinking, theory of mind development, or social cognition. While research regarding children's development through play with "old" technology (i.e., non-electronic toys) is extensive (see, Fromberg & Bergen, 2006), there has been only limited research on children's play with "new" technology—that is, electronically-enhanced toys and specially designed computer software, videos, or other media (also see, Fromberg & Bergen, 2006). Much of the research related to young children that does exist involves short-term studies in preschools or single case studies of toddlers. Thus, the published literature on effects of electronically-enhanced toys or child-consumer-directed media (i.e., "new" technology) is primarily based on opinions, not research, at the present time. In a recent SRCD Social Policy Report, Wartella, Caplovitz, and Lee (2004) assert that although "Interactive media have come of age...Little systematic research has been conducted to either legitimize or dispute claims about the impact of interactive media on children's cognitive and social development... [especially with media]...such as handheld devices, wireless technology, and interactive toys" (p. 1).

This review will focus on two particular types of technology-enhanced interactive media used by young children: robotic toys (toys with embedded computer chips that trigger verbal comments or sounds, movements, and/or facial/body changes designed to promote child/toy interaction) and computer software that promotes similar interactive features (including robot/computer interfaces and "child-friendly" learning programs). It will discuss initial research on effects of such "new" technology play on the development of four groups: infants and toddlers; preschoolers, early elementary schoolers, and young children with disabilities.

According to Luckin et al. (2003), technology-enhanced interactive media have the potential to "provide support to young learners" by playing a "collaborative partnership role" (p. 166). Many of them use specially designed programs that attempt to promote learning through some type of scaffolding approach. This review will evaluate potential effects of such media in relation to three affordance criteria suggested by Carr (2000) and three play qualities discussed by Kafai (2006). Carr's affordance criteria include the following: transparency, challenge, and accessibility. Transparency refers to the ability to understand the concepts inherent in the toy or object. Papert (1980) indicated that physical affordances of objects can create mental schemes or models that increase transparency of understanding in other domains. For example, the puzzle has immediate transparency because it signals to the player whether performance is accurate. An electronically-enhanced toy or computer software that signals the child's progress or success would also have transparency. The second criteria, challenge, involves having affordances that increase possibilities for action rather than narrowing options. Blocks and sand have extensive possibilities for action, while an electronically-enhanced toy that has only one opportunity for reaction or interaction would have little challenge. For example, if the toy makes one sound each time it is pressed and has no other manipulative devices or sounds, it would have low challenge. On the other hand, if it makes a number of sounds but they are random rather than activated by pressing particular places, then it would not have transparency. Accessibility is related to the amount and type of participation that a toy affords, such as parent-child or peer collaboration. Some types of toy technology afford extensive participation while others allow only one participator. Also, a toy might involve much child participatory interaction with the toy or be lacking in ways to enhance child participation in its use. All three of these qualities interface; for example, transparency is more likely to facilitate accessibility, and challenge is usually increased if the other two factors are present.

According to schema theory, young children construct schema (organizing designs that impose structure on the environment), and learning occurs when they "encounter environments with the kinds of affordances they need to elaborate these prepared structures" (Resnick, 1994, p. 476). Resnick suggests a "situated cognitive perspective," however, which emphasizes the influence of particular environments and the "knowledge attuned to those environments" (p. 476) rather than "built-in" general schema, and she also stresses the social nature of cognitive development. A major question therefore, is whether technology-enhanced play materials differentially affect both cognitive schema and situated cognition.

Kafai (2006) suggests that toys and software with possibilities for encouraging all types of play—practice, pretense, and games—are more likely to be of interest to children and promote developmental progress. Practice play involves the self-directed repetition and elaboration of actions until they are mastered. Symbolic play allows the child to enter into the "as if" world where the risks are only pretend and the child is powerful. Game play provides challenge and competition, either with a peer, with oneself, or with imaginary opponents, and, if the game is lost, there are no lasting consequences. These various aspects of play are especially relevant for the affordance of challenge because flexibility of response is a component of challenge. The more varieties of play that can be promoted through the electronically-enhanced technology, the more likely it is to engage children's interest and motivation. However, the types of play facilitated and the affordances provided by electronically-enhanced technology play materials vary widely in products designed for the early childhood years, and their effects on development may differ depending on the age of the child.

ELECTRONICALLY-ENHANCED PLAY OF INFANTS
AND TODDLERS

Although there have been educational publications pointing with alarm to the possible negative results for infants and toddlers of exposure to new technology, it is still unclear as to what the positive or negative effects of having technologically sophisticated very young children might be. Recently there was a mother's question in a newspaper parent advice column asking whether her husband's purchase of a computer for their 18-month-old child was a good idea (Brett, 2006). The advice included having the child sit on the parent's lap when it is used rather than having it be an "electronic babysitter." Parental reports of the amount of television, video, and computer exposure that children under three are experiencing have been reviewed by Jordan and Woodward (2001). In this study, parents indicated that their 2–3-year-olds averaged about 2½ hours of television watching and spent about 1½ hours with a VCR each day. These parents did report that their children averaged more time with books (46 minutes) than with computers (17 minutes). The American Academy of Pediatrics issued a recommendation in 1995, however, that children under two should not watch television and expressed concerns about ergonomic problems of young children at computers (Bergen, 2002).

Nevertheless, almost every new toy for infants and toddlers has computer chips that enable the toy to produce words, the alphabet, and songs. Many also have automated actions that can continue for extensive time periods without adult intervention. Manufacturers say that parents want to buy such toys because they will enhance their child's early literacy development, but there is presently no definitive research with these very young children that establishes this relationship, and there is at least some question as to how much the parental motivation is for an "electronic babysitter." Although many positive claims have been made by producers of the programs and software used in these technologies, there is scant research focusing on exploring cognitive, social, emotional, or even physical effects, and very little funding to encourage such research. Some toy companies are interested in this issue and are beginning to fund research of this type. This author is presently conducting collaborative research with a toy company to investigate the potential effect of one of their toys on early language and actions, as well as on its enhancement of parent-child interactions. Preliminary results indicate that the interactive toy promotes child exploratory and practice play behaviors but that when parents interact with the child and toy, there are more social games and sustained play activity (Bergen, 2006a).

There have been a few case studies showing how young children's behavior is affected by technology play. One of these is of a 2½–3½ year old who experienced long-term exposure to CD-ROM storybooks, as well as to other book reading (Smith, 2002). After learning how to manipulate the CD-ROM (Talking Books) activities using the "clicker," the child was able to activate the hypertext characters and change the presentations, which resulted in his generating various patterns of response in non-electronic situations. For example, the researcher documented not only the child's facility with the CD-ROM but also the "meaning making" of the child in other contexts, in which he used the actions and patterns derived from this media. For example, he pretended to "click" his father's actions and responded with appropriate actions when his father "clicked" him, and he reproduced patterns of response that fit the models shown on the CD-ROM. The author states that for this child, "it was just as typical to pretend to be a hypertext object on the computer screen as to pretend to be Bat-man" (p. 8). She concludes that this activity facilitated his language development and book-related dramatic play. The exact nature of the CD-ROM influence as compared to other book-related activity is unclear, however. What is clear from this report is that even very young children can use electronically-enhanced technology to elaborate on their play skills. The actions (and presumably the cognitive schema) related to the electronic toy were incorporated into the child's other play activities. Thus, the assimilative quality that Piaget discussed was as evident when the play materials were these electronically-enhanced toys as is usually the case with more traditional toys.

In regard to the criteria discussed by Carr and by Kafai, the infant/toddler toys are usually transparent (e.g., effects result from specific child actions) and involve extensive practice play (i.e., the actions are repeated to mastery). The challenge level of most is usually appropriate for a young child; however, many do not have "levels" of difficulty and thus may lose child interest because the elaborations typically seen in child practice play with less defined play materials may not be facilitated. If there is adult interaction that can model pretense or social game activities using the toy, the toys' interest life may be increased and the accessibility dimension promoted. Of course, many of these toys are recommended as parent-child interactive ones rather than ones children are to use on their own. Research is needed on whether toys that can be interactive with very young children are actually used with an adult present or whether they are more likely to serve as the "electronic baby-sitter." If they are part of a child care environment, this question is even more important. From a situated cognition perspective, the developmental value of such toys is likely to be very different with and without the dimension of human social interaction.

ELECTRONICALLY-ENHANCED PLAY OF PRESCHOOLERS

There has been more interest in studying preschool children's use of electronically-enhanced technology, but much of this has been focused on the ways children interact with peers and the social contexts of their interaction in play rather than on developmental effects. For example, studies of preschool children's computer play has shown that there is a period of discovery, which is then followed by involvement, self-confidence, and creativity (Haugland & Wright, 1997). A recent study of the social dimensions of computer play in preschools found that the preschoolers observed each other, commented on the actions, shared and helped with software-related problems, and also had conflicts over turn-taking (Heft & Swaminathan, 2002). Results from research on CD-ROM and other computer software activity with preschool age children have shown some positive results related to play activity. Focusing primarily on computer-related play, some researchers have found that all three types of play noted by Kafai occur at the computer and that the play is usually developmentally appropriate (Escobedo, 1992). Others have noted that vocabulary, language expression, and generally expanded symbol use results from such activities (Labbo, 1996). By preschool age, much of the research on technology focuses on how use of computer software may serve to mediate literacy and other academic "readiness" skills. However, even in regard to literacy the authors of a review of the research on literacy enhancement through new technologies conclude that it is "radically underresearched," (Lankshear & Knobel, 2003, p. 59), and many of the studies of computer facilitated literacy that are reported do not focus on preschoolers.

Another type of result reported at the preschool level has been that generated by constructivist theory. For example, Wright (1998) discusses integrating technology into the curriculum of a summer program by first giving children trips and other experiences and then engaging them in a variety of technology-related playful projects built on their interests. These included using an electronic mural maker to develop animal puppets after a farm visit, using cameras and multimedia software to design a presentation documenting a visit to the woods, and creating web pages and portfolios connecting children from two countries. No data are reported, however, on the concepts learned through these activities. A similar type of approach in a preschool using concepts from Reggio Emilia focused on documenting children's long-term projects using technology (Bergen, 2000; Trepanier-Street, Hong, & Bauer, 2001). This program has been a pioneer in showing how children can use technology to document their learning (a prime goal of the R-E philosophy). For example, pictures of ongoing project activities are taken with a digital camera, transferred to the computer, printed, scanned, or made into overhead transparencies so that children and teachers can discuss the actions and reflect on thinking processes that occurred during the project. Books that include these pictures and the stories children write about the activities in the pictures are made with computer software. Children's original drawings are scanned onto the computer for child and peers to view and discuss, and pictures from various other sources that relate to the project can also be incorporated. Children also draw pictures and write stories using computer software, and the authors report this method seems to be especially satisfying for children with fine motor disabilities because it can compensate for imprecise fine motor skills. They also use a video printer to capture particular segments of videotapes that show how children's actions have improved and this helps them find children's "zones of proximal development." Certain internet sites are also used and a classroom web page has been developed. This approach to the use of new technologies is an excellent example of a child active rather than reactive approach to new technology; however, research on the children's advances in cognitive or other domains is not included in this report.

A small body of research on children's play with electronically-enhanced toys that "talk" has been reported but this research also does not address long-term developmental gain issues. One recent study using plush toys that talked, giving directions and feedback to children while they used computers, reported that most children preferred human help rather than the toy's help (Luckin et al., 2003). This was partly due to the toy's "talk" not always being relevant to the task. Another study of preschool children's play with two types of action figures, some that had computer chips that allowed them to "talk" and some of similar appearance that did not talk, was conducted by this author (Bergen, 2004, 2006b). Overall, there were few differences in the children's play with the talking and non-talking toys, with the exception that there was a longer period of exploration (finding out what the toy did) before play (finding out what child can do with the toy) in the first session with the electronically-enhanced toys. This finding also occurred in a more recent study of an electronic book device, with more time being spent in exploratory behavior with the new technology book device than with books only (Strigen, Vonderhaar, & Wilson, 2006).

In the talking toys study, the affordances of both talking and non-talking toys were prominent in determining the children's initial actions with each set of toys. For example, pressing the "talk" buttons was a common activity with the talking toys, while activating the mechanical water-shooting device on a non-talking toy was common. As children played longer, however, their own cognitive "play schema" seemed to take over. Those children who had similar toys at home (primarily boys) played more of the themes the affordances of the toys promoted, while other children used the toys to enact other themes (e.g., building a house, jumping on a trampoline, going home to dinner) or elaborated on the "helper" themes the toys were designed to elicit (e.g., taking a nap after rescuing someone from a fire). The words the talking toys used were expressed more often by children who played with the talking toys; however, the language narratives of the children who played with a peer in both toy of the technology situations were richer and more elaborated than the narratives of the children who played alone (Bergen, 2006b). The presence of a peer increased the quality of play in many ways; thus, the best affordance seemed to be the presence of another child!

A recent study examining how children age 3 to 6 interacted with a robotic dog (AIBO) and a stuffed plush dog (nonrobotic) investigated the cognitive schema and the behaviors that were evident (Kahn et al., 2004). There were few differences in what children said about the two toys in regard to their biological properties (alive/not alive), mental states (aware/not aware), social rapport (friend/not friend), or moral standing (caring/not caring). However, the children's behavior differed in a number of ways; for example, they explored more, were more fearful, and more engage in reciprocity with the AIBO, while they were more likely to mistreat the stuffed dog and to make it be animated (e.g., talk or walk). The researchers concluded that the reciprocity children attempted with the robotic toy resulted in "impoverished" relationships, and they question whether these attempts to "replace children's interactions with sentient others . . . [when] . . . the robot only partially replicates the entire repertoire of its sentient counterpart . . . may impede young children's social and moral development" (p. 1452). They suggest that studies using robotic toys that look like humans need to be done to investigate this question further.

In regard to the three affordance criteria, transparency seems to be evident in play with both computer software and robotic toys, but a longer period of exploration seems to be necessary. The challenge affordance dimension varies with the type of computer software or the specificity of interaction elicited by the toys; in some cases the technology provides an appropriate set of challenge levels but in others the children may create challenge by using the toys in pretense that is unrelated to the toy affordances. In play with the electronically-enhanced toy figures, the accessibility dimension seemed to be promoted by "human interaction" with a peer more than by toy-initiated interaction. The progression of types of play thus goes from exploratory to practice to pretend activity, with pretense predominating in later sessions of toy exposure. Game play, which is promoted by much computer software, may not be as evident in electronically-enhanced toy play, although some of the robotic toys that give directions to children may elicit higher levels of interactive game play with the toy. This interaction is usually based on the robotic toy asking questions or giving directions and the child answering or taking appropriate action. Thus, it does not have the characteristics of a "sentient other."

ELECTRONICALLY-ENHANCED PLAY OF EARLY ELEMENTARY SCHOOLERS

As noted earlier, there is not an extensive body of research related to electronically-enhanced technology in the early elementary school either, and what there is often focuses on computer use related to literacy. Lankshear and Knobel (2003) report that in a review of 31 studies of new technologies and early literacy effects, "the corpus of studies is swamped by an emphasis on developing a generic capacity to encode and decode alphabetic print rather than to promote competence as "insiders" of practices and discourse communities..." (p. 77). Other than in the literacy area, most research has focused on the social behaviors children show when using computers, rather than on changes in their cognition or other development as a result of specific computer-child interactions.

There has been one rather extensive research-base amassed by designers of the programming software Logo and its spin-off products (Clements & Sarama, 1997), most of which, however, focuses on later elementary age children. Some of these studies show increases in children's creativity, metacognition, social skills, self esteem, and language/reading by using programming techniques. Very little of the software used presently in schools requires programming, however. The major difference in studies investigating effects of the use of programming types of technology is that in the interaction with the computer, the children are active initiators and the computer is reactive, not the reverse, which is the interaction model in most already programmed software. This programming approach only seems to be found in work with children older than third grade, however.

One of the most interesting and innovative approaches of this type in the "interactive character products" design field was used by Druin (2000). It involved having robotic pets designed by teams of 5th grade children and adults. The team selected from a variety of robotic animal parts, built their own pet, and programed the pet to act and say what the team determined. When the robot was hooked to the computer, the children could then control what it said and did. Since adult mentors guided the activity, it seems it could be a method that could be successful with 2nd and 3rd graders as well. There are some products for elementary age children presently advertised in the toy market that provide opportunities for making decisions about programming actions (e.g., robotic cars), but research data has not been collected on the effects of this type of play on developmental progress, and their use by children in early elementary grades is not extensive.

There are many potential playful approaches to achieving educational objectives through new technology use (Silvern, 2006). For example, according to Silvern, the "microworlds" of the computer can provide "a context that challenges children's skills and thoughts . . . [and] . . . no one observing the laughter and joy exuded by successful children could conclude that the activity was anything other than play" (p. 215). He describes play with computer games, computing tools, graphics, and engagement in the "internet playground." While many computer-enhanced learning models focus on literacy, one study that used an interactive program to promote science inquiry skills found that use of the science program supported children's social interaction and their ability to explain scientific phenomena. In the technology condition, the children's explanations were richer and connected to social contexts (Kumpulainen, Vasama, & Kangassalo, 2003). Another type of computer interface is one that elicits storytelling through interaction. It links stories to children's toys and makes them active in the story. Researchers report that this provides motivation for writing, editing, collaborating, and sharing stories, and seems to be especially appealing to girls (Glos & Cassell, 1997). Both of these approaches suggest that the children's cognitive schema were enhanced by the technology interaction.

While these types of technology-enhanced activities appear to be ones that could be used routinely in schools, other researchers have investigated why they are not being used more with early elementary children. For example, Turbill (2001) reports that the use of technology in a kindergarten literacy curriculum was hindered by teachers' narrow definition of literacy activities and by teachers' lack of time and expertise in the use of literacy-related software. Other authors in the United States and Asia have suggested ways that teachers can help children gain the technology skills outlined in curriculum standards (e.g., Gimbert & Cristol, 2004; Siu & Lam, 2005), and they suggest potentially playful projects and ways to make parents aware of the connection between interactive technology play and standards achievement.

Outside of school time, elementary age children are engaging in a wide range of playful activities that involve electronically-enhanced technology. Kafai (2006) describes how programmable building blocks, computational game tool kits, and virtual playgrounds are now available for children of this age. For example, the computational building blocks can "allow children to build computational objects that can interact independently with the world" (p. 212). She states, "electronic building blocks, and virtual playgrounds are materials and places as acceptable as wooden block, bricks, and sandboxes" (p. 213). Another recent addition to this technology is a video-camera specifically designed for children of early elementary age.

Most new technology for children, however, involves some type of adult-designed game software, played on a variety of small electronically-enhanced devices. These game-playing activities have been categorized depending on their purpose and the technology employed (Scarlett et al. (2005). These authors include real-time strategy games, first-person shooters, empire builders, simulations, adventure games, role-playing games, sports games, puzzles, and "massively-multiple" role-playing games that might involve many online participants (p. 117). Although a few studies have been published, early elementary age children's technology play remains mostly unresearched.

In regard to the affordance criteria of Carr (2000), the transparency, challenge, and accessibility of the new technological play varies greatly; those technologies with fewer of these affordance characteristics are probably not the ones played as often, however. Kafai (2006) suggests that the addictive nature of many of these interactive games can be explained by the fact that they usually incorporate all three of the basic types of play; that is, there are opportunities to practice skills to perform better, to bend reality through pretense, and to compete in games with oneself or with others. As yet most academic software and technological devices do not as successfully combine the opportunities for using play affordances as do the play devices elementary age children use out of school. Research on whether cognitive schema develop differently in children who spend extensive time with interactive technology has not yet been conducted.

ELETRONICALLY-ENHANCED PLAY OF YOUNG CHILDREN WITH DISABILITIES

Because constructivist theory has strongly emphasized the importance of children's active manipulation of their environment in play as a means of knowledge construction, one concern often found in the special education literature is how to enable children with physical, sensory, or cognitive impairments to engage actively with their environments. If electronically-enhanced technology can assist these children to be more initiating of action in their environment, it may be especially valuable. The general impetus for developing assistive technology came from PL 100-407 (Technology-Related Assistance for Individuals with Disabilities Act of 1988), which was further strengthened in PL-479 (Individuals with Disabilities Education Act of 1997). However, the use of such devices with young children has not always reached its potential (Judge, 2000). There are four main issues that need to be addressed, according to Judge: identifying the assistive devices that are available; determining what is most appropriate for particular children; finding funds to acquire them (cost may range from $500–$5000); and giving training to teachers and parents in how to facilitate children's use of the devices.

There are many types of assistive devices, not all of which require electronic-enhancement (Parette & Murdick, 1998). They include devices for mobility, communication, vision, hearing, positioning, independent living, and control manipulation. The electronically-enhanced types relevant for young children are ones that assist them in using computers and ones that enable them to engage in independent play; for example, using electronic hand-held toys or activating switch-controlled toys. These authors agree with Judge that cost can be a limiting factor but they stress that, "Assistive technology provides a means for including children with disabilities in a wide range of activities that might otherwise be unavailable or inaccessible to them" (p.197). This can be very important if the devices enable these children to play, especially to play with peers. There are some reports on how assistive technology can be helpful for infants and toddlers with disabilities (Wilds, 2001), but at present the research is limited, especially in regard to electronically enhanced play materials. For children who are able only to press a lever or nod their head, the range of actions that can be promoted through electronically-enhanced technology could extend their range of experiences dramatically; in fact, such toys could really allow them to play. Ironically, although there have been concerns that these types of technology may make children who are typically developing less actively engaged in their world, they may increase the active engagement of children who have disabilities that prevent them from initiating actions. There is a great need for longitudinal research on the effects of such technology on young children with disabilities, because at the present time, little is known about the specific way these toys might promote physical and sensory involvement, cognitive development, and more advanced social skills. One study testing assistive technology methodology that allowed children with motor disabilities to be actively engaged in play with toys has shown preliminary results indicating that this play enhanced their cognitive and social development (Besio, 2002).

Another goal of special education research has been to investigate effects of computer-assisted instruction in improving literacy skills of young learners with language or literacy disabilities. Studies done in a number of countries have consistently shown that literacy delayed children can gain reading skills, especially in the area of phonological awareness, with the use of a range of computer interactive software programs (e.g., Mioduser, Tur-Kaspa, & Leitner, 2000; Seger, & Verhoeven, 2002; Wise, Ring, & Olson, 2000). For example, in the Mioduser et al. study, Israeli special education kindergarteners improved in phonological awareness, word recognition, and letter naming; in the Segers and Verhoeven study, vocabulary gains were notable among immigrant children learning the Dutch language; and in the Wise et al. study, U. S. elementary age children who had computer-assisted phonological training gained more than children who had only computer-assisted reading in context. Thus, for the learning of specific skills, the computer in its "collaborative partnership role" appears to be helpful.

Robotic toys have also been hypothesized to help young children with autism because they are "socially intelligent agents" (Dautenhahn, 2003, p. 443). In this study, the robot had three roles: as a "persuasive machine," as a "social mediator," and as a "model social agent" (pp. 447–448). Although in the three case studies reported, the robot did seem to mediate play and interaction among children with autism, there was a range of interest levels, play styles, and behaviors modeled under the robot's direction. The researchers concluded that to be effective robots need to be "aware" of the social context in which they are embedded and if this can be achieved technically, they may be able to play the three desired roles. However, they caution that if the robots become "part of human society" (p. 449), they might also be used for commercial or manipulative rather than therapeutic purposes. Also, the mediating role of such toys in regard to situated cognition is one that needs further research.

The criteria of transparency, challenge, and accessibility are especially important in technology-enhanced toys for children with disabilities. Design features suggested by Parette and Murdick (1998) are relevant for increasing the affordance possibilities. Practice play has often been the goal of toys for children with disabilities; however, technology that fosters pretense and game play are especially needed for these children. The potential of interactive toys for these populations appears promising.

CONCLUSIONS

A few years ago, this author reported some words from a speech given by Dorothy Cohen, a prominent early childhood educator, entitled, "How do we keep children human in a technological age?" (Bergen, 2003). This talk is now more than 30 years old, and was given at a time when no one even imagined what marvels our "technological age" would bring us. However, the question is even more important today. Cohen cited three ways technology could negatively affect children's development of their "human" qualities, including the following (Bergen, 2003, pp. 251–242):

1. the technological gap between personal effort and observable productivity may result in loss of work satisfaction and reluctance to try
   tasks requiring human effort (shades of Dilbert?)
2. the increased pace of information transfer may result in loss of time
   for reflective thought and extended play and promotes a depen-
   dency on novelty (channel surfers?)
3. the inability to understand how technology works and connect that
   to what it means may promote a "magical" life quality that blurs reality and causes *images* of reality to substitute for reality (the virtual
   reality of videogames?).

Cohen's concern that children would be cut off from primary experiences as been echoed by others (e.g., Rivkin, 2006), as well as her lamenta-
tion that although technology might enhance human speed, physical
strength, and precision, it would not extend human powers of reflective
thinking, imagination, feeling, humor, or ethical/moral judgment. She
stressed that adults should be available to every child as reliable listeners,
observers, and explainers of the "real" world and "not leave them to
mechanical companions alone." Although at that time the technology was
"human-passive" rather than "human interactive," as much of today's technology is, it is still important to evaluate the effects of present technologies
on these important human qualities.

In summary, there have been a wide range of technology-enhanced play
materials developed in recent years and they may have potential for furthering cognitive schema development, specific skill learning, creative
inquiry, and socially mediated behaviors. Each should be evaluated, however, for its affordance possibilities: transparency, challenge, and accessibility, as well as for its richness in promoting a wide variety of play: practice,
pretense, and games. One action that would be helpful at this time is for
early childhood organizations to address these quality issues again. For
example, NAEYC technology standards are more than 10 years old and
need to be updated. As electronically-enhanced toys continue to develop,
they are likely to become more and more able to afford experiences that
give children the advantages that play with non-technological materials
and with other humans presently provide. Perhaps they will even extend
the play possibilities in ways that foster cognitive, language, social, physical,
and academic development. It is very important that systematic longitudinal research begins to examine some of these relationships and effects,
especially as electronically-enhanced technology toys are becoming pervasive in the early childhood years.

REFERENCES

Bergen, D. (2006a, July). *Laughing to learn: Parent-child play with a technology-enhanced toy.* Paper presentation at the 18th International Humor Conference, Copenhagen, Denmark.

Bergen, D. (2006b). Communicative actions and language narratives in preschoolers' play with technology-enhanced action figures. In O. Jarrett & D. Sluss (Eds.). *Play investigations in the 21st century. (Play and Culture Series, Vol. 7,* J. Johnson, Series Ed.) To be published by University Press of America.

Bergen, D. (2004). Preschool children's play with "talking" and "non-talking" rescue heroes: Effects of technology-enhanced figures on the types and themes of play. In J. Goldstein, D. Buckingham, & G. Brougere (Eds.) *Toys, games and media* (pp.195–206). Mahwah, NJ: Erlbaum.

Bergen, D. (2003). Technology in the classroom: Looking back and looking ahead. *Childhood Education, 79*(4), 251–252.

Bergen, D. (2002). Technology in the classroom: Using technology in inclusive classrooms. *Childhood Education, 78*(4), 251–252.

Bergen, D. (2001). Technology in the classroom: Learning in the robotic world: Active or reactive. *Childhood Education, 78*(1), 249–250.

Bergen, D. (2000). Technology in the classroom: Linking technology and teaching practice. *Childhood Education, 76*(4), 252–253.

Besio, S., (2002). An Italian research project to study the play of children with motor disabilities: The first year of activity. *Disability & Rehabilitation, 24*(1–3).

Brett, A. (2006, Mar. 30). Ask Mr. Dad. *Hamilton Journal News,* A9.

Carr, M. (2000). Technological affordances, social practice and learning narratives in an early childhood setting. *International Journal of Technology and Design Education, 10,* 61–79.

Clements, D. H., & Sarama, J. (1997). Research on Logo: A decade of progress. *Computers in the Schools, 14*(1–2), 9–46.

Dautenhahn, K. (2003). Roles and functions of robots in human society: Implications from research in autism therapy. *Robotica, 21,* 443–452.

Druin, A. PETS: *A personal electronic tell or stories.* Retrieved December, 2000 from http://www.umiacs.umd.edu/-allison/kidteam/robot-index.html.

Escobedo, T. H. (1992). Play in a new medium: Children's talk and graphics at computers. *Play and Culture 5*(2), 120–140.

Fromberg, D. P., & Bergen, D. (2006). *Play from birth to twelve: Contexts, perspectives, and meanings* (2nd ed.). New York: Routledge.

Gibson, E. J. (1969). *Principles of perceptual learning and development.* New York: Appleton-Century-Crofts.

Gibson, J. J. (1979). *The ecological approach to visual perception.* Boston: Houghton Mifflin.

Gimbert, B., & Cristol, D. (2001). Teaching curriculum with technology: Enhancing children's technological competence during early childhood. *Early Childhood Education Journal, 31*(3), 207–216.

Glos, J. W. & Cassell, J. (1997). *Rosebud: Technological toys for storytelling.* Paper presented at Conference on Human Factors in Computing Systems, Atlanta, GA.

Individuals with Disabilities Education Act. (1997) 20 U. S. C. ¶ 1400 et seq.

Haugland, S. W., & Wright J. L. (1997). *Young children and technology: A world of discovery.* Boston, MA: Allyn and Bacon.

Heft, T. M., & Swaminathan, S. (2002). Computer-assisted instruction of early academic skills. *Topics in Early Childhood Education, 20*(3), 145–158.

Jordan, A. B., & Woodard, E. H. (2001) Electronic childhood: The availability and use of household media by 2- to 3-year-olds. *Zero to Three, 22*(2), 4–9.

Judge, S. L. (2000). Accessing and funding assistive technology for young children with disabilities. *Early Childhood Education Journal, 28*(2), 125–131.

Kafai, Y. (2006). Play and technology: Revised realities and potential perspectives. In D. P. Fromberg & D. Bergen (Eds.), *Play from birth to twelve: Contexts, perspectives, and meanings* (2nd ed., pp. 207–213). New York: Routledge.

Kahn, P. H., Friedman, B., Perez-Granados, D. R., & Freier, N. G. (2004, April). *Robotic pets in the lives of preschool children.* Paper presented at CHI, Vienna, Austria.

Kumpulainen, K., Vasama, S., & Kangassalo, M. (2003). The intertextuality of children's explanations in a technology-enriched early years science classroom. *International Journal of Educational Research, 39*(8), 793–805.

Labbo, L. (1996). A semiotic analysis of young children's symbol making in a classroom computer center. *Reading Research Quarterly, 31*(4), 356–385.

Lankshear, C., & Knobel, M. (2003). New technologies in early childhood literacy research: A review of research. *Journal of Early Childhood Research Literacy, 3*(1), 59–82.

Luckin, R., Connolly, D., Plowman, L, & Airey, S. (2003). Children's interactions with interactive toy technology. *Journal of Computer Assisted Learning, 19,* 165–176.

Mioduser, D., Tur-Kaspa, H., & Leitner, I. (2000). The learning value of computer-based instruction of early reading skills. *Journal of Computer Assisted Learning, 16,* 54–63.

Newman, M. (1999, May). *Interactive Barney: Good or evil?* www.Post-gazette.com/businessnews/199052barney:1asp.

Norman, D. A. (1993). *Thing that make us smart: Defending human attributes in the age of the machine.* Reading, MA: Addison-Wesley.

Papert, S. (1980). *Mindstorms.* Brighton, MA: Harvester.

Parette, H. P., & Murdick, N. L. (1998). Assistive technology and IEP's for young children with disabilities. *Early Childhood Education Journal, 25*(3),193–198.

Resnick, L. B. (1994). Situated rationalism: Biological and social preparation for learning. In L. A. Hirschfeld & S. A. Gelman (Eds.), *Mapping the mind.* Cambridge: University of Cambridge.

Rivkin, M. (2006), Children's outdoor play: An endangered species. In D. P. Fromberg & D. Bergen (Eds.), *Play from birth to twelve: Contexts, perspectives, and meanings* (2nd ed., pp. 323–329). New York: Routledge.

Scarlett, W. G., Naudeau, S., Salonius-Pasternak, D., & Ponte, I. (2005). *Children's play.* Thousand Oaks, CA: Sage.

Segers, E. E., & Verhoeven, L. L. (2002). Multimedia support of early literacy learning. *Computers and Education, 39*(3), 207–221.

Silvern, S. (2006). Educational implications of play with computers. In D. P. Fromberg & D. Bergen (Eds.), *Play from birth to twelve: Contexts, perspectives, and meanings* (2nd ed., pp. 215–221). New York: Routledge.

Siu, C. K., & Lam, F. K. (2005). A cognitive tool for teaching the addition/subtraction of common fractions: A model of affordances. *Computers and Education, 45*(2), 245–265.

Smith, C. R. (2002). Click on me! An example of how a toddler used technology in play. *Journal of Early Childhood Literacy, 2*(1), 5–20.

Strigens, D., Vondrachek, S., & Wilson, J. (2006). *Comparisons of literacy effects of technology-enhanced and non-technology enhanced books.* Unpublished theses. Miami University, Oxford, OH.

Technology-Related Assistance for Individuals with Disabilities Act of 1988. P. L. 100-407. (1988, August 19). Title 29, U. S. C. ¶ 2201 et seq. U. S. Statutes at Large, 102. 1044–1065.

Trepanier-Street, M. L., Hong, S. L., & Bauer, J. C. (2001). Using technology in Reggio-inspired long-term projects. *Early Childhood Education Journal, 28*(3), 181–188.

Turbill, J. (2001). A researcher goes to school: Using technology in the kindergarten literacy curriculum. *Journal of Early Childhood Literacy, 1*(3), 255–279.

Wartella, E., Caplovitz, A. G., & Lee, J. H. (2004). From Baby Einstein to Leapfrog, from Doom to the Sims, from instant messaging to internet chat rooms: Public interest in the role of interactive media in children's lives. *Social Policy Report, 28*(4), 1–19.

What is technology? http:atschool.eduweb.co.uk/triity/watistec.html. Retrieved July, 2006.

Wilds, M. (2001). It's about time! Computers as assistive technology for infants and toddlers with disabilities. *Zero to Three, 22*(2). 37–41.

Wise, B. W., Ring, J., & Olson, R. K. (2000). Individual differences in gains from computer-assisted remedial reading. *Journal of Experimental Child Psychology, 77,* 197–235.

Wright, J. L. (1998). A new look at integrating technology into the curriculum. *Early Childhood Education Journal, 26*(2), 107–109.

CHAPTER 6

ENGINEERS
AND STORYTELLERS

Using Robotic Manipulatives to Develop
Technological Fluency in Early Childhood

Marina U. Bers

INTRODUCTION

Young children can be wonderful engineers and gifted storytellers. As caring adults, our role is to provide them with early experiences to enable them to flourish as both. We want children to discover the ways in which the man-made world comes to be, the design process involved in each tangible or digital object in our houses and neighborhood, as well as the underlying powerful mathematical ideas that enable engineers to design and build sturdy structures and complex machines. We want children to realize that physics is part of our everyday experience and that the scientific method is a useful tool not only for conducting experiments in a white coat lab, but also for testing our very own theories about the world.

But we also want children to fall in love with language. We want them to tell and listen to stories, to experience the pleasure of both written and oral texts and to understand the structural, grammatical and linguistic choices

Contemporary Perspectives on Science and Technology in Early Childhood Education, pages 105–125
Copyright © 2008 by Information Age Publishing
All rights of reproduction in any form reserved.

that are made every time one engages in the art of storytelling. We want them to understand that letters, words and sentences have meanings, as well as authors, audiences and contexts, and we also want them to become aware of different narrative genres and the power of the written world.

Storytelling and engineering are two ways of understanding, making sense of and contributing to the world around us (Brunner, 1986). In the spirit of Piagetian theory, young children are both little storytellers and little engineers. Early childhood educators have long recognized this. In most settings we can find books as well as building blocks. However, as children grow and move forward in their formal schooling, we soon start to see a division of labor. Some children, who in kindergarten had pleasure in building and counting with their fingers, begin to shy away from math and science. For example, even though many girls may academically outperform their male peers in math and science courses, girls often lose interest or confidence in their abilities to do mathematics and science in middle school (Campbell et al., 2002; Eccles, 1997). There are many reasons for this, and describing all of those is beyond the scope of this work. This paper suggests that one of the reasons of this separation between the "I am good/enjoy math and science" vs. "I am good/enjoy language" is that children cannot find a connection between those very first enjoyable concrete experiences they had in early childhood and the abstract activities of the mind that they encounter in later schooling.

The issue of abstract and concrete is not new in education and became prevalent with Piaget's view of children's intellectual growth as proceeding from the concrete operations stage to the more advanced stage of formal operations (Piaget, 1952). Furthermore, the emergence of the computer incited researchers, such as Sherry Turkle and Seymour Papert, to call for a "revaluation of the concrete" in both epistemology and education. In their breakthrough article in 1991, they identified how

> The computer stands betwixt and between the world of formal systems and physical things; it has the ability to make the abstract concrete. In the simplest case, an object moving on a computer screen might be defined by the most formal of rules and so be like a construct in pure mathematics; but at the same time it is visible, almost tangible, and allows a sense of direct manipulation that only the encultured mathematician can feel in traditional formal systems. (Turkle & Papert, 1991)

While Turkle and Papert were describing the manipulation of virtual objects in the screen, the same process happens, and becomes even more powerful, when children are provided with objects that are physically tangible as well as digitally manipulable, such as robotic manipulatives. This paper proposes that robotic manipulatives can promote learning by both little storytellers and little engineers. Furthermore, the physical characteristics of these "concrete" objects foster the development of sensorimotor skills that, in early childhood, are as important as intellectual ability.

However, using a concrete object to learn important ideas about language, mathematics, physics, etc., does not guarantee that ideas from these domains will become concrete for the child (Clements, 1999). Wilensky proposes that *"concreteness is not a property of an object but rather a property of a person's relationship to an object"* (Wilensky, 1990). Therefore, *"concepts that were hopelessly abstract at one time can become concrete for us if we get into the 'right relationship' with them."* According to Wilensky, the more relationships we can establish with an object, the more concrete it will become, since

> concreteness, then, is that property which measures the degree of our relatedness to the object, (the richness of our representations, interactions, connections with the object), how close we are to it, or, if you will, the quality of our relationship with the object.

This chapter suggests that robotic manipulatives can help children make personal relationships with ideas through the use of sophisticated objects that introduce them to complex concepts in a concrete way. For example, the gears and motors of robotic manipulatives can invite children to think about powerful ideas such as ratios. Although this concept might be new in early childhood, the use of a manipulative object for promoting learning is not.

Robotic manipulatives engage children in building and programming personally meaningful objects, while providing an open-ended environment that fosters "epistemological pluralism" diversity in ways of knowing and approaching problems and ideas (Turkle & Papert, 1991). Although traditionally conceived as purely mechanical kits, robotic manipulatives can be inviting to both little engineers and little storytellers if presented with the right educational philosophy and pedagogy. For example, while some children might make robotic creatures and enact a play, others might focus on building cars or lifting bridges. Robotic manipulatives allow children to follow their own interests, in storytelling or engineering, wile providing objects that invite them to form, very early on, personal relationships with ideas. These ideas will be encountered later on, as schooling progresses, in a more abstract form.

While concrete objects (i.e., robotic manipulatives) are important to help children establish early personal relationships with abstract ideas, people are as important. The adults in the lives of young children, parents and early childhood teachers are, knowingly or unknowingly, helping them to make personal relationships with knowledge. As soon as they are borne, or even before, children are immersed in a learning environment (both home and daycare or school) in which adults and objects help them to make sense of the abstractions of language and to form a special relationship with the spoken word. This early relationship is fundamental for later literacy.

Many adults already have deep relationships with language and find intuitive ways to help young children develop their own by encouraging them to talk, to sing, to play with rhymes, and as they grow, to recognize the letters of their name and read everything from cereal boxes to the newspaper. And for those adults who do not have the intuition or an already established relationship with written language, many early literacy programs and interventions provide them, with diverse degrees of success, with some of these tools and strategies (Goodling Institute for Research on Family Literacy, 2006; National Literacy Trust, 2001).

However, the situation is very different for mathematics, science and technology. Most adults did not form relationships with these areas of knowledge when they were young. Thus, it becomes harder for them to engage children in early explorations of numbers and data. As children grow and the complexities of the disciplines increase, it becomes even more difficult for adults to support children's learning and for children themselves to establish personal connections. This is amplified by the fact that mathematical and scientific awareness are not as embedded in our culture as literacy is. When the computers began to enter everyday lives, visionary educators realized that this new object could be fundamental in changing this. As educational software was developed, research showed that computers enabled children to make concrete connections with mathematical ideas by providing a rich and accessible object (Papert, 1996).

Robotic manipulatives extend the possibilities of the computer by providing an opportunity to relate to concrete objects and ideas, while respecting the plurality of ways of knowing of little engineers and little storytellers. In this paper, I suggest that the little storytellers and the little engineers can learn to form closer relationships with abstract mathematical and scientific concepts by engaging in the design of their own personally meaningful robotic projects. And at the same time, they can learn to develop technological fluency, a set of skills and attitudes that are increasingly needed in today's society.

ON THE SHOULDER OF GIANTS: FROM BUILDING BLOCKS TO ROBOTIC MANIPULATIVES

Robotics can be a powerful learning manipulative for young children. It can enable the early introduction of engineering and programming skills, as well as the understanding of abstract mathematical and science concepts in a concrete, playful and hands-on way. Since Froebel established the first kindergarten in 1837, and developed a set of toys (which became known as "Froebel's gifts") with the explicit goal of helping young children in learning concepts such as number, size, shape, and color, other educators, such as Maria Montessori, have created a wide range of manipulative materials that engage children in learning through playful explorations (Brosterman, 1997).

Nowadays, the use of manipulatives as a teaching tool is widespread. Most early childhood settings have building bricks, Pattern Blocks, Digi-Blocks, Cuisenaire Rods, etc. These manipulatives, not only can be used as teaching aids, but also as materials for fostering creativity. They enable students to build, to design, to experiment and to solve problems. "Digital manipulatives" are now supplementing these traditional manipulatives, because they also afford students the opportunity to explore ideas and concepts beyond what traditional manipulatives can provide, for example dynamic concepts such as feedback (Resnick, 1998). Robotic manipulatives, such as the ones this paper focuses on, extend the potential of digital manipulatives by enabling children to use their hands and develop fine motor skills, as well as hand-eye coordination. But even more important, they provide a concrete and tangible way to understand abstract ideas.

Robotic manipulatives engage children in the design of their own projects. Children can explore traditionally abstract concepts such as gears, levers, joints, motors, sensors, programming loops and variables in a concrete and fun manner, while engaging early on in most of the steps involved in the engineering design process (Erwin et al., 2000). This way of working with robotics in early childhood is strongly inspired by the constructionist philosophy of education, which conceives technology as a playful material to make personally and epistemologically meaningful projects (Papert, 1980).

Constructionism asserts that computers are powerful educational technologies when used as tools for supporting the design, the construction, and the programming of projects people truly care about (Papert, 1980; Renick et al., 1996). By constructing an external object to reflect upon, people also construct internal knowledge. Constructionism has its roots on Piaget's constructivism (Papert, 1991). However, while Piaget's theory was developed to explain how knowledge is constructed in our heads, Papert pays particular attention to the role of constructions in the world (i.e., robotic constructions in this case) as a support for those in the head. Thus, constructionism is both a theory of learning and a strategy for education that offers the framework for developing a technology-rich design-based learning environment, in which learning happens best when learners are engaged in learning by making, creating, programming, discovering and designing their own "objects to think with" in a playful manner.

Robotic manipulatives are powerful "objects to think with," when used in the context of a constructionist learning environment that gives the individuals the freedom to explore their natural interests using new technologies, with the support of a community of learners that can facilitate deeper understanding.

In the work described in this paper the robotic manipulative used is a commercially available robotics kit, called Lego Mindstorms Robotic Invention Kit. The kit contains a large Lego brick with an embedded microcomputer, called the RCX brick, an infrared USB tower that connects the RCX to the computer, so the programs that children create in the computer can be downloaded to the RCX, and a variety of Lego pieces in different sizes and shapes. Some of the pieces are familiar, such as beams, bricks, and plates. Others are unique to robotics such as motors, light sensors, touch sensors, wires, axles, and gears. The RCX has three input connections (for the touch and light sensors) and three output connections (for motors and lights). In addition, an LCD display provides information about the input and output connections as well as data stored in the processor (see Figure 6.1).

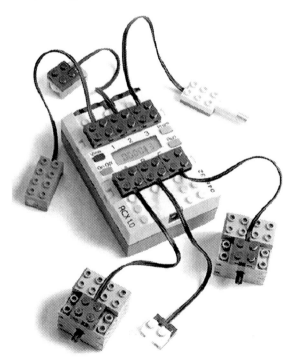

Figure 6.1. The RCX with sensors, motors and a light connected to inputs and outputs.

Figure 6.2.   A simple program in ROBOLAB built with two motors, A and B, that go forward for 4 seconds, then go backwards for 2 seconds, then stop.

Children can include the RCX in the building of their project. Since it does not need to be connected to the computer (the program can be downloaded through the tower), children have flexibility in the type of creations they can make, as well as in deciding the behaviors of their projects. They can create a moving car that follows the light or a merry-go-round that plays their favorite tunes. In order to program behaviors for their robotic creations, such as motion and reactions to stimuli (i.e., if there is light, then go forward; if the touch sensor is pressed, then play a sound), children can use ROBOLAB™, a software program developed at the Tufts University Center for Engineering Educational Outreach (CEEO), one of several educational software packages available (see Figure 6.2). ROBOLAB is a programming language that provides a drag-and-drop iconic interface that has several levels of difficulty, so the user can tailor the functions that are available to their personal programming skills (Portsmore, 1999).

TECHNOLOGICAL FLUENCY:
BEYOND TECHNOLOGICAL LITERACY

To make their robotic creations come alive, children manipulate the physical Lego pieces to build sturdy and efficient structures, and program the software to make the robotic project behave in the way they want. Building and programming engage children in learning about physics, math and engineering concepts. It also encourages them to start wondering about our surrounding world, which is populated by objects that, in the same spirit as robotic manipulatives, integrate bit and atoms (Gershenfeld, 2000). Most important, robotic manipulatives provide an opportunity for children to develop technological fluency very early on.

Papert has coined the term technological fluency to refer to the ability to use and apply technology in a fluent way, effortlessly and smoothly, as one does with language. For example, a technologically fluent person can use technology to write a story, make a drawing, model a complex simulation or program a robotic creature (Papert & Resnick, 1993). As with learning a second language, fluency takes time to achieve and requires hard work and motivation. In order to achieve technological fluency, it is imperative to develop technological literacy, or basic skills.

To express ourselves through a poem, we first need to learn the alphabet. In the same spirit, to create a digital picture or program a robot, we first need to learn how to use the keyboard and to navigate the interface. Technological literacy has sometimes come to be known as "computer literacy" and has a long history. It refers to the ability to use computer applications, such as a spreadsheet and a word processor, and to search the World Wide Web for information. However, skills with specific applications are necessary but not sufficient for individuals to prosper in the information age, where new skills are constantly needed because applications change rapidly and new tools emerge frequently, requiring new skills.

While learning the alphabet is required to write a poem, it is not enough. In the same spirit, knowing how to use some software packages is not enough to become technologically fluent. As stated by the Committee on Information Technology Literacy in 1999, *"the 'skills' approach lacks 'staying power'."* In this paper I am suggesting that technological literacy is a fundamental stepping stone toward technological fluency, but not a goal in and by itself. I am also proposing that, regardless of the age of the children and the challenge to create developmentally appropriate curriculum and software, the goal should be to promote technological fluency and not merely technological literacy.

Technological fluency is knowledge about what technology is, how it works, what purposes it can serve, and how it can be used efficiently and effectively to achieve specific personal and societal goals. The Committee identified at least four broad categories of rationale motivating the need of helping children develop an understanding of information technology: personal, workforce, educational, and societal (Committee on Information Technology Literacy, 1999).

Thirty states include technology education in their educational frameworks (Newberry, 2001). Massachusetts is leading the nation in declaring that technology and engineering are as important to the curriculum as science, social studies, and other key subjects. The Massachusetts Science and Technology/Engineering Curriculum Framework (Massachusetts Department of Education, 2001) mandates the teaching of technology and engineering for all students in grades PreK–12.

Robotic manipulatives provide a venue by which to engage children in developing technological fluency (Miaoulis, 2001; National Academy of Engineering & National Research Council, 2002; Roth, 1998; Sadler et al., 2000). They also offer a platform for project-based learning (Resnick et al., 2000) that promotes design processes such as iteration and testing of alternatives in problem solving, encompasses hands-on construction that can promote three dimensional thinking and visualization, offers design-based activities to engage students in learning by applying concepts, skills and strategies to solve real-world problems that are relevant, epistemologically and personally meaningful (Papert, 1980; Resnick et al., 1998). Robotic manipulatives also provide a wonderful opportunity to integrate different areas of the curriculum, such as math and science with the humanities and the social sciences (Benenson, 2001). Last but not least, robotic manipulatives can motivate students to engage in learning complex concepts, in particular in the areas of math and science, even when they label themselves as "not good at" or "not interested in" this (Bers & Urrea, 2000).

Although many high schools and middle schools have adopted some form of engineering education through robotics (Bayles & Aguirre, 1992; Jaramillo, 1992; Kreinberg, 1983; Metz, 1991), very few elementary schools actively do so (Benenson, 2001; Rogers & Portsmore, 2004) and a handful of early childhood settings are exploring the use of robotics in early childhood (Bers et al., 2002; Bers et al., 2004, Bers, 2004; Beals & Bers, 2006).

Robotic manipulatives provide opportunities for both little engineers and little storytellers to develop technological fluency, while respecting and engaging their epistemological styles and ways of knowing the world (Bruner, 1986). In the next section I present examples of this.

LITTLE ENGINEERS AND LITTLE STORYTELLERS

Robotic manipulatives can engage children in developing technological fluency. However, regardless of the tool, the best learning experiences happen when children are deeply invested in their own learning. Thus, as mentioned earlier, the pedagogy is as important as the technology. Within the constructionist approach, it is essential that children have the freedom to make projects they truly care about. Over years of conducting research and teaching children to use robotics, I have observed that some children tend to choose projects that reflect early engineering tendencies, while others tend to choose projects that engage their storytelling potential. Robotic manipulatives allow both types of children to create meaningful projects, and at the same time, to develop technological fluency while exploring both the physical and the digital worlds.

Max used robotic manipulatives in a combined first and second grade classroom in a small private school in MA. When given the choice to build a project he decided to make a "hoping Eskimo." In his journal, he wrote *"My Eskimo hops and runs away from a polar bear. I built this because I am an Eskimo."* Max wanted to use the technology to tell a story, a story about himself and his cultural heritage (see Figure 6.3). The open-ended nature of the technology enabled Max to work on this project. But it wasn't only the technology that made this possible. It was also the constructionist pedagogy that Max's teacher used when introducing robotics.

Figure 6.3.   Max's hoping Eskimo.

Max was not as interested in exploring the potential of the technology as an end in itself, as many of the children that I classify as "little engineers" were, but he wanted to tell a story. When Max recounts his work on the project, this priority is also expressed by the order of the steps he describes. "*First I built a platform. Then I built the background. Then I built the Eskimo and the trees and then the motor for the Eskimo. I put a lot of slow motion into the motor of the Eskimo. And then I put a lot of fast speed into the wheels. I learned that is mostly very hard to support the car.*" The last thing Max did was working with the motor and program its speed. He first needed to have the setting for the story (the platform, the background and the trees), and the main character (the Eskimo). Then he could focus on the motor. As I will later describe, this approach differs from the one taken by children in the group which I classify as "little engineers." These children tend to first explore and make use of most of the fancy toys and pieces such as wheels, gears, motors and sensors.

Max used a motor and learned a few things about motion and programming. He had fun and he expressed that he enjoyed most "*to learn how to make things jump.*" However, using motors wasn't what got Max hooked into his project. He had a story to tell. He put the engineering skills and his evolving technical fluency to the service of storytelling.

I started with Max's story because Max is a boy and, his choice of storytelling, instead of engineering, is counter intuitive with traditional views that see boys as little engineers and girls as little storytellers. Girls and boys approach problem solving differently; for example, boys seem to be better at tasks involving spatial relations, while girls seem to be better at verbal problems (Helgeson, 1992). However, some work started to explore what happens when the task is open-ended, such as the constructionist philosophy proposes, and children can choose a personally meaningful project to work that is holistic and relevant to real-world situations (Margolis & Fisher, 2002).

Very little education research has looked at how very young children use robotic manipulatives for learning. However, since research shows that attitudes about science and math start to form during the early elementary school years, it is expected that the same is true for engineering education. However, there is no research in this area yet. Elementary school girls are less confident in their math abilities than boys (Eccles, 1997), and both girls and boys perceive that science is male dominated as early as second grade (Andre et al., 1997).

While research has shown that there is a gender gap in technological fluency and a lack of women in engineering or technologically challenging professions (Thom, 2001), this paper hopes to suggest that the early use of robotic manipulatives can serve to bridge the gap between gender stereotypes and engage both girls and boys in developing technological fluency, while respecting their own epistemological styles and their interest in both building sturdy structures and telling stories.

Caroline, a classmate of Max, is also interested in stories. She was fascinated by the Nutcracker, not only because of the popularity of the ballet, but also because, in her own words, "*the Nutcracker represents Christmas.*" Caroline celebrates and truly enjoys Christmas. She chose to make a Nutcracker out of Legos for her final project. The doll opens and closes its mouth and its eyes light up. In her on-line design journal, with the help of a teacher, Caroline wrote: "*Some important parts of the building were getting the mouth attached to the head. The gears made the mouth go up and down. We had to put it on the platform or it would be tilted to one side. I programmed it to go one way, stop, and go the other way, and that made the mouth go up and down. . . .*"

Caroline spent a long time tinkering with engineering concepts to make the Nutcracker's mouth move the way she wanted. Her persistence and determination to succeed in her goals were not guided by her fascination with gears, but by her desire to have a working Nutcracker. Caroline can be classified as a "little storyteller"; however, in order to tell her story and build her doll, she first needed to master some engineering concepts.

During a conversation with a teacher Caroline said: "*. . . the hardest part was programming because first the motor went spinning around and got tangled in the wires but then we put on this fuel thing and it stopped shaking, but you still have to hold it. I learned a lot about computers and how things work.*" We do not know if Caroline will choose, as she grows up, to engage with disciplines that are closely related to engineering or to storytelling. By exposing her early on to robotic manipulatives, she can explore powerful ideas that she wouldn't have explored otherwise. She learned that, as much as she likes stories and characters, she can also enjoy building and programming, thus developing both competence and confidence regarding technological fluency.

Readiness to learn and self-confidence in our own abilities are not new ideas. However, although there is general consensus about the importance of "readiness" in literacy and mathematics, it is not clear what does it mean to achieve early readiness in engineering, programming and technological fluency. In this paper I am proposing that readiness is intimately associated with our ability to engage in the design and implementation of a personally meaningful project. For some children, in particular for the little storytellers, their interest in something else, other than technology, is likely to lead them to learn about the technology.

Kate is a first grader who loved music and bunnies. She started her project with a very clear goal: to make a rabbit. She did not like to build with Legos, neither was she interested in giving motion to her bunny. She was happy with paper and pencil. The challenge, with children like Kate, is to help them move beyond their comfort zone, while respecting their interests. Had Kate's teacher forbidden her to use paper and pencil for her bunny, it is most likely that Kate would have lost interest in the project. Little by little, while encouraging Kate to explore other materials to create a stand for her bunny, her teacher introduced her to the many possibilities that a robotic bunny could offer. Kate became interested in this and built a Lego car to support her paper and pencil bunny (see Figure 6.4).

Figure 6.4.   Kate's bunny.

After hard work, Kate wrote in her on-line journal:

The Easter Bunny spins around and sings songs and it drives forward and backwards. My family celebrates Easter. It's important because it's my favorite holiday and it's my mom's favorite holiday. I had an idea. I drew a picture of an Easter Bunny and some flowers. Then I started working on it.... B. helped me program it. It goes forward, stops, and then it spins around and then you flash a light on it and it goes backwards and then it sings a song, an Easter song, and then stops. The wheels kept falling off, so I was very frustrated. Then B. said, "You need an axel extender." I got two axel extenders and it worked and the wheels stopped falling off. That was the only problem. I learned how to program. I learned how to make it spin around, play music, and stop.

By helping Kate move beyond her comfort zone of using paper and pencil, the teacher helped her to adventure into the realm of technology in which the child had no previous interest. Kate saw an opportunity in the many possibilities and flexibility of robotic manipulatives. Kate's emerging technological fluency was fostered by her interest in making digital music, not in building with the Legos or engineering.

In contrast with Kate, Max, and Caroline, the three "little storytellers" mentioned earlier, Marcos is a "little engineer." He loves to build. His project, called "speedy legs," spins and charges against another robot (see Figure 6.5). His goal was "to build a robot that would never break." This goal is an example of what differentiates little engineers from little story-

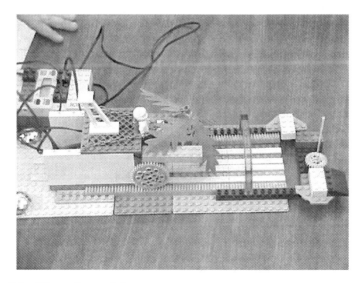

Figure 6.5.   Marcos's speedy legs.

tellers. While the engineers want something sturdy that won't break, the storytellers want a story, a context, a character. Marcos explains:

> I like building. I designed it by looking at how the pieces would go together and I asked a friend when I had a problem. I programmed it by putting the speed the highest it could be. And then I did the programming and I tried it out. Then I built more and it worked. It broke when pieces fell off and that helped me learn a lot. Sometimes the blocks need to be strong. Sometimes it goes slow and sometimes it goes fast because of how I build it.

For children like Marcos, robotic manipulatives provide an early gateway into a way of thinking and a set of skills that are not learned in school until much later, if ever. Beyond providing opportunities for exploring with building sturdy structures and completing programming challenges, robotic manipulatives also offer opportunities for collaboration and teamwork, skills that will also be much needed as children grow up.

James, a first grader who is an engineer at heart, described his collaboration to make a robot with one of his classmates in the following way (see Figure 6.6):

> The big robot fighter fights and waters plants by dumping a big bucket! The big robot moves and it spins the rocket like crazy. The wheels move. It is important to Mike because almost everybody in Mike's family went in the war. It is important to me because I water the grass every summer.... We really worked hard. I did the bucket and Mike did the rocket and we worked together on the wheels and the motors. It took a really long time. We needed a little help with the motors. We worked together to decide how it would move and how it would spin the rocket and how it would stop. We took turns putting stuff on the screen when we programmed. We had problems with the rocket and the wheels and how to straighten it out. The rocket was the hardest thing. We didn't know how to attach it. We learned we had to attach the wires to the brain and the motors. We learned how to attach the rocket to a motor. We kept trying to get bigger wheels. Mike said, "Hey...Aren't we missing something?" Then we both said, "We need the big wheels!" Someone took the wheels off and we got bigger wheels. We had lots of lots of lots of fun.

Mike and James formed a productive team. In James' description of their collaboration, we can see that they sometimes chose to work together and sometimes did independent tasks. These very young children were able not only to collaborate, but also to manage their collaboration to achieve higher productivity and...fun. In the process, they learned how to program their robot, how to debug it (i.e., discover and solve problems in the code), and how engineering can be an engaging and fun experience.

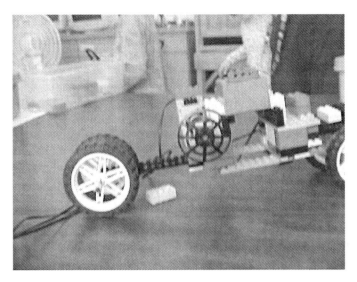

Figure 6.6.   Mike and James' robot

Children like Marcos, James and Mike enjoyed using robotic manipulatives because they had an interest in engineering, although they did not know it. They engaged in the engineering design process and took upon themselves challenges to solve problems. In contrast, the little storytellers described earlier, enjoyed the work with robotic manipulatives because they could tell their stories. Both groups of children learned similar content and skills. However, had the learning environment not been set up so they could make personally meaningful projects, it is very likely that the little storytellers would have lost interest and lack motivation.

CHILDREN AND PARENTS: LESSONS FROM THE FAMILY LITERACY MOVEMENT

As shown in some of the stories presented before, children can be little storytellers and little engineers. While some tend to favor one way of knowing over the other, most young children are comfortable in both and can switch back and forth between the two roles. As children grow, some little engineers begin to label themselves as enjoying and being good at math/ science and technology, while some little storytellers chose language arts and social sciences. Slowly, the gap between both ways of knowing starts to emerge and it becomes harder to help children transition with ease.

The early years are important because they set the foundation, the motivation and the readiness to later learning. However, during those early years, the role of schooling is limited in the children's lives. Learning at home is as important as learning in school. The stronger the home-school connection through parental involvement, the higher likelihood of ensuring educational success (Fan & Chen, 2001). Literacy education has been aware of this and family literacy is a growing movement in the US and abroad (National Literacy Trust, 2001; Goodling Institute, 2006). Research has shown that the practice of parents reading with their young children is a significant contributor to young children's learning to read (Teale, 1984). Some of the lessons learned from literacy education are having an impact in technology education (Wright & Church, 1986). However, while most parents are comfortable helping their children to develop literacy, the same is not true for technological fluency. How do we conceive programs to promote technological fluency in both parents and children? The family literacy movement can provide useful insights.

In the 60s, most of the studies were done following the "parent impact model" which consisted in having a teacher visit the homes and present the pedagogy and materials to the parents. Although this model proved to be successful, criticism said that this method operates in a deficit model assuming that parents lacked basic skills and methods of teaching. Later on, the success of parental involvement in Head Start led to the emergence of the Parent Education Fellow through programs that promoted diverse parental participation. The goal was for parents to become genuine partners in their child's education in whatever role suited them better (i.e., teachers, volunteers, decision makers, etc.) (Wright & Church, 1986). This approach informs my own work on Project Inter-Actions, a research program developed to understand, amongst other things, how to help parents develop technological fluency along with their children (Bers, 2004, Beals & Bers, 2006). Project Inter-Actions offers a unique opportunity to conduct research to investigate how parents can become learners at the same time as their children, while they are also providing support and guidance to them (Bers et al., 2004). Looking at parents as learners is not unique to the field of technological education and can also be found in studies of immigrants' acculturation (Jones & Trickett, 2005).

Project Inter-Actions examines the many interactions that exist when parents and young children are brought together in a learning environment fostered by new technologies that enable programming and building a robotic toy with Lego pieces and art materials to represent an aspect of the family's cultural heritage. The project's name stems from the different types of interactions looked at throughout the project: 1) interactions between adults and children together learning something that is new for both, such as robotic technology, and something that they are immersed into, such as their own cultural background, 2) interactions between abstract programming concepts and concrete building blocks, 3) interactions between ideas of what is developmentally appropriate and what children can and cannot do with technology at such early age, and 4) interactions between technology, art, and culture, areas of the curriculum that computers have the potential to integrate.

Project Interactions has been running for the last four years in the context of after-school weekend workshops for families. More than one hundred and eighty people participated so far and, amongst the many projects that were developed by the young learners and their families, it is possible to identify little storytellers and little engineers, as well as "big" ones. However, all of them, young and old, developed technological fluency by learning how to build and program their robotic projects, regardless of their favored way of knowing.

When conducting the initial background survey, 46% of the participating young children claimed that their favorite subjects at school are math and science. But only 3% declared themselves as good in math and science. Since children involved in Project Inter-Actions are first and second graders, this data is both alarming and inspirational. On the one hand, what is going on in the way math and science are taught in early childhood education, that children of such young age are already experiencing difficulties? On the other hand, almost half of the sample stated that math and science are their favorite subjects in school. This shouldn't be that surprising, given that researchers such as Piaget had long ago proclaimed that young children are "little scientists and little mathematicians." However, these first results from Project Inter-Actions suggest the need of designing educational programs to help children learn better math and science at this early age. This can be done by providing opportunities for them to make connections between abstract concepts and concrete ideas, and to help them establish personal relationships with knowledge, through the use of robotic manipulatives. Another way is to help their parents develop confidence in these areas as well, so they can support their children's early learning.

CONCLUSION

This paper suggests that we can tap the potential of young children as both little storytellers and little engineers to help them develop technological fluency. It also shows how robotic manipulatives can be used to support this work because, in the tradition of most well-known early childhood manipulatives, they engage children in learning by making, by building, by creating. They also add the programming aspect, which in today's world of integrated bit and atoms, is necessary to help young children understand how our everyday objects work, including, but not limited to, computers.

We go to the bathroom to wash our hands and the faucets "know" when to start dispensing water and when we are done. The elevator "knows" when someone's little hands are in between the doors and shouldn't close. Our cell phones "know" how to take pictures, send e-mails and behave as alarm clocks. Even our cars "know" where do we want to go and can take us there without getting lost. Robotic manipulatives provide a concrete material to start experimenting with and modeling some of these complex objects.

In the spirit of manipulative materials that has been in early childhood since Fröebel invented kindergarten in the 1800s, robotic manipulatives provide materials for children to learn about sensors, motors and the digital domain in a playful way by building their own cars that follow the light or elevators that work with a touch sensor. But even more important, robotic manipulatives are a gateway for helping children learn about abstract mathematical and science concepts in a concrete way and for helping them to develop early on technological fluency through the introduction of engineering and programming.

However, as shown in this paper, early fluency is best achieved when there is a strong home-school connection and when parents, as they do with language by reading and singing to their children before they learn these skills in school, start to immerse their very young children in a world of technology. Although multimedia applications and educational software are available and can be used to teach children new things, technological fluency is not measured by how much children learn with computers and how many new skills they develop, but by children's ability and confidence to use computers and other technologies (such as robotic manipulatives) to be able to create their own personally meaningful projects. On the way, they will probably be learning new concepts and skills, but most important, they will be able to see themselves as good learners. With the continuous advances in new technologies and applications, learning how to learn is the only viable recipe for success.

This paper also suggests that the field of technological education in early childhood has much to learn from the family literacy movement to involve parents in the early years. However, if the work is done without respecting the different ways of knowing, in both children and adults, it is very likely that we will lose the little storytellers in the way and only attract the little engineers. Early childhood is a time of fluidity and experimentation between roles and epistemological styles. While most ways of using technological tools such as robotics, focus on little engineers who will grow into big engineers, this paper advocates for the importance of respecting and inviting different ways of knowing and motivations while working with robotic manipulatives. But the pedagogy with which the tools are used is as important as the tools themselves. Thus this paper has focused on the constructionist philosophy of learning and its tenet that people learn better while using technology to build concrete meaningful projects to establish personal connections with abstract ideas.

REFERENCES

Andre, T., Whigham, M., Hendrickson, A., & Chambers, S. (1997). *Science and mathematics versus other school subject areas: Pupil attitudes versus parent attitudes.* Paper presented at the National Association for Research in Science Teaching, Chicago, IL.

Bayles, T. M., & Aguirre, F. J. (1992). Introducing high school students and science teachers to chemical engineering. *Chemical Engineering Education, 26*(1).

Beals, L., & Bers, M. (2006). Robotic technologies: When parents put their learning ahead of their child's. *Journal of Interactive Learning Research, 17*(4), 341–366.

Benenson, G. (2001). The unrealized potential of everyday technology as a context for learning. *Journal of Research in Science Teaching, 38*(7), 730–745.

Bers, M. (2004, April). *Parents, children and technology: Making robots, exploring cultural heritage and learning together.* Presentation given at American Educational Research Association (AERA), Los Angeles, CA.

Bers, M., New, B., & Boudreau, L. (2004). Teaching and learning when no one is expert: Children and parents explore technology, *Journal of Early Childhood Research and Practice, 6*(2).

Bers, M., Ponte, I., Juelich, K., Viera, A., & Schenker, J. (2002). Integrating robotics into early childhood education. *Childhood Education.* Annual AACE: pp. 123–145.

Bers, M., & Urrea, C. (2000). Technological prayers: Parents and children working with robotics and values. In A. Druin & J. Hendler (Eds.), *Robots for kids: Exploring new technologies for learning experiences* (pp. 194–217). New York: Morgan Kaufman.

Brosterman, N. (1997). *Inventing kindergarten.* New York: Harry N. Adams Inc.

Bruner, J. (1986). *Actual minds, possible worlds.* Cambridge, MA: Harvard University Press.

Campbell, P. B., Jolly, E., Hoey, L., & Perlman, L. K. (2002). *Upping the numbers: Using research-based decision making to increase diversity in the quantitative disciplines.* Newton, MA: Campbell-Kibler Associates, Inc. & Education Development Center, Inc.

Clements, D. H. (1999). 'Concrete' manipulatives, concrete ideas. *Contemporary Issues in Early Childhood, 1*(1), 45–60

Clements, D. H. (2002). Computers in early childhood mathematics. *Contemporary Issues in Early Childhood, 3*(2).

Committee on Information Technology Literacy. (1999). *Being fluent with information technology.* Washington, DC: National Academy Press. Retrieved April 11, 2003, from http://www.nap.edu/html/beingfluent/

Eccles, J. (1997). Female friendly science and mathematics: Can it interest girls and minorities in breaking through the middle school wall? In D. Johnson (Ed.), *Minorities and girls in schools* (pp. 66–104). Thousand Oaks, CA: Sage.

Erwin, B., Cyr, M., & Rogers, C. B. (2000). LEGO engineer and ROBOLAB: Teaching engineering with LabVIEW from kindergarten to graduate school. *International Journal of Engineering Education, 16*(3).

Fan, X., & Chen, M. (2001, March). Parental involvement and students'' academic achievement: A meta-analysis. *Educational Psychology Review, 13*(1), 1–22.

Gershenfeld, N. (2000). *When things start to think.* New York: Owl Books.

Goodling Institute for Research on Family literacy. (2006). *Annotated bibliography,* Penn State, PA

Helgeson, S. L. (1992). *Problem solving research in middle/junior high school science education.* Columbus, OH: ERIC Clearinghouse for Science.

Jaramillo, J. A. (1992). *Ethnographic evaluation of the MESA program at a south-central Pheonix high school.* Tempe, AZ: Preparation for Project Prime.

Jones C., & Trickett, E. (2005, August). Immigrant adolescents behaving as culture brokers: A study of families from the former Soviet Union. *Journal of Social Psychology, 145*(4): 405–427.

Kreinberg, N. (1983). EQUALS: Working with educators. In S. M. Humphreys (Ed.), *Women and minorities in science: Strategies for increasing participation* (p. 218). Boulder, CO: Westview Press.

Margolis, J., & Fisher, A. (2002). *Unlocking the clubhouse: Women in computing.* Cambridge, MA: The MIT Press.

Martin, F., Mikhak, B., Resnick, M., Silverman, B., & Berg, R. (2000). To mindstorms and beyond: Evolution of a construction kit for magical machines. In A. Druin, & J. Hendler (Eds.), *Robots for kids: Exploring new technologies for learning.* San Francisco: Morgan Kaufmann.

Massachusetts Department of Education. (2001). *Massachusetts science and technology/engineering curriculum framework.* Malden: Author.

Metz, S. S. (1991). ECOES: A summer engineering and science program for high school women. *Gifted Child Today (GCT), 14*(3).

Miaoulis, I. (2001). Introducing engineering into the K–12 learning environments. *Environmental Engineering, 37*(4), 7–10.

National Academy of Engineering, & National Research Council. (2002). *Technically speaking: Why all Americans need to know more about technology.* Washington, D.C.: National Academy Press.

National Literacy Trust. (2001). *Parental involvement and literacy achievement: The research evidence and the way forward. A review of the literature.* London, UK.

Newberry, P. (2001). Technology education in the U.S.: A status report. *The Technology Teacher, 61.*

Papert, S. (1996). An exploration in the space of mathematics educations. *International Journal of Computers for Mathematical Learning, 1*(1), 95–123.

Papert, S. (1980). *Mindstorms: Children, computers, and powerful ideas.* New York: Basic Books.

Papert, S. (1991). Situating constructionism. In I. Harel & S. Papert (Eds.), *Constructionism.* Norwood, NJ: Ablex.

Papert, S., & Resnick, M. (1993). *Technological fluency and the representation of knowledge.* Proposal to the National Science Foundation, MIT Media Laboratory.

Parkinson, E. (1999). Re-constructing the construction kit—re-constructing childhood: A synthesis of the influences which have helped to give shape and form to kit-based construction activities in the primary school classroom. *International Journal of Technology and Design Education, 9,* 173–194.

Piaget, J. (1952). *The origins of intelligence in children.* New York: International University Press.

Piaget, J. (1971). The theory of stages in cognitive development. In D. R. Green (Ed.), *Measurement and Piaget* (pp. 1–11), New York: McGraw

Portsmore, M. (1999, Spring/Summer). ROBOLAB: Intuitive robotic programming software to support life long learning. *APPLE Learning Technology Review.*

Resnick, M. (1998). Technologies for lifelong kindergarten. *Educational Technology Research and Development, 46*(4).

Resnick, M., Berg, R., & Eisenberg, M. (2000). Beyond black boxes: Bringing transparency and aesthetics back to scientific investigation. *The Journal of the Learning Sciences, 9*(1).

Resnick, M., Bruckman, A., & Martin, F. (1996). Pianos not stereos: Creating computational construction kits. *Interactions, 3*(6).

Resnick, M., Martin, F., Berg, R., Borovoy, R., Colella, V., Kramer, K., & Silverman, B. (1998, April). Digital manipulatives. *Proceedings of the CHI '98 conference,* Los Angeles.

Rogers, C., & Portsmore, M. (2004). Bringing engineering to elementary school. *Journal of STEM education, 5*(3–4), 17–28.

Roth, W. M. (1998). *Designing communities.* Boston: Kluwer.

Sadler, P. M., Coyle, H. P., & Schwartz, M. (2000). Engineering competitions in the middle school classroom: Key elements in developing effective design challenges. *Journal of the Learning Sciences, 9*(3), 299–327.

Senechal, M., & LeFevre, J. (2002). Parental involvement in the development of children's reading skill: A five-year longitudinal study. *Child Development, 73*(2), 445–460.

Teale, W. H. (1984). Reading to young children: its significance for literacy development. In H. Goelman, A. Oberg, & F. Smith (Eds.), *Awakening to literacy* (pp.110–121). Portsmouth, NH: Heinemann.

Thom, M. (2001). *Balancing the equation: Where are the women and girls in science, engineering, and technology?* New York: National Council for Research on Women.

Turkle, S., & Papert, S. (1991). Epistemological pluralism and the revaluation of the concrete. *Journal of Mathematical Behavior.*

Wilensky, U. (1990). Abstract meditations on the concrete and concrete implications for mathematics education. In I. Harel & S. Papert (Eds.), *Constructionism.* Norwood, NJ: Ablex.

Wright, J., & Church, M. (1986). The evolution of an effective home-school microcomputer connection. *Education & Computing, 2,* 67–74.

Wright, J. L. (1998). Computers and young children: A new look at integrating technology into the curriculum. *Early Childhood Education Journal, 26*(2).

CHAPTER 7

MATHEMATICS
AND TECHNOLOGY

Supporting Learning for Students
and Teachers[1]

Douglas H. Clements and Julie Sarama

Computer technology has the potential to make multiple contributions to early childhood education, particularly in core areas such as language, literacy, and mathematics (Clements & Sarama, 2003b; Sarama & Clements, 2002; Seng, 1999). Whether this potential is realized depends on which technology is used and how the technology is used. We begin this chapter by considering recent criticisms of computers in childhood. Next, we review research and offer suggestions drawn from that literature on using technology to support the learning first of young children and second, their teachers.

TECHNOLOGY IN CHILDHOOD—ISSUES AND DEBATES

More than a decade ago, we argued that "we no longer need to ask whether the use of technology is 'appropriate'" in early childhood education (Clements & Swaminathan, 1995). The research supporting that statement was, and remains, convincing. However, social and political

Contemporary Perspectives on Science and Technology in Early Childhood Education, pages 127–147
Copyright © 2008 by Information Age Publishing
All rights of reproduction in any form reserved.

movements often cycle back to issues that research has closed. For example, some publications say that computers have no place in the early childhood classroom because they pose serious hazards—physical, emotional, intellectual, and developmental—to children (Cordes & Miller, 2000). The authors do not discriminate between violent video games and educational software in their broad attack on technology. They quote one negative finding from a study on creativity, but fail to report the many positive affects of using computers on other areas of development from the same study and ignore the many studies showing positive affects of computers on children's creativity. (For a full report on such misinterpretations, and a review of the research, see Clements & Sarama, 2003a.) Such conclusions ignore or misinterpret most of the research on technology in early education. Young children show comfort and confidence in using software. They can understand, think about, and learn from their computer activity (Clements & Nastasi, 1993; Clements & Sarama, 2003a; Wang & Ching, 2003). Here we emphasize one criticism that *is* valid: In practice, reality often falls short of realizing the promise of technology (Cuban, 2001; Healy, 1998).

It is not that technology is underused in general (cf. Cuban, 2001). Children age 6 years and under spend an average of two hours a day using screen media, about the same amount of time they spend playing outside, and well over the amount they spend reading or being read to—about 40 minutes a day (Rideout, Vandewater, & Wartella, 2003). For two-thirds of children, the TV is left on at half the time or more, even if no one is watching, and for one-third the TV is on "always" or "most of the time." A fourth have TVs in their bedrooms.

The problem is that technology is underused for its positive contribution to children's development (Cuban, 2001). Would other forms of media make such contributions? Children using computers show greater levels of concentration than they do watching television (Hyson & Eyman, 1986).

Nearly half of children 6 years and under have used a computer, 31% of 0–3 year-olds and 70% of 4–6 year-olds (Rideout et al., 2003). In a typical day about one in four 4–6 year-olds uses a computer, and those who do spend an average of just over an hour. More than a third of 4–6 year-olds use a computer several times a week or more; 37% in this age group can turn the computer on by themselves, and 40% can load a CD or DVD program (Rideout et al., 2003). About a third of 2 to 5-year-olds are on the Internet, with that group's use increasing at a rate five times that of older children (Grunwald Associates, 2003). So, children can and do use computers. Although children using computers are more active than those watching TV, producing far more active, positive, and emotionally-varied facial expressions than they do watching television (Hyson & Eyman, 1986), it may not be that this time is wisely spent. For example, just under a third have played video games, 14% of 0–3 year-olds and 50% of 4–6 year-olds (Rideout et al., 2003). Further, equity problems remain (Rathbun & West, 2003).

Computer technology can help children learn (Clements & Sarama, 2003a; Sarama & Clements, 2002). Whether it fulfills that potential is largely determined by the approach the software takes and the quality and quantity of professional development their teachers receive. We address each in turn.

APPROACHES TO TEACHING AND LEARNING MATHEMATICS WITH TECHNOLOGY

Young children can use computers and software to support their learning from at least the age of four years on (Clements & Nastasi, 1992; Sarama & Clements, 2002). The nature and extent of technology's contribution depend on what type of technology they use and how it is blended into the curriculum they experience.

Computer-Assisted Instruction (CAI)

Children can use CAI, in which the computer presents information or tasks and gives feedback, to develop their skills and learn some concepts. For example, drill-and-practice software can help young children develop competence in such skills as counting and sorting (Clements & Nastasi, 1993). Indeed, some reviewers claim that the largest gains in the use of CAI have been in mathematics for preschool (Fletcher-Flinn & Gravatt, 1995) or primary-grade children, especially in compensatory education (Lavin & Sanders, 1983; Niemiec & Walberg, 1984; Ragosta, Holland, & Jamison, 1981). This CAI approach may be as or more cost effective than traditional instruction (Fletcher, Hawley, & Piele, 1990) and other instructional interventions, such as peer tutoring and reducing class size (Niemiec & Walberg, 1987). Mathematics CAI appears especially effective in remedial situations and with students from schools serving lower socioeconomic populations (Corning & Halapin, 1989; Hotard & Cortez, 1983; Lavin & Sanders, 1983; McConnell, 1983; Ragosta et al., 1981).

Such results are not guaranteed, but research provides straightforward guidelines for effective use. CAI should be integrated into instruction, so that children are working on content that corresponds closely with the rest of the mathematics curriculum. Children need to have adequate time to work on the software. Ten or more minutes a day proved sufficient time for significant gains; twenty minutes was even better (Lavin & Sanders, 1983; Niemiec & Walberg, 1984; Ragosta et al., 1981).

CAI should include interpretable text, graphics, and sound, appropriate to the age and abilities of the children. It should provide well-sequenced instruction, corrective feedback and positive reinforcement, a high frequency of student response opportunities, and the opportunity for extended remediation through branching when needed (Watson, Chadwick, & Brinkley, 1986).

Finally, CAI should provide individualization for all children, including branching based on children's work and reporting to teachers (Clements, 1994). In one study, the software did not do that, and low-performing children progressed slowly than above-average students (Hativa, 1988). Lower-performing children were hampered by numerous "child-machine" errors; that is, hardware and software difficulties such as switching digits, pressing wrong keys, and pressing keys too long. They had trouble determining the solution algorithm from the final answers presented briefly on the screen. In this case, such difficulties overpowered attempts at remediation. Thus, this system was not individualized for students, and those students most in need suffered for it.

However successful, CAI work that is exclusively drill should be not be used exclusively. Some children may be less motivated to perform academic work or less creative following a steady diet of only drill (Clements & Nastasi, 1985; Haugland, 1992). There are several complements to the CAI approach; one is the computer manipulative.

Computer Manipulatives

Most of us think of "manipulatives" as physical objects. Surprisingly, manipulating shapes and other mathematical objects on the computer can be just as or more effective in supporting learning (Clements & McMillen, 1996). For example, in one study, the first time children reflected on, and planned, putting together shapes to make new shapes, they were working on a computer, not with physical blocks (Sarama, Clements, & Vukelic, 1996). In a similar vein, children who explore shapes on the computer learn to understand and apply concepts such as symmetry, patterns, and spatial order (Wright, 1994). In a study comparing the use of physical bean sticks and onscreen bean sticks, children found the computer manipulative easier to use for learning (Char, 1989).

One of the reasons for this finding is that computer manipulatives can help children to connect different representations. In Figure 7.1a, for example, children manipulate base-ten blocks on screen. They can add or take away any numbers of blocks of different values (1, 10, 100 . . .). Notice,

(a)

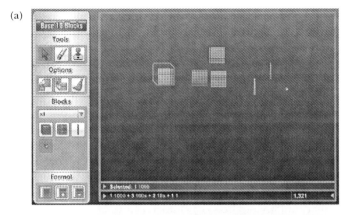

(b)

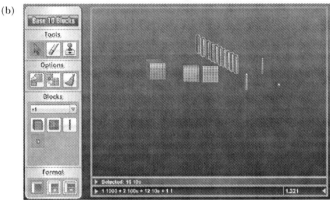

Figure 7.1. Children drag base ten blocks to the work area to create quantities. The software automatically provides different numerical representations. In (b), children have used the "trade" tool to decompose 1 hundreds block into 10 tens.

at the bottom of the screen how, automatically, the software generates different numerical representations. On the left, we see 1 1000 + 3 100s + 2 10s + 1 1. At the right 1,321.

Another reason that computer manipulatives help children is that they allow them to perform specific mathematical transformations on objects on the screen. For example, whereas physical base-ten blocks must be "traded" (when subtracting, children may need to trade 1 ten for 10 ones), children can break a computer base-ten hundreds block directly into 10 tens. For example, in Figure 7.1b a child has broken apart a hundreds block into 10 tens. Such actions are more in line with the *mental actions* that we want children to carry out. The computer also *connects* the blocks to the symbols. For example, the number represented by the base-ten blocks is dynamically connected to the children's actions on the blocks, so that when the child changes the blocks, the number displayed is automatically changed as well. In Figure 7.1b, as the child breaks the 100s block, the amount 210 is the same of course, but the display shows the new number of hundreds and tens. Similarly, if the child removes 3 tens, the display automatically adjusts. Such features can help children make sense of their activity, the numbers, and the arithmetic.

Thus, computer manipulatives can offer unique advantages (Clements & Sarama, 1998; Sarama et al., 1996). They can allow children to save and retrieve work (and that work doesn't get "bumped" and "ruined" or "put away") and thus work on projects over a long period (Ishigaki, Chiba, & Matsuda, 1996). Computers can offer a flexible and manageable manipulative, one that, for example, might "snap" into position. They can provide extensible manipulatives, allowing children to resize shapes, for example, or other manipulations impossible with physical manipulatives. Computer manipulatives can also help connect concrete and symbolic representations by means of multiple, linked representations and feedback. In a similar vein, computers can help bring mathematics to explicit awareness, by asking children consciously to choose what mathematical operations (turn, flip, scale) to apply (Sarama et al., 1996). Children learned more about those operations, and about shapes and composing shapes, than they did working with physical manipulatives.

As an example, Mitchell started making a hexagon out of triangles. After placing two, he counted with his finger on the screen around the center of the incomplete hexagon, imaging the other triangles. He announced that he would need four more. After placing the next one, he said, 'Whoa! Now, three more!' Whereas off-computer, Mitchell had to check each placement with a physical hexagon, the intentional and deliberate actions on the computer lead him to form mental images (decomposing the hexagon imagistically) and predict each succeeding placement (Sarama et al., 1996).

In another study, kindergartners made a greater number of patterns with computer manipulatives than with physical manipulatives or drawing (Moyer, Niezgoda, & Stanley, 2005). They used more elements in their patterns using computer manipulatives. With physical manipulatives, children often lost the pattern after laying down 13 to 16 blocks. They also created shapes by partially occluding one shape with another (which they could not do with physical manipulatives). Creative behavior was more prevalent with the computer manipulatives. All these are consistent with the unique advantages of computer manipulatives.

Finally, technology may also foster deeper conceptual thinking, including a valuable type of "cognitive play" (Steffe & Wiegel, 1994). For example, to develop concepts of length and measurement, children engaged in drawing onscreen sticks, changing the color of a stick, marking a stick, breaking it along the marks, joining the parts back together, and cutting off pieces from a stick. Children adopted a playful attitude as they repeatedly engaged in these activities, and they learned considerable mathematics.

Combining CAI and Computer Manipulatives

The advantages of each of these two types of software can be combined. This is especially important because without computer manipulatives, learning from CAI can be limited. Children do not always learn to manipulate mathematical objects to solve problems independently. Without CAI, children often do not learn to use the features of computer manipulatives, or they explore their surface characteristics only in a trivial manner.

The Building Blocks project was designed to combine CAI and manipulative software. For example, one goal was to help children develop the ability to identify and apply various transformations to two-dimensional shapes. The Building Blocks activities follow a research-based learning trajectory for shape composition (Clements, Wilson, & Sarama, 2004). Children move through levels of thinking in developing the ability to compose two-dimensional figures.

At the earliest level, children have little competence in composing geometric shapes. For example, they cannot complete a pattern block shape puzzle without leaving gaps. They pass through several levels as they learn to combine shapes—initially through trial and error and gradually by attributes—into pictures, and finally synthesize combinations of shapes into new shapes (composite shapes).

In the first suite of activities, "Mystery Pictures," children learn about shapes and see examples of how they can be combined to make pictures. The specific task for children is matching shapes to congruent outlines and hearing their names as they guess what the eventual picture will be (Figure 7.2). The next level is similar, but children have to identify the shapes given their names, instead of a matching outline. Later, children have to solve actual composition problems.

Later in the year, a series of "Piece Puzzler" activities asks children to manipulate shapes to fill puzzles, learning to compose shapes themselves, first without and then with the rigid motions of slide, flip, and turn. The puzzles follow the learning trajectory from simple, highly guided puzzles (Figure 7.3a) to those demanding significant composition competencies (Figure 7.3b). Then, children have to solve similar puzzles, but they only get one shape to use; thus, they must decompose that shape with transformations. One, the axe tool, decomposes shapes into their canonical components (e.g., symmetrical halves). In later problems in the in "Super Shape" suite, children use the scissors tool, which requires them to cut the

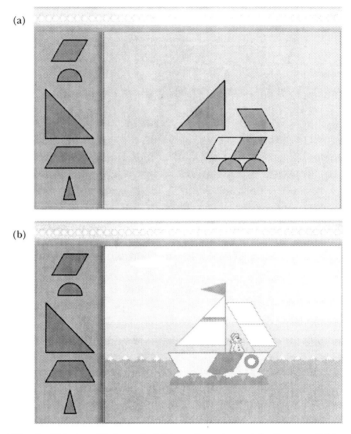

Figure 7.2.   In "Mystery Pictures," children have to match shapes, clicking on the shape in the palette that matches the outlined shape (a). When they finish the task, the full picture is revealed (b).

shape from one vertex or midpoint to another. Thus, they have to create shapes they have not seen before.

Finally, children use the "Create a Scene" program, in which children create their own pictures using the mathematical ideas and skills they have developed. That is, they turn, flip, resize, glue, and even cut shapes to create objects for their pictures (see Figure 7.4). Thus, these are examples of *extensible* manipulatives in a CAI progression, based on learning trajectories.

These *Building Blocks* activities illustrate effective software (empirical support can be found in Clements & Sarama, 2004, in press; Sarama, 2004, and at UBBuildingBlocks.org). To evaluate software, teachers should request empirical evidence, as well as applying general criteria for effective software (Grover, 1986; Haugland & Shade, 1990; Haugland & Wright, 1997), such as providing meaningful contexts, appropriate interface (including reading level), and high-quality feedback.

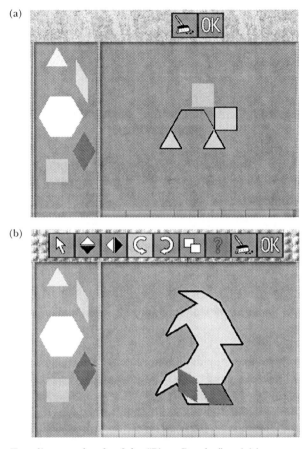

Figure 7.3.   Two disparate levels of the "Piece Puzzler" activities.

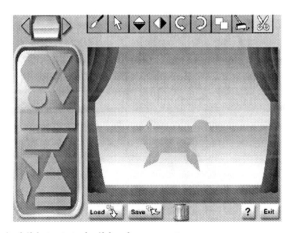

Figure 7.4.   A child starts to build a dog on a stage.

This is not meant as an exhaustive list. Other approaches, such as computer games and the computer programming language Logo, have also shown to be effective, but have been reviewed in previous publications (Clements, 2002; Yelland, 2002a,b).

TEACHERS, TECHNOLOGY, AND PROFESSIONAL DEVELOPMENT

There is evidence that the more teachers receive support using computers, the more their children learn, especially if the support is targeted at effective use of computers with children (Fuller, 2000; Schaffer & Richardson, 2004). Research has described features of effective professional development. Here we summarize this research in three categories: professional development, research-based programs for professional development, and using technology for professional development.

Professional Development in Early Childhood Educational Technology

Many agree on the general characteristics of effective professional development. For example, professional development should be multifaceted, extensive, ongoing, reflective, focused on common actions, problems of practice, and especially children's thinking, grounded in particular curriculum materials, and, as much as possible, situated in the classroom (Cohen, 1996; Darling-Hammond & McLaughlin, 1995; Fullan, 1992; Garet et al., 2001; Kaser et al., 1999; Rényi, 1998; Richardson & Placier, 2001; Sarama & DiBiase, 2004; Swaminathan, 2000). With regard to technology, professional development must be "characterized by access to high-quality software, ongoingness, curriculum and instruction embeddedness, a variety of learning partners (e.g., coordinators, other teachers), a variety of learning formats (e.g., visits, workshops, meetings, group, one-to-one), opportunities for practice-practice-practice and feedback, and data on the impact" (Fullan, 1992, p. 46). It should also involve participants in teams from the same school, model constructivist approaches to learning, and promote ongoing conversations and reflections about practice, theories of learning, and ways that classroom practice might change in the context of technology (Dwyer, Ringstaff, & Sandholtz, 1991). Technology is a particularly challenging field because the learning task is daunting, the vision of high-quality use is not clear, and well-designed, intense, relevant, sustained assistance is critical (Fullan, 1992).

Research has established that less than ten hours of training in technology can have a negative impact (Ryan, 1993). It is thus unfortunate that only 15% of teachers in the U.S. report receiving up to 9 hours of training (Coley, Cradler, & Engel, 1997). This may not easily change because, although college faculty in the U.S. reported being comfortable with computers, they were not satisfied with their ability to integrate this technology into their courses (Sexton et al., 1999). Teachers say that computer courses can be effective, but a third had never taken such a course. U.S. teachers' most preferred method of learning about software is from a tutor; their least preferred is to learn from a manual (Mowrer-Popiel, Pollard, & Pollard, 1993). Courses or workshops should emphasize repeated experiences and discussions regarding the integration of computers into the curriculum, including determining the objectives and contributions of software (Swaminathan, 2000; Swaminathan et al., 2004).

What motivates teachers to learn about and use technology? In one study, the primary reasons Head Start teachers learned about computers were to improve their skills, teach children how to use computers and make teaching easier. The least motivating reason was "others said I should" (Bewick, 2000). Also revealing is that most of these teachers learned about technology by "messing about." In the following section, we examine some models of professional development stemming from large projects that address both motivation and learning systematically and successfully.

Research-based Programs for Professional Development

We begin with a brief overview of programs not specialized in early childhood. In general, these programs indicate that successful programs (a) should emphasize comfort and familiarity with computers and emphasize integration into subject-matter curricula; (b) benefit from support from administrative personnel and outside experts; (c) should provide ongoing, on site technical support, and educate parents and school boards so they understand the demands technology makes on teachers (Ferris & Roberts, 1994). As an example, Gilmore (1995) evaluated a teacher development program that involved teachers in school-based, action-research projects supported by visits from resource personnel who provided one-on-one attention. Clusters of teachers attended meetings to evaluate their experiences, share ideas, and discuss relevant issues. This program led to dramatic increases in teacher confidence in and commitment to using technology and, to a somewhat smaller extent, competence in using computers. Finally, they reported noticeable cognitive and social benefits for their children.

The TICKIT program (Ehman & Bonk, 2002) has documented its success in providing high-level professional development within teachers' schools. The researchers credit TICKIT's effectiveness to its duration (1–2 years), collaborative approach (participants help determine their program), and embeddedness (teachers work in their own classrooms to invent, teach, and reflect upon their technology integration and daily teaching practices). The researchers offer several recommendations in the form of lessons: avoid including teachers who are not volunteers; ensure teachers have a reasonable technology environment in which to work; teach technology use in the teacher's computing environment; ensure a local leader for a cohort of teachers in a school; provide challenge and high expectations; and require projects in a graduate course framework.

A similar comprehensive program, but in the early childhood realm, is the Early Childhood Comprehensive Technology System (ECCTS, Hutinger et al., 1998; Hutinger & Johanson, 2000). The ECCTS was a 3-year collaborative project designed to implement and maintain a comprehensive technology system based on combining four components of nationally recognized demonstration models and peer-reviewed outreach models funded by the Early Education Program for Children with Disabilities in the U.S. Department of Education. The models incorporated (a) ongoing training, follow-up, and technical support for teachers and an on-site technology support team (Tech Team), with an emphasis on hands-on work with computers, software, and adaptive devices; (b) team-based technology assessments for children with moderate to severe disabilities; (c) technology integration into the classroom curriculum; and (d) transition into public school kindergartens and other programs. ECCTS components were effective in establishing, maintaining, and institutionalizing computer technology in a large preschool program.

The ECCTS curriculum experiences, which provide activities involving equalized play, communication, and most subject areas, enhance problem solving and higher-order thinking. Results pointed to the efficacy of an on-site Tech Team, to conditions that promoted maintenance of the system, to increased technology skills between teachers, and to positive outcomes for families and children. When technology was used to support learning, children achieved success; they could accomplish an activity. Further, children made substantial progress in all developmental areas, including social-emotional, fine motor, gross motor, communication, cognition, and self-help. The evaluation demonstrated that computers, when employed according to the ECCTS model, were efficient in promoting attending behaviors, cause and effect reasoning, emergent literacy, and engagement. As a result of computer use, children's social skills increased, such as sharing, turn taking, and communicating. Children also increased in self-confidence, attention span, fine motor skills, and visual-motor skills (e.g., tracking). Results on adults showed that teachers, parents, and administrators were more likely to use computers when they learned to use adult productivity software such as word processing, databases, and spreadsheets, in addition to the software applications for children.

What helped the program achieve these results for children and adults? Effective technology use depended on establishing a functional, well-trained, on-site Tech Team at the school, which provided leadership and support that held the system together. This led to an institutionalization of the program even after the end of external funding. ECCTS findings indicated the teachers were more likely to adopt changes when they observed positive child outcomes and when they had opportunities to see others using the innovation. The program also "started small and grew."

Other early childhood projects produce consistent findings. For example, a project trained teacher facilitators to introduce technology to young children, instruct their peers in the use of early childhood computer programs, and improve family literacy and computer literacy through parent education (Ainsa, 1992). These efforts, which emphasized language arts skills, holistic approaches to computing, "hands-on" activities, and software for young children, led to significant improvements in the use of technology. As a final example, a research-based model for technology integration workshops improved preschool teachers' confidence and comfort in using technology, as shown by a doubling in their interaction with children at the computer and significant increases in children's skill and appropriate use of technology, as well as their performance in problem solving and literacy, including letter identification, word recognition, and concepts of print and phonemic awareness, maintained over the course of three years (Swaminathan et al., 2004; Swaminathan, Trawick-Smith, & Barbuto, 2006). However, the teachers' actual integration of technology into the curriculum remained limited (Swaminathan et al., 2004). It may be that curricula that already carefully integrate software will be most successful.

Using Technology for Professional Development

Sarama (2002) conducted a survey of hundreds of early childhood professionals and found that 71% of the respondents had access to the Internet and 80% would be interested in some sort of distance learning. Thus, professional development may be able to reach many individuals through non-traditional means. There are several projects that have used technology to extend professional development experiences of teachers, however, some have not focused on early childhood. For example, one study reported that collaboratively produced network-based communication was significantly more reflective than face-to-face discourse between teachers (Hawkes, 2001).

Our TRIAD project enhances professional development with a variety of technologies, including discussion boards, e-mail, distance learning centers, and Web sites and applications, enhancing the scalability of the professional development. The most important of these is the *Building Blocks Learning Trajectories* web application.

Building Blocks Learning Trajectories provides scalable access to the learning trajectories via descriptions, videos, and commentaries. Each aspect of the learning trajectories—*developmental progressions* of children's thinking and connected *instruction*—are linked to the other. For example, teachers might choose the ⟨ instruction ⟩ (curriculum) view and see the screen on the left of Figure 7.5. Clicking on a specific activity provides a description. Clicking on ⟨ more info ⟩ slides the screen over to reveal descriptions, several videos of the activity "in action," notes on the video, and the level of thinking in the learning trajectory that activity is designed to develop, as shown below on the right.

Alternatively, the user may have been studying developmental sequences. After choosing ⟨ development ⟩, teachers see a list of the mathematical topics and the developmental sequences. If they had chosen "Count-

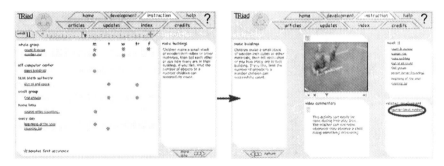

Clicking on the related developmental level, or child's level of thinking, ringed above, switched to the ⟨ development ⟩ view *of that topic and that level of thinking.* This, likewise, provides a description, video, and commentary on the developmental level—the video here is of a clinical interview task in which a child displays that *level of thinking.*

Figure 7.5. The Building Blocks Learning Trajectories web site application (© Clements & Sarama, 2006).

ing," then the "Counter (Small Numbers)" level, and then "More Info," they would see the same screen as above. The video commentary shown is just one of three commentaries. Commentaries are by researchers, assessors, and teachers. Further, the level of thinking is illustrated by both video of clinical interview assessments *and* video of classroom activities in which children show that level of thinking (the icons above the video allow the selection of alternative video), an approach that has received empirical support (Klingner, Ahwee, Pilonieta, & Menendez, 2003).

Of course, the *Building Blocks Learning Trajectories* application is only a tool. All TRIAD teachers are provided a full range of professional development opportunities, based on the research previously described. They participate in a credit-bearing course with five components: (a) a 5-day institute in the summer and 2-day follow up after the winter break, (b) 3-hour classes after school once per month, (c) out-of-class assignments, (d) electronic communications, and (e) coaching and mentoring within each teacher's classroom. All of these components use the web application as a tool.

Similar to the TICKIT and ECCTS programs, the *Building Blocks* has been tested at various phases of development, from one-on-one interviews with children during early phases, to multiple classrooms randomly assigned to treatment or control conditions. In the first summary research study, *Building Blocks* classrooms significantly outperformed the control classrooms on tests of number and geometry (including measurement, patterning, etc.), with effect sizes from 1 to 2 standard deviations, up to double what is considered a strong effect (Clements & Sarama, in press). In a larger study involving 36 classrooms, using the TRIAD model for curriculum implementation on a large scale, the *Building Blocks* curriculum was compared to an alternate, intensive, Pre-K Mathematics Curriculum and control classrooms with standard curricula. Building Blocks classrooms significantly outperformed both other groups in mathematics achievement, with effect sizes above 1 standard deviation compared to the control group and about a half of a standard deviation compared to the alternate intensive curriculum. They also significantly outperformed the control group in classroom observations of the mathematics environment and teaching. These results are consistent with those of the other studies reviewed here and support the use of technology in educating students and teachers.

CONCLUSIONS

We believe that research such as that reviewed here offers substantial guidance in teaching effectively with technology. Children, their parents, and their teachers have considerable and growing access to all types of technology. If high-quality media is selected on the basis of children's educational needs, technology can make a substantive contribution to children's learning. CAI materials, connected consistently in to ongoing instruction and including features such as sequencing and feedback, can lead to significant gains in mathematics. Computer manipulatives, integrated into mathematics curricula, present several unique advantages that, when capitalized upon by teachers, can allow children make mathematical ideas more accessible and more salient. Last, the advantages of these can be combined in software that uses a CAI format to introduce concepts and computer manipulatives, which can become tools for solving a range of mathematical problems.

To take advantage of such educational computer software, teachers need substantial professional development. This work should be long-lasting, hands-on, practical, grounded in the instructional integration of software, and multifaceted, including demonstrations, practice, feedback, and in-classroom coaching and support. Finally, technology can help teachers understand and use technology-based curricula by providing professional development that can be easily accessed and therefore used in workshops, classes, or in early childhood classrooms (e.g., as a quick "reminder").

Every aspect we have described needs committed people working actively at the core. Computers can contribute significantly, but that contribution may be maximized when they are used as a tool by knowledgeable, supported educators working with a research-based curriculum and software.

NOTE

1. This chapter was based upon work supported in part by the National Science Foundation under Grant No. ESI-9730804 and the U.S. Education Department's Institute of Educational Sciences Grant No. R305K05157. Any opinions, findings, and conclusions or recommendations expressed in this material are those of the author(s) and do not necessarily reflect the views of these agencies.

REFERENCES

Ainsa, P. A. (1992). Empowering classroom teachers via early childhood computer education. *Journal of Educational Computing Research, 3*(1), 3–14.

Bewick, C. J. (2000). *The adoption of computers as an instructional tool by Michigan Head Start teachers.* Unpublished Dissertation, Michigan State University.

Char, C. A. (1989). *Computer graphic feltboards: New software approaches for young children's mathematical exploration.* San Francisco: American Educational Research Association.

Clements, D. H. (1994). The uniqueness of the computer as a learning tool: Insights from research and practice. In J. L. Wright & D. D. Shade (Eds.), *Young children: Active learners in a technological age* (pp. 31–50). Washington, D.C.: National Association for the Education of Young Children.

Clements, D. H. (2002). Computers in early childhood mathematics. *Contemporary Issues in Early Childhood, 3*(2), 160–181.

Clements, D. H., & McMillen, S. (1996). Rethinking "concrete" manipulatives. *Teaching Children Mathematics, 2*(5), 270–279.

Clements, D. H., & Nastasi, B. K. (1985). Effects of computer environments on social-emotional development: Logo and computer-assisted instruction. *Computers in the Schools, 2*(2–3), 11–31.

Clements, D. H., & Nastasi, B. K. (1992). Computers and early childhood education. In M. Gettinger, S. N. Elliott & T. R. Kratochwill (Eds.), *Advances in school psychology: Preschool and early childhood treatment directions* (pp. 187–246). Hillsdale, NJ: Lawrence Erlbaum Associates.

Clements, D. H., & Nastasi, B. K. (1993). Electronic media and early childhood education. In B. Spodek (Ed.), *Handbook of research on the education of young children* (pp. 251–275). New York: Macmillan.

Clements, D. H., & Sarama, J. (1998). *Building blocks—Foundations for mathematical thinking, pre-kindergarten to grade 2: Research-based materials development* [National Science Foundation, grant number ESI-9730804; see www.gse.buffalo.edu/org/buildingblocks/]. Buffalo, NY: State University of New York at Buffalo.

Clements, D. H., & Sarama, J. (2003a). Strip mining for gold: Research and policy in educational technology—A response to "fool's gold". *Educational Technology Review, 11.*

Clements, D. H., & Sarama, J. (2003b). Young children and technology: What does the research say? *Young Children, 58*(6), 34–40.

Clements, D. H., & Sarama, J. (2004). *Building Blocks* for early childhood mathematics. *Early Childhood Research Quarterly, 19*, 181–189.

Clements, D. H., & Sarama, J. (in press). Effects of a preschool mathematics curriculum: Summary research on the *Building Blocks* project. *Journal for Research in Mathematics Education.*

Clements, D. H., & Swaminathan, S. (1995). Technology and school change: New lamps for old? *Childhood Education, 71*, 275–281.

Clements, D. H., Wilson, D. C., & Sarama, J. (2004). Young children's composition of geometric figures: A learning trajectory. *Mathematical Thinking and Learning, 6*, 163–184.

Cohen, D. K. (1996). Rewarding teachers for student performance. In S. H. Fuhrman & J. A. O'Day (Eds.), *Rewards and reforms: Creating educational incentives that work.* San Francisco: Jossey Bass.

Coley, R. J., Cradler, J., & Engel, P. K. (1997). *Computers and classrooms: The status of technology in U.S. schools.* Princeton, NJ: Educational Testing Service.

Cordes, C., & Miller, E. (2000). *Fool's gold: A critical look at computers in childhood.* Retrieved November 7, 2000, from http://www.allianceforchildhood.net/projects/computers/computers_reports.htm

Corning, N., & Halapin, J. (1989). *Computer applications in an action-oriented kindergarten.* Wallingford: Connecticut Institute for Teaching and Learning Conference.

Cuban, L. (2001). *Oversold and underused.* Cambridge, MA: Harvard University Press.

Darling-Hammond, L., & McLaughlin, M. W. (1995). Policies that support professional development in an era of reform. *Phi Delta Kappan, 76,* 597–604.

Dwyer, D. C., Ringstaff, C., & Sandholtz, J. H. (1991). Changes in teachers' beliefs and practices in technology-rich classrooms. *Educational Leadership, 48,* 45–52.

Ehman, L. H., & Bonk, C. J. (2002). *A model of teacher professional development to support technology integration.* New Orleans: American Educational Research Association.

Ferris, A., & Roberts, N. (1994, Autumn/Winter). Teachers as technology leaders: Five case studies. *Educational Technology Review,* 11–18.

Fletcher, J. D., Hawley, D. E., & Piele, P. K. (1990). Costs, effects, and utility of microcomputer assisted instruction in the classroom. *American Educational Research Journal, 27,* 783–806.

Fletcher-Flinn, C. M., & Gravatt, B. (1995). The efficacy of computer assisted instruction (CAI): A meta-analysis. *Journal of Educational Computing Research, 12,* 219–242.

Fullan, M. G. (1992). *Successful school improvement.* Philadelphia, PA: Open University Press.

Fuller, H. L. (2000). First teach their teachers-Technology support and computer use in academic subjects. *Journal of Research on Computing in Education, 32,* 511–537.

Garet, M. S., Porter, A. C., Desimone, L., Birman, B. F., & Yoon, K. S. (2001). What makes professional development effective? Results from a national sample of teachers. *American Educational Research Journal, 38,* 915–945.

Gilmore, A. M. (1995). Turning teachers on to computers: Evaluation of a teacher development program. *Journal of Research on Computing in Education, 27,* 251–269.

Grover, S. C. (1986). A field study of the use of cognitive-developmental principles in microcomputer design for young children. *Journal of Educational Research, 79,* 325–332.

Grunwald Associates. (2003). *Connected to the future.* Retrieved April 16, 2003, 2003, from http://www.cpb.org/stations/reports/connected/

Hativa, N. (1988). Computer-based drill and practice in arithmetic: Widening the gap between high- and low-achieving students. *American Educational Research Journal, 25,* 366–397.

Haugland, S. W. (1992). Effects of computer software on preschool children's developmental gains. *Journal of Computing in Childhood Education, 3*(1), 15–30.

Haugland, S. W., & Shade, D. D. (1990). *Developmental evaluations of software for young children.* Albany, NY: Delmar.

Haugland, S. W., & Wright, J. L. (1997). *Young children and technology: A world of discovery.* Boston: Allyn and Bacon.

Hawkes, M. (2001). Variables of interest in exploring the reflective outcomes of network-based communication. *Journal of Research on Computing in Education, 33*, 299–315.

Healy, J. (1998). *Failure to connect: How computers affect our children's minds—for better or worse.* New York: Simon and Schuster.

Hotard, S. R., & Cortez, M. J. (Cartographer). (1983). *Computer-assisted instruction as an enhancer of remediation.*

Hutinger, P. L., Bell, C., Beard, M., Bond, J., Johanson, J., & Terry, C. (1998). *The early childhood emergent literacy technology research study. Final report.* Macomb: Western Illinois University.

Hutinger, P. L., & Johanson, J. (2000). Implementing and maintaining an effective early childhood comprehensive technology system. *Topics in Early Childhood Special Education, 20*(3), 159–173.

Hyson, M. C., & Eyman, A. (1986). Approaches to computer literacy in early childhood teacher education. *Young Children.*

Ishigaki, E. H., Chiba, T., & Matsuda, S. (1996). Young children's communication and self expression in the technological era. *Early Childhood Development and Care, 119*, 101–117.

Kaser, J. S., Bourexis, P. S., Loucks-Horsley, S., & Raizen, S. A. (1999). *Enhancing program quality in science and mathematics.* Thousand Oaks, CA: Corwin Press.

Klingner, J. K., Ahwee, S., Pilonieta, P., & Menendez, R. (2003). Barriers and facilitators in scaling up research-based practices. *Exceptional Children, 69*, 411–429.

Lavin, R. J., & Sanders, J. E. (1983). *Longitudinal evaluation of the C/A/I Computer Assisted Instruction Title 1 Project: 1979–82*: Chelmsford, MA: Merrimack Education Center.

McConnell, B. B. (Cartographer). (1983). *Evaluation of computer instruction in math. Pasco School District. Final Report.*

Mowrer-Popiel, E., Pollard, C., & Pollard, R. (1993). An investigation of preservice education students' perceptions of computer technology. In N. Estes & M. Thomas (Eds.), *Rethinking the roles of technology in education* (Vol. 1, pp. 180–182). Cambridge, MA: Massachuseets Institute of Technology.

Moyer, P. S., Niezgoda, D., & Stanley, J. (2005). Young children use of virtual manipulatives and other forms of mathematical representations. In W. Masalski & P. C. Elliott (Eds.), *Technology-supported mathematics learning environments: 67th Yearbook* (pp. 17–34). Reston, VA: National Council of Teachers of Mathematics.

Niemiec, R. P., & Walberg, H. J. (1984). Computers and achievement in the elementary schools. *Journal of Educational Computing Research, 1*, 435–440.

Niemiec, R. P., & Walberg, H. J. (1987). Comparative effects of computer-assisted instruction: A synthesis of reviews. *Journal of Educational Computing Research, 3*, 19–37.

Ragosta, M., Holland, P., & Jamison, D. T. (1981). *Computer-assisted instruction and compensatory education: The ETS/LAUSD study.* Princeton, NJ: Educational Testing Service.

Rathbun, A. H., & West, J. (2003). *Young children's access to computers in the home and at school in 1999 and 2000, NCES 2003-036.* Washington, DC: U.S. Department of Education, National Center for Education Statistics.

Rényi, J. (1998). Building learning into the teaching job. *Educational Leadership, 55,* 70–74.

Richardson, V., & Placier, P. (2001). Teacher change. In V. Richardson (Ed.), *Handbook of research on teaching* (4th ed., pp. 905–947). Washington, DC: American Educaitonal Research Association.

Rideout, V. J., Vandewater, E. A., & Wartella, E. A. (2003). *Zero to six: Electronic media in the lives of infants, toddlers and preschoolers.* Washington, DC: Henry J. Kaiser Foundation.

Ryan, A. W. (1993). The impact of teacher training on achievement effects of microcomputer use in elementary schools: A meta-analysis. In N. Estes & M. Thomas (Eds.), *Rethinking the roles of technology in education* (Vol. 2, pp. 770–772). Cambridge, MA: Massachusetts Institute of Technology.

Sarama, J. (2002). Listening to teachers: Planning for professional development. *Teaching Children Mathematics, 9,* 36–39.

Sarama, J. (2004). Technology in early childhood mathematics: *Building Blocks™* as an innovative technology-based curriculum. In D. H. Clements, J. Sarama, & A.-M. DiBiase (Eds.), *Engaging young children in mathematics: Standards for early childhood mathematics education* (pp. 361–375). Mahwah, NJ: Lawrence Erlbaum Associates.

Sarama, J., & Clements, D. H. (2002). Learning and teaching with computers in early childhood education. In O. N. Saracho & B. Spodek (Eds.), *Contemporary perspectives in early childhood education* (pp. 171–219). Greenwich, CT: Information Age Publishing, Inc.

Sarama, J., Clements, D. H., & Vukelic, E. B. (1996). The role of a computer manipulative in fostering specific psychological/mathematical processes. In E. Jakubowski, D. Watkins, & H. Biske (Eds.), *Proceedings of the 18th annual meeting of the North America Chapter of the international group for the psychology of mathematics education* (Vol. 2, pp. 567–572). Columbus, OH: ERIC Clearinghouse for Science, Mathematics, and Environmental Education.

Sarama, J., & DiBiase, A.-M. (2004). The professional development challenge in preschool mathematics. In D. H. Clements, J. Sarama, & A.-M. DiBiase (Eds.), *Engaging young children in mathematics: Standards for early childhood mathematics education* (pp. 415–446). Mahwah, NJ: Lawrence Erlbaum Associates.

Schaffer, S., & Richardson, J. (2004). *Looking at barriers to educational technology integration in schools from a performance support systems approach.* San Diego, CA: American Educational Research Association.

Seng, S.-H. (Cartographer). (1999). *Enhancing learning: Computers and early childhood education* [Information Analysis].

Sexton, D., King, N., Aldridge, J., & Goodstat-Killoran, I. (1999). Measuring and evaluating early childhood porspective practitioners' attitudes toward computers. *Family Relations, 48*(3), 277–285.

Steffe, L. P., & Wiegel, H. G. (1994). Cognitive play and mathematical learning in computer microworlds. *Journal of Research in Childhood Education, 8*(2), 117–131.

Swaminathan, S. (2000). Integrating technology within the curriculum: Teachers' challenges and teacher educators' insights. *Journal of Early Childhood Teacher Education, 21*(2), 289–294.

Swaminathan, S., Barbuto, L. M., Trawick-Smith, J., & Wright, J. L. (2004). *Technology training for preschool teachers: Study of the training model, pedagogical changes and student learning.* Paper presented at the American Educational Research Association, San Diego, CA.

Swaminathan, S., Trawick-Smith, J., & Barbuto, L. M. (2006). *Technology training for preschool teachers: Effects on children's computer competence, longitudinal impact on literacy development.* Paper presented at the American Educational Research Association, San Fransicso, CA.

Wang, X. C., & Ching, C. C. (2003). Social construction of computer experience in a first-grade classroom: Social processes and mediating artifacts. *Early Education and Development, 14*(3), 335–361.

Watson, J. A., Chadwick, S. S., & Brinkley, V. M. (1986). Special education technologies for young children: Present and future learning scenarios with related research literature. *Journal of the Division for Early Childhood, 10,* 197–208.

Wright, J. L. (1994). Listen to the children: Observing young children's discoveries with the microcomputer. In J. L. Wright & D. D. Shade (Eds.), *Young children: Active learners in a technological age* (pp. 3–17). Washington, DC: National Association for the Education of Young Children.

Yelland, N. J. (2002a). Creating microworlds for exploring mathematical understandings in the early years of school. *Journal of Educational Computing Research, 27*(1&2), 77–92.

Yelland, N. J. (2002b). Playing with ideas and games in early mathematics. *Contemporary Issues in Early Childhood, 3*(2), 197–215.

CHAPTER 8

VOCABULARY LEARNING BY COMPUTER IN KINDERGARTEN

The Possibilities of Interactive Vocabulary Books

Eliane Segers and Anne Vermeer

Vocabulary knowledge is an important factor for school success; early differences in vocabulary knowledge appear to have a strong impact on such success (Baker, Simmons, & Kame'enui, 1998). Especially immigrant children often enter school with limited knowledge of the second language, and research by Verhoeven and Vermeer (1992, 2001, 2006), for example, has shown the Dutch vocabularies of immigrant children in the Netherlands (i.e., children learning Dutch as a second language) to be much smaller than those of native children. Moreover, this difference tends to increase during the elementary school years, a phenomenon referred to as the Matthew effect (Stanovich, 1986).

Vocabulary can be acquired through independent reading. Children often learn the meaning of new words via the context (Kuhn & Stahl, 1998; Sternberg, 1987). However, when children cannot yet read, they are dependent on others to read to them. Storybook reading in Kindergarten plays a significant role in children's vocabulary development (Elley, 1989). Read-

Contemporary Perspectives on Science and Technology in Early Childhood Education, pages 149–166
Copyright © 2008 by Information Age Publishing
149

ing stories aloud impacts children's learning, helps them to gain insight into the meanings of words, and thereby promotes vocabulary growth (see Bus, Van IJzendoorn & Pellegrini, 1995, for a review). This effect has been observed both at home and in the school environment. Particularly when the teacher or parent elaborates on the story and interacts with the children, the learning gains can be quite high. When entering schools, first language learners are sometimes called 'the 1000-story children', since their parents have read about one story per day to them. This is a lot to catch up with for second language learners, and new ways to enhance their vocabulary are being sought. For second language learning children, reading books is not enough. Not only do they have more difficulties in understanding the stories read by the teacher in Kindergarten because of their limited vocabulary in their second language (Dutch), but, as a consequence of that limited vocabulary, they learn fewer words from those stories than their Dutch peers. Native Dutch children are able to guess the correct meaning of unknown words on the basis of the other—already known—words in the context. For their second language learning peers, the relative number of words known to them in a story is often too low to make a correct guess of the unknown words.

It has often been argued that the computer can be used to supplement reading to children but not replace the teacher (De Jong & Bus, 2002). In recent years, the computer has become very common in schools and books on computers have become available. These are books presented on the computer that include such features as animations or karaoke text. These computer books allow children to interact with the story (Anderson, 1992; Underwood & Underwood, 1998). They are very motivating, combine both audio and visual elements, and can thus, besides contribute to literacy development, enhance vocabulary (Stine, 1993). Recent developments also include speech recognition into the books on the computer, so children can read with the computer (Aist, 2002). Some have high expectations as regards the (positive) effects on the skills of all pupils, but others (e.g., Wood, 2001) question whether the medium in question is suitable for everything and everybody.

The present chapter is about vocabulary learning from books on computers in Kindergarten. Kindergartners cannot yet read and therefore learn new words from stories being read to them. The chapter will have a special focus on the effects of books on computers on the vocabulary learning for second language learners. First, a general review on books on computers will be given. Then we turn to vocabulary learning. After a short introduction on learning and teaching of vocabulary, we will present books on computer that are specifically designed for vocabulary learning. Research on this type of software is scarce, but will be described with the help of two Dutch examples. The software will be compared, after which suggestions can be made on how to optimize vocabulary learning in Kindergarten by the use of interactive vocabulary books.

BOOKS ON THE COMPUTER

De Jong and Bus (2003) distinguish three types of books on computer: talking books (with a minimum of multimedia and interactivity), living books (multimedia combined with limited activity) and interactive books (stories that combine multimedia with interactivity). The three types have been studied in several experiments by these researchers. De Jong and Bus (2002) compared adult book reading to computer book reading in Kindergarten. They found that both computer and human reading supported early literacy learning, although the regular format did have some advances. They concluded that books on computers can be a supplement to, but not a replacement of, the teacher. De Jong and Bus (2004) focused on the use of hot-spots in books on computers. These are often not story related and are therefore thought to interfere with learning. The researchers, however, found no effects of the hot spots on story understanding. These studies did not focus on the vocabulary learning possibilities of books on computers. Two other studies comparing adult book reading and computer reading did include vocabulary learning.

The first study was performed by Terrell and Daniloff (1996). They compared children's vocabulary development after live adult reading, listening to stories with still pictures presented on a computer (talking books), or watching an animated video version of the same stories on television, and found a small significant advantage for live reading. In a second study (Segers, Takke, & Verhoeven, 2004), the same advantage for live reading was found as compared to living books. These researchers compared a story read to children by the computer with little animation and little interaction, to a story read by the teacher showing pictures and interacting normally with the children. Vocabulary gains were found in both conditions; for immigrant children, however, the gains were larger when the teacher read the story.

Yet another study on living books was performed by Johnston (1997), but this study did not compare adult reading to computer reading. Johnston did not investigate vocabulary gain exclusively. The control group in this experimental study was engaged in regular classroom activities. Johnston trained kindergartners using living books for 300 minutes across a period of seven weeks. A learning gain was found on the combined variable of "verbal abilities," which included pictorial and verbal memory, word knowledge, verbal fluency, and opposite analogies.

One can conclude from the above examples that book reading by computer is feasible, and gives children a learning opportunity. As stated often though, the computer should not be a replacement for the teacher or parent. As far as this type of research is concerned, we think Reinking (2001) is right in arguing that since the computer will not disappear from schools, it is more fruitful to study what type of computer environment offers the best effects, instead of comparing real books versus books on computers.

Ricci and Beal (2002) conducted such an experiment in which they compared different conditions: audio only story presentation, audiovisual presentation (television), interactive presentation on the computer with the child clicking hot spots in the story pictures (living books), and children observing the interactive computer group. The researchers found the inclusion of visual stimuli to have additional value for story comprehension and recall. No differences were found among the three groups of children receiving direct visual input, and the children receiving the computer version were neither hindered nor helped by the hot spots. Unfortunately, vocabulary development was not considered in this study.

Verhallen, Bus and De Jong (2006) conducted an experiment in which vocabulary was studied in Kindergartners using books on computers. They compared different presentation formats of a story (multimedia, static, or combinations) and single to quadruple presentations and found that exposure to the multimedia format four times caused the highest vocabulary gain.

The studies presented above elaborated mostly on the already known positive effects of storybook reading on vocabulary development (Bus et al., 1995), and others did not have vocabulary learning as an explicit goal. Based on this overview on research on the effect of books on computers for pre-reading children, we share the statement by Blachowicz and Fisher (2000) that surprisingly little research has addressed the possibilities of extending children's vocabularies using the computer. The computer has more possibilities than presenting interactive multimedia stories. To further enhance vocabulary learning by the computer, especially by second language learners, additional materials in the form of explicit games can be made available, in which special attention is being paid to vocabulary learning. Vocabulary learning then becomes a goal instead of a positive side effect. This leads to an extended version of interactive books: software that offers all kinds of vocabulary games that are connected to a story that is being told, we will call these *interactive vocabulary books*. In interactive vocabulary books, words are presented in a more explicit manner. Thus, these books potentially offer far more possibilities to enhance vocabulary learning. Children who lag behind may be able to catch up with their peers.

These types of books on computers offer a new concept, and scientific research on the effects is scarce. There is considerable entertainment software, but this software is designed for the home-market and often lacks a solid educational basis (Schacter & Fagnano, 1999), and claims about learning effects are most often not tested (Wood, 2001).

For many of the words offered in entertainment software, it is not clear what concept or part of a concept is intended by the picture presented, and, by consequence, words are consequently semanticized incorrectly (Strating & Vermeer, 2001). For example: for the computer to say "tree" if you move over a tree would be a logical example, but unfortunately, the child hears "on top" when moving over a chest, "to flourish" when moving over a magic wand, or "to dress up" when moving over a magician (as in *Babbelbij,* a Dutch software program for young children). This, of course, also occurs in ordinary teaching, but the computer environment offers far fewer opportunities for checking and feedback, followed by the clearing up of the misunderstandings, than the presence of a teacher with whom the meaning of a word can be negotiated. It is especially because of these limited possibilities that computer material should pay far more attention to unambiguous interpretations. The fact that the vast majority of the exercises programmed can only be solved if there is already sufficient knowledge of the language brings Wood (2001) in her review to the conclusion that software products often are offering merely drill and practice routines, rather than helping students really know a word. They often appeal to knowledge that still has to be acquired by the language learner. The review suggests caution in relying on computers alone to foster vocabulary growth.

We present two Dutch examples of interactive vocabulary books in this chapter that try to overcome this problem. To the best of our knowledge, these are the only examples of such interactive vocabulary books for kindergartners that have been studied in scientific experiments. Both software programs were developed in cooperation between a university and a publisher, by using funds of the Dutch government, and designed for Kindergarten with a special focus on second language learners. In the Netherlands, Kindergarten starts at age 4, and lasts two years. Formal reading education starts after Kindergarten in first grade.

The first interactive vocabulary book is called *Schatkist met de muis* ("*Treasure Chest with the mouse*") and was released in 1999. The software not only focuses on vocabulary acquisition, but on the broad range of learning goals in Kindergarten such as metalinguistic awareness, beginning literacy and becoming familiar with books and stories. The software includes, in other words, more than an interactive vocabulary book. The second program is called *Woorden Vangen* ("*Catching words*") and was released in 2003. The program focuses solely on vocabulary acquisition and offers the children more in depth learning of the words in an adaptive manner. Both software programs will be described below and research results will be presented. To build the context for the research results a brief discussion on vocabulary learning and teaching is presented first.

TWO DUTCH EXAMPLES OF INTERACTIVE VOCABULARY BOOKS

Background: Learning and Teaching of Vocabulary

In learning a word, three principles play a role: *labeling, categorizing,* and *network building.* Labeling refers to the activity in which a word form (*label*) is attached to a certain object or action (Aitchison, 1994). The child learns that the label *chair* refers to the object CHAIR. Next, the child learns to categorize: he or she learns that his or her own little chair, but also the chair of the teacher, and the chair in the kitchen at home, etcetera, belong to the category of *chair,* but not the bench or the stool. Network building refers to relations between words, as between *to sit, chair* and *stool.* The existence of such networks is very important in the use, retrieval, and understanding of words in actual speech (Schmitt, 2000).

In teaching new words and labels, four phases can be distinguished: *preparation, semantization, consolidation* and *evaluation* (Verhallen & Verhallen, 1994). In the phase of preparation a context is offered in which new words and labels can easily be linked with already existing experiences and knowledge, which enhances links between new words and already known words and concepts. Semantization refers to learning the different aspects of the meaning of a word: by illustrations, synonyms or antonyms, by defining or translating, by giving examples of use in different contexts, by showing or hearing, by tasting or feeling. A new word is best learned if it is semanticized in as many as possible ways. In the phase of consolidation, the newly learned word and its meanings are anchored in the mental lexicon by exercising and repeating in different contexts. In the last phase, evaluation, is it controlled whether the word is really acquired. In the two software programs described below, we have incorporated these requirements for learning and teaching vocabulary (see for more information on learning vocabulary, Nation, 2001).

Schatkist met de muis ("Treasure chest with the mouse")

Background (more elaborately described in Segers & Verhoeven, 2002). *Schatkist met de muis* (SmdM) is a child-friendly computer software program designed to enhance the early literacy skills of Kindergarteners in the Netherlands, with a special focus on immigrant children. SmdM is part of a program used by the vast majority of teachers in Kindergarten that is a primer, linked to the reading program *Veilig Leren Lezen* ('Learning to read safely'; Mommers, Verhoeven, & Van der Linden, 1990) typically used in grade one. The Kindergarten program has four main literacy objectives: (a) becoming familiar with books and stories, (b) enlarging vocabulary, (c) enhancing metalinguistic awareness, and (d) discovering the alphabetic principle. SmdM also covers these four areas, however, the present chapter only deals with the first two objectives.

Description of the software. In the computer program, a story with story pictures as anchors is presented (Bransford et al., 1990). When children first play with one of the five CD-ROMs and choose to play with the story/vocabulary part of the program by clicking on the little book, they listen to a story. The story is short, about 300 words, and consists of high-frequency words that Kindergarteners with a limited vocabulary can be expected to understand. The story was intentionally kept short in order not to lose the children's attention. At the end of each story fragment, a parrot puppet at the bottom of the screen asks a question, which the children can then answer by clicking somewhere in the picture. In such a manner, the children are actively involved in the story and their understanding is enlarged.

If a child cannot hear or understand the question, he or she can click on the parrot to have the question repeated. When the child provides an incorrect answer, the little pirate next to the parrot helps them. First by telling the child that the answer was not correct and that he or she should try to answer the question again. If the second answer is incorrect, four large green arrows then point at the correct object in the picture. If the child still does not click in the right area, the program takes control of the cursor and points to the correct answer. In this way, children can never get 'stuck' in the program. The children can also ask the pirate for help by clicking on it; the four green arrows then point at the correct object.

At the end of the story, the child is asked to arrange the pictures in the correct order. This is a difficult task, but pilot research showed that the pictures could be correctly ordered in a maximum of five attempts. The next time the child enters the storybook, he or she can choose to listen to the story again or immediately start playing with the vocabulary games, which are described below.

After the child has listened to the story at least once, vocabulary games can be played using the story pictures. The story pictures all represent a fairly "high knot" in the semantic network and thus have numerous relations: a bakery, a living room, a forest, or a supermarket. With each picture, many words can be learned by playing several types of vocabulary games.

Figure 8.1.   Vocabulary game SmdM: Can you place the elf among the mushrooms? (SmdM, CD-ROM 2).

The first type of vocabulary game is the pointing game, which requires children to point at the objects the parrot asks for. As usual, the pirate provides help when needed. The second type of vocabulary game is the shifting game, which requires the child to move an object to a particular place in the picture. The parrot asks the child, for example, to place the cup of coffee on the kitchen table. This game is of special interest for learning prepositions, which can be particularly problematic for young children (see Figure 8.1 for an example). The third vocabulary game is a yes/no game. The child must decide whether an object belongs in the picture or not. The parrot asks, for example, whether you can buy a carrot in a bakery or not. The fourth vocabulary game is a coloring game in which objects in the picture have to be painted or decorated. The parrot asks the child, for example, to paint the curtains red or make the curtains flowered.

When the child demonstrates no problems with these games, two other vocabulary games become successively available. The first game is a pointing game in which the parrot chops the words into syllables (e.g., Can you point to the kit-chen ta-ble?). The second game involves a word being written on the screen and the graphemes lighting up as the parrot slowly pronounces the word. These two games stimulate not only vocabulary acquisition but also metalinguistic awareness of the ability to reflect on the units of language.

As can be seen in the upper left above the picture in Figure 8.1, the child has to answer five questions per session. The figures above the picture turn green, yellow, or red depending on how many attempts it takes the child to answer a question. The answering of the five questions cannot be interrupted, so the child is not encouraged to switch from one thing to the next. Each of the five available CD-ROMs contains 200 questions with 50 questions per picture.

Research on SmdM. The effects of the software on vocabulary learning has been elaborately studied. In two first pilot studies, Segers and Verhoeven (2002) studied immigrant children in their first (n = 20) or second (n = 30) year in Kindergarten. The youngest children worked six times 15 minutes with the story and vocabulary games, the older children worked three times 25 minutes. Significant learning gains were found ($p < .001$).

Segers and Verhoeven (2003) implemented the software in a regular school setting with 67 native and immigrant children in their first and second year in Kindergarten. Children worked with the computer under supervision of volunteer parents in fifteen-minute sessions, twice a week during half a school year. The parents provided little assistance; they answered questions of the children (cf. Klein & Darom, 2000). A significant effect of the computer intervention was found in comparison to a control group ($p < .05$). However, no effect on a standardized vocabulary test was found. It was observed that especially second language learners who came to Kindergarten with little or no knowledge of the Dutch language had difficulties in working with the software in the beginning. Native children had higher learning gains in their first school year, whereas immigrant children had higher learning gains in their second year in Kindergarten, when they had a basic Dutch vocabulary.

The software was also studied in other populations: Segers and Verhoeven (in press) showed how children in special education enhanced their vocabulary with this type of software, and Segers, Nooijen and De Moor (2006) also found learning effects in children with special needs, although the effects were less clear-cut. These latter children need software that is better designed for their needs.

Woorden Vangen ("Catching Words")

Background (more elaborately described in Van de Guchte & Vermeer, 2004). *Woorden vangen* (WV) has been released in two themes ("school" and "playing"). Both consist of a large picture book for the teacher with a story, a CD-ROM cassette with an audio CD with the story, together with a small picture book with the same illustrations, and a CD-ROM with the story and various vocabulary games. The purpose of the program is vocabulary learning, especially for children with Dutch as a second language. Each theme has 140 target words, on four levels of difficulty (35 words each level). From a curriculum-developmental point of view, the main characteristic of WV is that the different games are built as "empty frames" in such a way that, as soon as the child chooses a specific game, that game is filled with the learning content (the words) from a database, depending on the level of vocabulary of the child and his past performance in the games. In this way, it is possible that the program builds a user model, on the basis of which a choice is made with respect to the next interaction form, or the content items that are next in line. In the eleven different games on the CD-ROM, there is no programmed order, so the child can choose his preferred game. That choice does not influence which words are offered: all words are offered in almost all games. The variation in games meets the different preferences of children: some adapt more to motor skills (the child has to catch objects with a bird's beak), others more to cognitive skills (the child has to find out which illustration is newly added to an earlier presented series), and a third kind, more to associative skills (categorizing words: which of these ones do you see in the school-yard?). The games also meet the different learning styles of children: in some games they have to compare silhouettes (visual), in others they have to connect objects of actions to descriptions (verbal), and in the "parrot-game" they have to connect the sound (e.g., of a bell, or the sound of tear-ing up a paper) to the object or action (auditive).

Description of the activities. In the classroom, the teacher reads the story aloud, showing the pictures to the children. On the back of the (very large) pictures two versions of the story are printed out for the teacher—an original, and a simplified version. As in SmdM, the story creates a meaning-ful context for the target words, with twelve pictures as anchors. After the story has been read, the children can listen to the story again on the CD, at home or at school. They can also use the CD-ROM on the computer, and choose between listening to the story or playing different games. In the story on the CD-ROM, the children can go back and forth in the twelve pic-tures, so they can skip fragments or repeat parts of the story again. In each picture the children can move the mouse over details. That object then becomes bigger, and at the same time the label is pronounced (e.g., "the clock"). Some words have an accompanying sound (ticking of the clock) or an animation (the hands of the clock turn around).

The child can also choose to play games. At first, they can choose between seven different types of games, and if they have learned more words in the games, four more types of games become available. During these games, children can earn different stamps to play a rewarding game with. There are also verbal rewards if the child gives a correct response, in the form of many different kinds of feedback: from "well done" to "there is nothing wrong with your ears."

Figure 8.2.   WV: The bat game (silhouette) and pelican game.

Most of the games are semanticizing in nature, meant to acquire the meaning of words. In the "bat-game" (see Figure 8.2), the child has to match a given picture with one of the silhouettes shown. Every time as he moves the mouse over a picture, he hears the word. In the "pelican-game" (see Figure 8.2) the child has to search for a word (auditory given) in a pile of cards with pictures. Every time he moves a particular card aside, he or she hears the word of the object on that card. Thus, in most games the object or action in the picture is directly connected to its spoken word.

Next to these semanticizing games, in some games the child's knowledge of a word is tested. In all games, if the child makes a mistake, feedback is given in the form of a description of the word. Thus, if the child delivers the bench to the pelican, instead of the heater that the pelican asked for, then he hears: "No, that is not the heater. A heater is used to make it warm inside, if it is cold outside." Other ways of semanticizing words in WV are provided in categorizing games, in which the child has to put together words that belong to a certain domain, e.g., in the "monkey-game" he has to choose from many pictures on a wheel he can turn around, three objects that are associated with "to draw": a paper, a pen, a pencil. Next to this game, children can look up words in a 'dictionary' (in fact, a pictionary), in which next to the word and its picture, a context sentence and a definition are given, the translation of the word in Turkish, Moroccan Arabic or English is provided, and four other words that belong to the same domain. After every three mistakes the child makes, the dictionary opens automatically with the picture of that word, and gives a context sentence, e.g., "That is a beautiful pencil. You can make a nice drawing with that pencil." The child himself can also open the dictionary and ask for a translation or description of a picture, by moving a spider's web to that picture.

As the child is playing the games, the program automatically selects the words for a particular child from the database. First, words are chosen from level one, the easiest words. If the child shows to know the words on this level, the program automatically selects words of level two, the more difficult words, and so forth, to level three and four. However, if the child misses too many words on level three, the program switches back to level two, and so on. After three times correct, a word is tagged as "known" and will no longer be selected. All children start at level one, but a child that has a vocabulary equivalent to level three, quickly arrives at that level after three or four games. Words are only tagged as "known" on the basis of games that are apt to do so. If, by chance, a child chooses semanticizing games only, the program forces him or her to play a game in which testing his knowledge is possible. This system of evaluation and testing knowledge does not interfere with the system of rewarding a child with stamps and new games. The child does not know that knowledge is tested, nor does he or she know anything about levels. If all words are tagged as "known", the child is advised to ask the teacher for the next CD-ROM.

Research on Woorden Vangen. On two different schools in Tilburg (a medium-sized town in the south of The Netherlands), 27 Dutch L2 speaking children (mean age 5;6 years; 12 girls and 15 boys) were selected to participate in an experiment in a pre-test-treatment-post-test design. For the curriculum dependent pre-test and post-test 52 items were randomly selected from the 140 targets words of WV, each level 13 items. It was a receptive test, individually administered, in which four pictures were presented, the experimenter said the word (item) which was tested, and the child had to point to the correct picture. The maximum score was 52. The reliability was good, Cronbach's alpha being .83 and .88 in the pre-test and post-test, respectively.

In one Kindergarten, the teacher read the story first in the class, and after that the children played the games on the CD-ROM. In the other Kindergarten, the story book was not presented by the teacher, but the children listened to the story on the computer. In both groups, the children played the games during four weeks, each child in 10 sessions of about 20 minutes (mean time spent = 225 minutes). After that period of four weeks, the children were tested again. Analyses showed that all children made considerable progress in vocabulary ($p < .001$). Surprisingly, the children who listened to the story on the computer only made more progress than the children who heard the story from both the teacher and the computer (interaction pre-test/post-test * condition: $p = .05$).

Comparison of SmdM and WV

In comparing the two examples, the effects of the WV study can best be compared to the pilot study with immigrant children in their second year in Kindergarten done with SmdM, because the two settings are most equal.

The learning gain (defined as the words known in the post-test as a per-
centage of the words not known in the pre-test) of SmdM in this study
(Segers & Verhoeven, 2002) was 23,08% for the second language learners
in their second year in Kindergarten, whereas the learning gain of WV was
51%. The learning gain of WV is almost twice as much as the learning gain
of SmdM and of comparable gains in other vocabulary studies with children of that age (Appel & Vermeer, 1998; McKeown & Curtis, 1987). The
difference can be explained by the fact that the children in the WV study
worked for 225 minutes with the software, in which 140 different words
had to be learned, and the children in the SmdM study for 75 minutes, in
which about 100 different words were offered. In future research we plan
to do better comparisons. For now, we will focus on similarities and differences between the two examples.

SmdM and WV both adapt the principle of learning new words via the
context of a story: preparation. With regards to semantization, the shifting
games and the yes/no games in SmdM help children to learn words, without them having to know how to label the words. WV does the same in several semanticizing games, tracking down each word individually, and uses
more alternatives than SmdM, in particular in building networks around
words. Consolidation is found in the pointing and coloring games in
SmdM and evaluating is attached to this. WV has special games in which
each word is tested to see if the child knows that particular word.

Because of its adaptive character of "empty" games that are filled with
words from a database, WV is able to present games tailored to the different vocabulary levels of the children. If words of a certain level of difficulty
are known, more games and more difficult words become available. SmdM
also has an adaptive component, but in this software, if children show a
certain degree of vocabulary knowledge, vocabulary games aiming at
emerging literacy, too, become available. In other words, whereas WV is
more varied in different aspects of vocabulary learning (semantization,
consolidation), and the exercises are often less 'testing', SmdM aims at a
broader learning spectrum.

DISCUSSION AND CONCLUSION

The present chapter gave an overview about research on books on computers in Kindergarten, with a special focus on their effects on vocabulary
learning. Most research on books on computers elaborated on the already
known positive effects of storybook reading on vocabulary. Second language learners need more than storybook reading to have a chance to
catch up with their peers, as they have a lower background knowledge and
fewer experiences in the second language. Talking books, living books and

interactive books do not have a special interest in vocabulary learning. "Interactive vocabulary books" offer more opportunities to enhance vocabulary for kindergartners. These are books that combine a story with interactive vocabulary games. In these books and their software, attention is being paid to the four basic principles of vocabulary learning: preparation, semantization, consolidation, and evaluation (Nation, 2001), and the interactive and adaptive possibilities of the computer are elaborated upon.

Two Dutch examples were presented in this chapter, and research on this type of software was described. The results of these interactive vocabulary books are promising; the vocabulary of young children is enhanced with this type of software. However, Segers and Verhoeven (2003) showed that the gap between second language learners and their peers was not bridged with an SmdM intervention. Whether the new generation of software such as WV is able to show effects on independent vocabulary tests remains a question for future research.

Based on the two studies on WV and SmdM presented in this chapter, we suggest that software aiming at vocabulary learning should firstly include the four principles: preparation, semantization, consolidation and testing. Preparation can best be done by presenting the children with an *interactive* story on the computer. Then, semantization games should become available to become familiar with the new words in a playful and meaningful manner. The words in these games should be presented unambiguously. Consolidation can adaptively be connected to the semantization as well as the testing phase. The software has to take into account the general principles of (first and second) vocabulary learning and teaching with respect to the selection of words, text coverage, repetition, and so on (e.g., Baumann & Kame'enui, 2004; Beck, McKeown, & Kucan, 2002; Graves, 2006; Schmitt, 2000).

Adaptivity is the second important feature that should be included in software aiming at vocabulary learning, as evidenced by the high learning gains found with WV. The computer then not only serves as an extra exercise medium for repeating, but the software also makes use of the interactive and adaptive possibilities of the medium. By tracking the knowledge and the outcomes of exercises of the learner, an adaptive program can continuously tailor the curriculum to the pupil on the basis of the interaction that is going on. In such a case, the program builds a user model, on the basis of which a choice is made with respect to the next interaction form, or the content items that are next in line. This may mean that the presentation of the content is adapted (this may concern the adding or skipping of auditory or visual information); that the order in which the teaching material is presented is variable; or that various types of help or feedback are given to the learner. This way, the learners can be prevented from jumping ahead to the next learning content although they have not yet sufficiently practiced the preceding one. In addition, it can be ascertained whether all relevant links have been activated by the child, and remedying feedback can be given selectively and individualized.

Thirdly, software should not be used on its own. It is important to have an integration of what is going on in the classroom and what can be learned with the computer. WV uses books that have to be read by the teacher first and SmdM also emphasizes that the stories on the computer should also be read by the teacher. SmdM is even embedded in the language curriculum course most used in Kindergarten in the Netherlands, and WV made sure to use themes that are often used in Kindergarten. In this way, children encounter an enormous amount of new words both on the computer and in the classroom in many different settings and many different dimensions, and this is the best way to consolidate. To optimize vocabulary learning by computer in Kindergarten, good educational software in other words needs to be embedded in a good educational environment. We agree with Roschelle et al. (2000) that educational technology can be effective when viewed as an integral aspect of larger, ongoing educational reform, and, as Honey, Culp, and Carrigg (1999) state, that it can serve as catalyst for innovation of approaches to teaching and learning.

The educational value of books on computers for kindergartners is promising, but more research is this area is needed. Very little is known, for example, about the design of computer programs for young children. Druin and Solomon (1996) address some of the relevant issues, and Segers and Verhoeven (2002) and Bus, De Jong, and Verhallen (2006) make some suggestions. Besides good contents, software should look attractive and be challenging for children, to keep them motivated.

The role of the teacher is also important when using software. The teacher is the glue between computer activities and what goes on in the classroom, and more learning occurs when they use a mediating interaction style (encouraging, regulating behavior, affecting, etc.) (Klein & Darom, 2000) as opposed to only answering children's questions or, even worse, only providing technical assistance. Research on the role of the teacher during software interventions for young children is scarce and was also not studied in the present chapter. The interaction between child (and child characteristics), software (and software characteristics) and teacher is an interesting and important ongoing topic for future research.

REFERENCES

Aist, G. (2002). Helping children learn vocabulary during computer-assisted oral reading. *Educational Technology & Society,* 5, (2). Online at http://ifets.ieee .org/periodical/vol_2_2002/aist.html

Aitchison, J. (1994). *Words in the mind: an introduction to the mental lexicon*. Oxford: Blackwell.

Anderson, J. (1992). Living books and other books without pages. *Unicorn, 18,* 64–67.

Appel, R., & Vermeer, A. (1998). Speeding up second language vocabulary acquisition of minority children. *Language and Education, 12* (3), 159–173.

Baker, S. K., Simmons, D. C., & Kame'enui, E. J. (1998). Vocabulary acquisition: Research Bases. In D. C. Simmons & E. J. Kame'enui (Eds.): *What reading research tells us about children with diverse learning needs: basics and bases* (pp. 183–217). Mahwah, New Jersey: Lawrence Erlbaum Associates.

Baumann, J. F., & Kame'enui, E.J. (eds.) (2004). *Vocabulary instruction: research to practice*, New York: Guilford Press.

Beck, I., McKeown, M., & Kucan, L. (2002). *Bringing words to life: robust vocabulary instruction*. New York: Guilford Press.

Blachowicz, C. L., & Fisher, P. (2000). Vocabulary instruction. In: M. L.Kamil, P. B. Mosenthal, P.D.Pearson, & R. Barr (Eds.). *Handbook of reading research III* (pp. 503–523). Mahwah, New Jersey: Lawrence Erlbaum Associates.

Bransford, J. D., Sherwood, R. D., Hasselbring, T. S., Kinzer, C. K., & Williams, S. M. (1990). Anchored instruction: why we need it and how technology can help. In: D. Nix & R. Spiro (Eds.) *Cognition, Education and Multimedia: Exploring Ideas in High Technology*. Hillsdale, New Jersey: Lawrence Erlbaum.

Bus, A. G., Van IJzendoorn, M. H., & Pellegrini, A. D. (1995). Joint book reading makes for success in learning to read. A meta-analysis on intergenerational transmission of literacy. *Review of Educational Research, 65,* 1–21.

Bus, A. G., De Jong, M. T., & Verhallen, M. (2006). CD-ROM talking books: a way to enhance early literacy? In: M. McKenna, L.D. Labbo, R.D. Kieffer & D. Reinking (Eds.), *International Handbook of Literacy and Technology Volume II* (pp. 41–53). Mahwah, NJ: Lawrence Erlbaum.

De Jong, M. T., & Bus, A.G. (2002). Quality of book-reading matters for emergent readers: an experiment with the same book in a regular or electronic format. *Journal of Educational Psychology, 94,* 145–155.

De Jong, M. T., & Bus, A. G. (2003). How well suited are electronic books to supporting literacy? *Journal of Early Childhood Literacy, 3,* 147–164.

De Jong, M. T., & Bus, A. G. (2004). The efficacy of electronic books in fostering Kindergarten children's emergent story understanding. *Reading Research Quarterly, 39,* 378–393.

Druin, A., & Solomon, C. (1996). *Designing multimedia environments for children*. New York: John Wiley & Sons.

Elley, W. B. (1989). Vocabulary acquisition from listening to stories. *Reading Research Quarterly, 23,* 174–187.

Graves, M. (2006). *The vocabulary book: Learning and instruction*. New York: Teachers College Press.

Honey, M., Culp, K., & Carrigg, F. (1999). *Perspectives on technology and education research: lessons from the past and present*. New York: Center for children and technology.

Johnston, C. B. (1997). Interactive storybook software: effects on verbal development in Kindergarten children. *Early Child Development and Care, 132,* 33–44.

Klein, P. S., & Darom, N. E. (2000). The use of computers in kindergarten, with or without adult mediation; effects on children's cognitive performance and behavior. *Computers in Human Behavior, 16,* 591–608.

Kuhn, M. R., & Stahl, S. A. (1998) Teaching children to learn word meanings from context: A synthesis and some questions. *Journal of Literacy Research,* 30(1), 119–138.

McKeown, M. G., & Curtis, M. E. (Eds.) (1987). *The Nature of Vocabulary Acquisition.* Hillsdale, New Jersey: Lawrence Erlbaum Associates.

Mommers, M. J. C., Verhoeven, L., & Van der Linden, S. (1990). *Veilig leren lezen [Learning to read safely].* Tilburg: Zwijsen.

Nation, I. S. P. (2001). *Learning vocabulary in another language.* Cambridge: Cambridge University Press.

Reinking, D. (2001). Multimedia and engaged reading in a digital world. In: L. Verhoeven & C. Snow (Eds.), *Literacy and Motivation* (pp. 195–221). Mahwah, NJ: Lawrence Erlbaum.

Ricci, C. M., & Beal, C. R. (2002). The effects of interactive media on children's story memory. *Journal of Educational Psychology, 94,* 138–144.

Roschelle, J., Pea, R., Hoadley, C., Gordin, D., & Means, B. (2000). Changing how and what children learn in school with computer-based technology. *Children and Computer Technology,* 10, 2, 76–101.

Schacter, J., & Fagnano, C. (1999) Does computer technology improve student learning and achievement? How, when, and under what conditions? *Journal of Educational Computing Research, 20,* 329–343.

Schmitt, N. (2000). *Vocabulary in language teaching.* Cambridge: Cambridge University Press.

Segers, E., Nooijen, M., & De Moor, J. (2006). Vocabulary training with the computer in kindergarten children with special needs. *International Journal of Rehabilitation Research.*

Segers, E., Takke, L., & Verhoeven, L. (2004). Teacher-mediated versus computer-mediated storybook reading to children in native and multicultural classrooms. *School Effectiveness and School Improvement, 15,* 215–226.

Segers, E., & Verhoeven, L. (2002). Multimedia support in early literacy learning. *Computers & Education, 39,* 207–221.

Segers, E., & Verhoeven, L. (2003). Effects of vocabulary computer training in Kindergarten. *Journal of Computer Assisted Learning, 19,* 559–568.

Segers, E., & Verhoeven, L. (in press). Educational software to support teaching in Kindergarten. A focus on second language learners and children in special education. In L. Verhoeven & C. Kinzer (Eds.), *Interactive literacy education.* Mahwah, NJ: Erlbaum.

Stanovich, K. E. (1986). Matthew effects in reading: Some consequences of individual differences in the acquisition of literacy. *Reading Research Quarterly, 21,* 360–407.

Stine, H. (1993). *The effects of cd-rom interactive software in reading skill instruction with second grade Chapter 1 students.* Doctoral dissertation, George Washington University.

Sternberg, R. J. (1987). Most vocabulary is learned from context. In: M. G. McKe-own, & M. E. Curtis (Eds.). *The Nature of Vocabulary Acquisition* (pp. 89–105). Hillsdale, New Jersey: Lawrence Erlbaum Associates.

Strating, H., & A. Vermeer (2001). De digitale klas: over (in-)efficiëntie van het inzetten van multimediale software in het tweede-taalonderwijs. [Digital class-rooms: on the (in)efficiency of multimedia software in second language edu-cation]. *Spiegel* 17/18, 3/4: 151–162.

Terrell, S. L., & Daniloff, R. (1996). Children's word learning using three modes of instruction. *Perceptual and Motor Skills, 83,* 779–787.

Underwood, G., & Underwood, J. D. M. (1998). Children's interactions and learn-ing outcomes with interactive talking books. *Computers and Education, 30,* 95–102.

Van de Guchte, C., & Vermeer, A. (2004). Woorden Vangen: woordenschatonder-wijs met de computer [Catching words: vocabulary learning on the computer]. In: R. Aarts, P. Broeder, & A. Maljers (eds.), *Jong geleerd is oud gedaan. Talen leren in het basisonderwijs* (173–182). Den Haag: Europees Platform Onderwijs.

Verhallen, M. J., Bus, A. & De Jong, M. (2006). The promise of multimedia stories for Kindergarten children at risk. *Journal of Educational Psychology, 98,* 2, 410–419.

Verhallen, M., & Verhallen, S. (1994). *Woorden leren woorden onderwijzen* [Vocabulary learning and teaching]. Amsterdam: Universiteit van Amsterdam

Verhoeven, L., & Vermeer, A. (1992). Woordenschat van leerlingen in het basis- en MLK-onderwijs [Vocabulary of students in primary and special education]. *Pedagogische Studiën, 69,* 218–234.

Verhoeven, L., & Vermeer, A. (2001). *Taaltoets Alle Kinderen [Language Test for All Children]*. Arnhem: Cito.

Verhoeven, L., & Vermeer, A. (2006). Sociocultural variation in literacy achieve-ment, to appear in *British Journal of Educational Studies,* 54 (2). (to appear)

Wood, J. (2001). Can software support children's vocabulary development? *Lan-guage Learning & Technology,* 5, 166–201.

MATERIALS

Babbelbij, Wolters-Noordhoff (http://www.wolters.nl/)

Schatkist met de muis : Verhoeven, L., Segers, E., & Mommers, C. (1999) *Schatkist met de muis.* Tilburg: Zwijsen.

Woorden Vangen: Boot, I., Van de Guchte, C., Van der Linden, W., & Vermeer, A. (2003). *Woorden vangen. Woordenschat voor kleuters.* Tilburg: Zwijsen (http://www.zwijsen.nl/

CHAPTER 9

A FUTURE RESEARCH AGENDA FOR EARLY CHILDHOOD SCIENCE AND TECHNOLOGY

Olivia N. Saracho and Bernard Spodek

Literacy in science, mathematics, and technology is a future requirement for all children. Researchers, theorists, policy makers, and educators need to be involved in defining what this will involve. Worldwide knowledge about science and technology has increased in importance. In addition, an increased number of professions require knowledge of science and technology. Thus, society's future depends on the decisions that need to be based on scientific knowledge. Attention to these two important areas has led to the creation of the present volume. The first section of the volume has focused on science, while the second section has focused on technology. The role of science and technology as well as any research and educational implications are addressed in the volume.

SCIENTIFIC KNOWLEDGE

Many countries have established the challenging goal of "science for all" (American Association for the Advancement of Science, 1990) to include science instruction for a wide range of groups in the school-aged popula-

Contemporary Perspectives on Science and Technology in Early Childhood Education, pages 167–181
Copyright © 2008 by Information Age Publishing
All rights of reproduction in any form reserved.

tion (Lee & Luykx, 2007), including young children. Current educational research suggest that even very young children are able to understand the world from a scientific perspective. According to French (2004), infants and young children are biologically ready and motivated to acquire knowledge about the world around them. Beginning in infancy, children process their personal experiences to produce "generalized event representations" (or "scripts") consisting of information about the temporal/causal system of a condition, its essential and optional elements, and the related roles and props (Nelson, 1986). Such mental representations establish the young children's understanding of and involvement in their everyday world. In addition, young children are able to (a) identify regularities, (b) understand their everyday experiences, (c) anticipate the individuals' behavior in a variety of situations, and (d) behave properly (French, 2004).

Several studies showed that even three-year-old children have the capacity to learn theoretically-based concepts, although Nelson (1996) found that children need to be four- or five-years-old to be able to learn mental representations through listening. In addition, children need the language to be able to communicate their mental representations. Several researchers have shown that very young children are able to produce representations and understand their symbolic functioning. As early as two years of age, children are able to recognize familiar objects in pictures (DeLoache & Burns, 1994), while four-year-olds are able to produce effective graphic symbols to communicate with an interlocutor when solving a problem (Callaghan, 1999). Young children between four and seven years of age tend to be intellectually realistic based on their understanding of the object that they are representing. These children usually believed that the objects have a few essential characteristics (Cox, 1992; Piaget & Inhelder, 1966/1978).

Four-year-olds respond to critical feedback about their representations, directing them to include more detail, discover a variety of representational choices, and specifically represent them in a domain (Callaghan, 1999). Conceptual structures differ by both domain and task. Even within a domain, children differ in the information they use for each context according to the task or function at hand (Gelman, 1999). Five- and six-year-olds are able to provide relevant details in a given representation (Tversky, Kugelmass, & Winter, 1991). Danish and Enyedy (2007) found that five- and six-year-old children were able to create and use representations. They examined the children's representational practices and capabilities to understand the various factors that influence their creation and discussion of representations. Their results showed that the children created their representations and the existence of several key mediators in the children's representational activities, such as peers, task constraints, teachers, and local norms for what constituted a "good representation." Danish and Enyedy (2007) also found that these norms changed over time when new content was presented in the class and children interacted with their peers. When children created their representations, they frequently encountered competing constraints, but they solved such constraints through a complex set of negotiations. They concluded that children need to be allowed to select their representations and include content details that they understand, which gives them a feeling of ownership and individuality of their representations.

Research in child development indicates that young children assign the characteristics of animate objects to natural phenomena. Malcolm (1999) reported how her four-year-old daughter formulated a hypothesis, which was based on a question that was important to her and was followed by an explanation that assisted her in making sense of the world. Science experiences would assist her in formulating and refining her theories. Young children need to take advantage of their daily science experiences and be provided with additional experiences that are developmentally appropriate for all as well as individual children.

Research and theory development have emerged as science studies support the children's alternative conceptions of various natural phenomena and have recommended instructional strategies that can assist young children to modify their prior perceptions and accept scientific ideas (e.g., Scherz & Oren, 2006; Solomonidou & Kakana, 2000). According to Osborne and Brady (2002),

> When asking children to "do" science we also ask them to explore the nature of science, thinking on a meta-level about acts of design and personal agency in science. We provided many different materials for making the stepping-stones and we asked questions about the qualities of the materials and the relationships between those and their resulting designs. The activities were shaped by the children's desires, aesthetic, and their past histories, which were in turn altered by their experiences in this class. (p. 328)

This understanding of science learning in early childhood education integrates aesthetics and science, explanation and emotion, and gives a new and different definition to early childhood science. Osborne and Brady's (2002) approach offers young children a feeling of wonder, relatedness, and fascination. When they experience a novelty effect, young children are able to become creative in science. Osborne and Brady (2002) state,

> We would like to argue, as they point out, that rather than increased test scores or vague concepts such as scientific literacy, the outcomes of education should be more ambiguous.... We would argue that instead of increased test scores, science education should concern itself with the transformation

of both the teacher's and learner's roles and this entails a transformation of subject matter. (pp. 330–331)

The science goal consists of providing "developmentally appropriate" experiences where young children develop their cognitive understanding in science (Hadjigeorgiou, 2001). Piaget and Vygotsky have contributed to research a theory on science learning, although contemporary researchers have acknowledged the integration of cognitive and social/affective processes (Dai & Sternberg, 2004). For example, Ravanis and Bagakis (1998) address the socicognitive perspective of several didactic strategies for science education at the kindergarten level. They provide examples where children understand the scientific phenomenon through their social, cognitive, and emotional abilities. The affective domain in science education is in its initial stages, but it is important to include this domain in teaching science interventions with young children (Zembylas, this volume).

For young children, the *Benchmarks for science literacy* (American Association for the Advancement of Science, 1993) determined that young children had to learn about the Scientific World View, Scientific Inquiry, and Scientific Enterprise. During the last few years, research has supported the *Benchmarks for science literacy* (American Association for the Advancement of Science, 1993) and the areas of early childhood science and technology education.

TECHNOLOGICAL KNOWLEDGE

Children today are growing up in the presence of technology. Even before young children enter school, technology has usually been part of their life. They experience digital technology even before they experience books. Young children usually observe their parents use computer technology more frequently than reading books and they often use computers themselves. Digital technology attracts the young children's interest with color, movement, sound, and interaction. In addition, it provides them with immediate responses and give the children the power to make things happen instantaneously. The nature of technology and its importance demands that children be provided with sufficient opportunities and appropriate experiences in its use (Cooper, 2005). These types of experiences are easy to provide in early childhood settings since almost all early childhood programs have a computer. According to Clements (1999), in 1997 the ratio of computers to students in an early childhood classroom was one to ten, which is a favorable ratio for social interaction (Clements & Nastasi, 1993).

Electronic Media

Research showed that even the youngest children in the United States use multiple types of screen media, which have been found to be at highest levels than are considered developmentally appropriate (Rideout, Vandewater, & Wartella, 2003). During the last few years, there has been an outburst of electronic media that has been targeted directly to the youngest children in our society. In the United States, children from birth are growing up immersed in media; they spend many hours a day watching television and videos, using computers and playing video games. Television, movies, videos, music, video games, and computers are essential to both work and play. An increase is occurring in early childhood television programming, computer software for toddlers, and video series for infants (Schmidt et al., 2005). Rideout et al. (2003) conducted a national study of more than 1,000 parents of children ages six months through six years to examine the role of electronic media in the young children's lives. They found that children from birth to six years spent as much time with television, computers, and video games as playing outside. Their results showed that almost half (48%) of the children less than six years of age used a computer (31% of 0–3 year olds and 70% of 4–6 year olds) and almost one-third (30%) played video games (14% of 0–3 year olds and 50% of 4–6 year olds). Even two-year-olds had experiences with electronic media where 43% watched television every day and 26% had a television in their bedroom. Two-thirds (68%) of the children less than two years of age watched a screen media, for a little more than two hours (2:05). In relation to computers, 25% of four to six-year-olds used a computer, spending more than an hour (1:04) each day at the keyboard. Four- to six-year-olds spent 39% using a computer several times a week or more, where 37% were able to turn on the computer by themselves and 40% were able to load a CD-ROM.

Pediatricians, educators, researchers, and policymakers are concerned about the use of electronic media among very young children. Developmental science indicates that children between birth and school age are the most vulnerable to a negative impact on the use of media. Therefore, educational programming is necessary to protect children from their vulnerability (Schmidt et al., 2005). Technology has generated developmentally appropriate components that rely on formal characteristics and symbol systems of media that it has prompted the researchers' interest who have explored the relationship between techniques and the individuals' cognitive skills (Krendal & Warren, 2004).

Developmentally Appropriate Implications

Many early childhood educators have challenged the appropriateness of computers with young children. Clements and Nastasi (1993) believe that the use of technology is "developmentally appropriate." They assume that very young children are comfortable and have confidence using the software. In addition, they are able to follow pictorial instructions as well as use situational and visual cues to understand their activity. Clements (1999) adds that typing on the keyboard seems to be easy and becomes a source of pride.

Studies of young children and technology have investigated the implications on the use of technology in early childhood education. Liu's (1996) study showed that children as young as three years of age were able to use computers. Ruff, Capozzoli, and Weissberg (1998) found that from infancy through the toddler years, children process information by differentiating objects on the screen through salient visual (e.g., motion, color, shapes, graphics) and auditory (e.g., music, voices, sound effects) cues. During this stage, children perceive and comprehend the perplexing code structure of television that creates a sense of story grammar. Young children integrate novel stimuli with existing knowledge structures (assimilation) and simultaneously learn the dual process requirements of visual and verbal information.

In relation to technology, Piaget (1970, 1972) also supports the results of contemporary studies. He disclosed a hierarchy of progressively abstract viewing skills that guide children's message processing. From infancy through the toddler years, young children differentiate objects on the screen through perceptually salient visual (e.g., motion, color, shapes, graphics) and auditory (e.g., music, voices, sound effects) cues. At this age, they can perceive and understand the complex code system of television and develop an awareness of story grammar. Their job is to combine novel stimuli with existing knowledge structures (assimilation), while simultaneously they acquaint themselves with the binary processing demands of visual and verbal information.

During this development stage, children pay more attention to the television screen (Ruff et al., 1998), since visual cues are more perceptually salient. Six to twelve-year-old children, who are in Piaget's concrete operations stage, are able to monitor both video and audio information from a screen. Children in ages ranging from six to twelve years (Piaget's concrete logical operations stage) are more proficient in monitoring both video and audio information from a screen. At this stage, they focus more on monitoring the audio content than viewing the screen (Baer, 1994) for relevant cues.

Relevancy relates to personal components (e.g., the use of familiar voices or music) rather than perceptual ones (e.g., novel music, sound effects). Therefore, children learn to discriminate patterns because they are familiar with the medium. They can distinguish between relevant and irrelevant information, focus on dialogue, and process video and audio information independently (Field & Anderson, 1985). Baer (1997) showed that these children spend more time monitoring the audio content for salient cues rather than looking at the screen. They focused on personally relevant features (e.g., the use of familiar voices or music) rather than perceptual features (e.g., novel music, sound effects). The children's familiarity with this medium increases their discriminating viewing patterns. They can differentiate between relevant and irrelevant information, focus on dialogue, and process video and audio information independently (Field & Anderson, 1985).

Addressing Technological Issues

Advocates on the future of children's education are pressuring the appropriate use of instructional content and strategies for young children. Toward the end of the twentieth century, education has dramatically shifted in organizing their thoughts concerning the world, its resources, and their relationships with each other. According to Bowman (1999), the new revolution has the following characteristics:

- the reorganization of knowledge systems through the use of high-powered computers;
- increased access to inexpensive audiovisual and computer hardware and software, worldwide computer networks, and interactive technologies;
- new symbol systems (computer programming) and the use of old systems in new ways (word processing, calculators, etc.); and
- new models for understanding the world (artificial intelligence and problem simulations).

Bowman (1999) believes that as a result of these changes, children have multiple opportunities to learn through the media, books, and computers and children who have knowledgeable family members and preschool teachers may be better prepared for school than children without this reinforcement.

The National Science Teachers Association (NSTA) has raised two issues: (1) it is important to understand how and why young children learn, and (2) it is important to identify programs and learning experiences that are effective in meeting the young children's needs. A future undertaking is to build technology education into the curriculum and to employ technology in the students learning. This process can assist the students in learning about nature, powers, and boundaries of technology.

Children need to learn to use computers as tools to extend their ability to solve problems instead of simply learning ways to perform specific skills from preprogramed problems and solution. Children also need to participate in meaningful experiences where they function as doers and thinkers instead of recipients of information from teachers (Bowman, 1999).

SCIENTIFIC AND TECHNOLOGICAL KNOWLEDGE

Young children informally and intuitively acquire knowledge of concepts in science and technology as they interact with people and things. In their world, children observe physical phenomena, utilize technologically driven equipment (e.g., telephones, television), and generate hypotheses about cause and effect. Sometimes very young children construe incorrect concepts but even three-year-old children can practice science and use technology (Bowman, 1999).

Contemporary educational research indicates that very young children are able to understand their world from a scientific perspective. Several studies provide evidence that three-year-old children are able to learn theoretical concepts, including how young children can learn science and technology. Knowledge in science and technology can help young children succeed in society. They need to acquire knowledge and skills in these two important areas to become literate in science and technology and to be prepared for the future (American Association for the Advancement of Science, 1999).

Research shows that preschool children's knowledge, skills, and dispositions in science and technology can be developmentally appropriate. Many early childhood educators have challenged the appropriateness of "too early" instruction, but contemporary research support that the foundation for educational opportunities in science and technology can promote the young children's learning and development in these areas. Spodek (1986, 1991) also proposed that the developmental perspective, as well as the cultural and social contexts, need to be considered in all early childhood education programs, which includes science and technology. Malcolm (1999) suggested that educators take advantage of the children's daily experiences and extend them with additional experiences that are developmentally appropriate and meet the children's individual needs. David Hawkins (1983) described the importance of this approach in an article in the Spring 1983 issue of *Daedalus*:

The kind of experiential background in children's lives before schooling begins or along the way is more uniformly adequate to math and science than to most other school subjects. The poverty or richness of social background matter less here in the early years than in other school subjects. Math and science should therefore be the great equalizer, whether they are now seen to be or not. (Hawkins, 1983)

Regrettably, science and technology have become the major dividers instead of providing a balance, which excludes students from education opportunities and experiences that influence their role in society and personal fulfillment.

Thinking about science and technology for young children is not a novel concept. A number of projects in the curriculum reform movement of the 1960s, including the American Association for the Advancement of Science's *Science—A process approach*, the Educational Development Center's *Elementary school science*, and Karplus' *Science curriculum improvement study*, all included content for kindergarten (Spodek, 1985). In addition, there is now a growing awareness that young children who participate in science and technology experiences can obtain both short and long-term benefits, which can insure that all young children have a basis for future learning. It has become apparent that science and technology can provide young children with knowledge about the world, while their experiences can help them later to become ready for the formal study of science and technology (Malcolm, 1999). For example, Scherz and Oren (2006) examined the students' images of science and technology. They described how an instructional initiative affected images and stated that "investigation into Science and Technology" (IST), was designed to introduce students to science and technology in the "real life" (p. 965). Their results showed that before the IST intervention, the students' images of the scientific or technological environments were superficial, unreal, and incorrect. The intervention (IST) program modified the students' images. Their prejudgments changed from superficial and vague to precise and correct, from stereotypic to rational and open-minded, and from negative to positive attitudes. Based on these results, they recommend that researchers examine the relationship between the students' images and attitudes toward science and technology, that the IST program be tested with all types of students including those from both lower and upper socioeconomic backgrounds, and with science teachers. Scherz and Oren (2006) concluded that science programs at school need to provide learning opportunities that relate meaningful and well-designed experiences in the real world of science and technology.

Our previous discussion is based on the assumption that schools can take advantage of the complementary qualities of science and technology in society through the interaction between design and inquiry. The science and technology education communities are beginning to accept that the content standards of science literacy and technological literacy are intertwined. In addition, Lewis (2006) has shown that both science and technology educators have been teaching instructional units that can assist students to understand science through design. Lewis (2006) concluded that both science and technology education teachers are able to learn from each other, but they need to disregard that separation in schools, which has caused them to function as two independent cultures. Positive attitudes toward science and technology are critically important in the development of scientific literacy. A logical process in developing positive attitudes would be for both science and technology teachers to deal with both the students' as well as the teachers' knowledge, understanding, and attitudes toward science and technology.

CONCLUSION

Technology has a separate history and identity from science, although it has drawn on science knowledge in learning how the natural world works and how to control what happens in the world. Technology has become increasingly associated with science, which motivated the American Association for the Advancement of Science (1993) to generate goals and establish guidelines in designing curricula that included content standards for *Science for all Americans* (American Association for the Advancement of Science, 1990), also designed for children ranging from kindergarten to the second grade. These standards and guidelines led the American Association for the Advancement of Science (1993) to create the *Benchmarks for science literacy,* which characterizes the students' (a) progress toward science literacy, (b) knowledge that they are required to learn, and (c) abilities for each grade level. Both of these publications offer guidelines for reforming science and technology education. Guidelines and recommendations for science and technology education are also discussed in Saracho and Spodek's chapter titled, *Scientific and Technological Literacy Research: Principles and Practices.* They refer to the above reports in their discussion. In addition, they also discussed the National Association for the Education of Young Children [NAEYC], 1996) statement on developmentally appropriate ways to use technology with young children whose ages range from three to eight.

The American Association for the Advancement of Science and the National Research Council of the National Academy of Sciences are challenging the young children's achievement in science and technology to emphasize problem solving, direct experiences, and understanding as the major goals of early childhood education. The National Council of Teachers of Mathematics (NCTM) has established a separate standard emphasizing that the students' need to relate science and technology through first-hand experiences with technological products, including such machines as zippers, coat hooks, and can openers.

Concerns about teaching science and technology have usually focused on the fairness of access and opportunities to engage in cognitive experiences. However, the recent reforms in the early childhood curriculum have addressed the importance of science and technology education in relation to the children's socialization. For example, these areas offer young children opportunities to share, cooperate, and solve problems in small groups. They are able to generate and test hypotheses, leading them to participate in the scientific process of observation, hypothesis generation, hypothesis testing, and encounter the challenge of comparing their own understandings with those of their peers (New, 1999).

Reforming the early childhood curriculum in teaching science and technology has been based on the developmental perspective about how young children learn as well as their need to understand their role in a pluralistic and democratic society. It is essential that young children develop conceptual understandings in science and technology within that role. Three, four, and five-year-old children are able to achieve these goals. The National Research Council (1996), in its *National Science Education Standards*, established that combined and continued support of all Americans can facilitate the achievement of such goals, because it needs more than one group to implement the Standards. Everybody in the education system needs to be involved, including teachers, administrators, science and technology educators, curriculum designers, assessment specialists, local school boards, state departments of education, and the federal government. In addition, individuals outside the education system, including students, parents, scientists, engineers, businesspeople, taxpayers, legislators, and other public officials, can affect science and technology education.

There is broad support for this integration. For example, the scientific and engineering communities acknowledge the importance of having young children become technologically literate (e.g., Bybee, 2000; Institute of Electrical and Electronics Engineers, 2002). The proposed alignments between science and technology education in the curriculum. During the last decade, the National Science Foundation has actively promoted technology education as a school subject and has funded science projects that included the Standards for Technological Literacy (International Technology Education Association, 2000) and the National Center for Engineering and Technology Education (see www.NCETE.org). The National Academy of Engineering has also supported technology education as a part of the curriculum. In addition, the National Association for the Education of Young Children (1996) proposed developmentally appropriate ways to use technology with young children whose ages range from three to eight.

The interest in science and technology education led the National Science Foundation and the American Association for the Advancement of Science to convene educators, scholars, and researchers to discuss ways to teach developmentally appropriate science, mathematics, and technology to pre-kindergarten children. In February 1998, the National Science Foundation (NSF) invited, to Washington, DC, a multidisciplinary group of experts for a Forum on Early Childhood Science, Mathematics, and Technology Education. According to Johnson (1999), the purpose of the forum was to:

- merge three constituencies—representatives from the mathematics, science, and technology communities, early childhood educational practitioners, and the educational equity community—to enhance mathematics, science, and technology education in early childhood;
- consider what the goals of such education should be and to begin to articulate strategies for achieving these goals;
- review what is know about this area of education;
- identify promising subject areas or programs worthy of outside funding.

The discussions at the forum led to the publication of a book titled, *Dialogue on early childhood science, mathematics, and technology education* (American Association for the Advancement of Science, 1999). This volume has attempted to facilitate the research conducted by both novice and expert researchers in this area. The volume consists of reviews of critically analyzed research in science and technology education that is useful in advancing the field by stimulating additional research and recommendations for both researchers and educators in science and technology.

REFERENCES

American Association for the Advancement of Science. (1990). *Science for all Americans: Project 2061.* New York: Oxford University Press.

American Association for the Advancement of Science. (1993). *Benchmarks for science literacy.* New York: Oxford University Press.

American Association for the Advancement of Science, Project 2061. (1999). *Dialogue on early childhood science, mathematics, and technology education.* Cary, NC: Oxford University Press.

Baer, S. A. (1997). Strategies of children's attention to and comprehension of television. Doctoral dissertation, University of Kentucky, 1996. *Dissertation Abstracts International, 57*(11-B), 7243.

Bowman, B. T. (1999). Policy implications for math, science, and technology in early childhood education: A context for learning. In American Association for the Advancement of Science, Project 2061, *Dialogue on early childhood science, mathematics, and technology education.* Cary, NC: Oxford University Press.

Bybee, R. W. (2000). Achieving technological literacy: A national imperative. *The Technology Teacher, 60,* 23–28.

Callaghan, T. C. (1999). Early understanding and production of graphic symbols. *Child Development, 70*(6), 1314–1324.

Clements, D. (1999). Young children and technology. In American Association for the Advancement of Science, Project 2061, *Dialogue on early childhood science, mathematics, and technology education.* Cary, NC: Oxford University Press.

Clements, D. H., & Nastasi, B. K. (1993). Electronic media and early childhood education. In B. Spodek (Ed.), *Handbook of research on the education of young children* (pp. 251–275). New York: Macmillan.

Cooper, L. Z. (2005). Developmentally appropriate digital environments for young children. *Library Trends, 54,* 286–302.

Cox, M. V. (1992). *Children's drawings.* Harmondsworth: Penguin.

Dai, D. Y., & Sternberg, R. J. (Eds.). (2004). *Motivation, emotion, and cognition: Integrative perspectives on intellectual functioning and development.* Mahwah, NJ: Erlbaum.

Danish, J. A., & Enyedy, N. (2007). Negotiated representational mediators: How young children decide what to include in their science representations. *Science Education, 91*(1), 1–35.

DeLoache, J. S., & Burns, N. M. (1994). Early understanding of the representational function of pictures. *Cognition, 2*(52), 83–110.

Field, D. E., & Anderson, D. R. (1985). Instruction and modality effects on children's television attention and comprehension. *Journal of Educational Psychology, 77,* 91–100.

French, L. (2004). Science as the center of a coherent, integrated early childhood curriculum. *Early Childhood Research Quarterly, 19*(1), 138–149.

Gelman, S. A. (1999). Concept development in preschool children. In American Association for the Advancement of Science, Project 2061, *Dialogue on early childhood science, mathematics, and technology education.* Cary, NC: Oxford University Press.

Hadjigeorgiou, Y. (2001). The role of wonder and 'romance' in early childhood science education. *International Journal of Early Years Education, 9,* 63–69.

Hawkins, D. (1983, Spring). Nature closely observed. *Daedalus, 111*(2).

Institute of Electrical and Electronics Engineers. (2002). *Proceedings of technological literacy counts workshop: A collaboration of educators and engineers.* Baltimore, October 9–10, 1998. Piscataway, NJ: Author.

International Technology Education Association. (2000). *Standards for technological literacy: Content for the study of technology.* Reston, VA: Author.

Johnson, J. R. (1999). The Forum on early childhood science, mathematics, and technology education. In American Association for the Advancement of Science, Project 2061, *Dialogue on early childhood science, mathematics, and technology education.* Cary, NC: Oxford University Press.

Krendal, K. A., & Warren, R. (2004). Communication effects of noninterative media: Learning in out-of-school contexts. In D. H. Jonassen (Ed.), *Handbook of research on educational communications and technology* (pp. 59–78). Mahwah, NJ: Erlbaum.

Lee, O., & Luykx, A. (2007). Science education and student diversity: Race/ethnicity, language, culture, and socioeconomic status. In S. K. Abell, N. G Norman, & G. Lederman (Eds.), *Handbook of research on science education* (pp. 171–197). Mahwah, NJ: Erlbaum.

Lewis, T. (2006). Design and inquiry: Bases for an accommodation between science and technology education in the curriculum? *Journal of Research in Science Teaching, 43,* 255–281.

Liu, M. (1996). An exploratory study of how pre-kindergarten children use the interactive multimedia technology: Implications for multimedia software design. *Journal of Computing in Childhood Education, 7,* 71–92.

Malcolm, S. (1999). Making sense of the world. In American Association for the Advancement of Science, Project 2061, *Dialogue on early childhood science, mathematics, and technology education.* Cary, NC: Oxford University Press.

National Association for the Education of Young Children. (1996). Position statement: Technology and young children: Ages three through eight. *Young Children, 51*(6), 11–16.

National Research Council. (1996). *National science education standards.* Washington, DC: National Academy Press.

National Research Council. (2000). *Inquiry and the national science education standards: A guide for teaching and learning.* Washington, DC: National Academy Press.

Nelson, K. (1986). *Event knowledge: Structure and function in development.* Hillsdale, NJ: Erlbaum.

Nelson, K. (1996). *Language in cognitive development: The emergence of the mediated mind.* New York: Cambridge University Press.

New, R. S. (1999). Playing fair and square: Issues of equity in preschool mathematics, science, and technology. In American Association for the Advancement of Science, Project 2061, *Dialogue on early childhood science, mathematics, and technology education.* Cary, NC: Oxford University Press.

Osborne, M. D., & Brady, D. J. (2002). Imagining the new: Constructing a space for creativity in science. In E. Mirochnik & D. Sherman (Eds.), *Passion and pedagogy: Relation, creation, and transformation in teaching* (pp. 317–332). New York: Peter Lang.

Piaget, J. (1970). *Genetic epistemology.* New York: Viking.

Piaget, J. (1972). *The principles of genetic epistemology* (trans. W. Mays). New York: Basic Books.

Piaget, J., & Inhelder, B. (1966/1978). *Mental imagery in the child.* New York: Routledge.

Ravanis, K., & Bagakis, G. (1998). Science education in kindergarten: Socio-cognitive perspective. *Journal of Early Years Education, 6,* 315–327.

Rideout, V. J., Vandewater, E. A., & Wartella, E. A. (2003). *Zero to six: Electronic media in the lives of infants, toddlers, and preschoolers* (Report). Washington, DC: Kaiser Family Foundation. Retrieved on February 6, 2007, from http://www.kff.org/

entmedia/upload/Zero-to-Six-Electronic-Media-in-the-Lives-of-Infants-Toddlers-and-Preschoolers-PDF.pdf

Ruff, H. A., Capozzoli, M., Weissberg, R. (1998). The effect of television and radio on children's creativity. *Human Communication Research, 11*, 109–120.

Scherz, Z., & Oren, M. (2006). How to change students' images of science and technology. *Science Education, 90*(6), 965–985.

Schmidt, M. E., Bickham, D., King, B., Slaby, R., Banner, A.C., & Rich, M. (2005). *The effects of electronic media on children ages zero to six: A history of research.* Prepared for the Kaiser Family Foundation by the Center on Media and Child Health (http://www.kff.org). Washington, DC: Kaiser Family Foundation. Retrieved on February 6, 2007, from: www/kff.org/entmedia/upload/The-Effects-of-Electronic-Media-on-Children-Ages-Zero-to-Six-A-History-of-Research-Issue-Brief.pdf

Solomonidou, C., & Kakana, D. (2000). Preschool children's conceptions about the electric current and the functioning of electric appliances. *European Early Childhood Education Research Journal, 8*(1), 95–111.

Spodek, B. (1985). *Teaching in the early years* (3rd ed.). Englewood Cliffs, NJ: Prentice-Hall.

Spodek, B. (1986). Development, values and knowledge in the kindergarten curriculum. In B. Spodek (Ed.), *Today's kindergarten: Exploring the knowledge base, expanding the curriculum* (pp. 32–47). New York: Teachers College Press.

Spodek, B. (1991). Early childhood curriculum and cultural definitions of knowledge. In B. Spodek & O. Saracho (Eds.), *Issues in early childhood curriculum* (pp. 1–20). New York: Teachers College Press.

Tversky, B., Kugelmass, S., & Winter, A. (1991). Cross-cultural and developmental-trends in graphic productions. *Cognitive Psychology, 23*(4), 515–557.

ABOUT THE CONTRIBUTORS

Doris Bergen is a Distinguished Professor of Educational Psychology at Miami University, Oxford, Ohio. She received her Ph.D. from Michigan State University. Her research interests have focused on cross-cultural programs for young children, play and humor in early and middle childhood, effects of technology-enhanced toys, adult memories of childhood play, social interactions of children with special needs, effects of early phonological awareness levels on later reading, and gifted children's humor development. She has published eight books, over 40 refereed articles, and 25 book chapters. In 2000, she was recognized as a Miami University Distinguished Scholar. She was selected as a National Academy of Science visiting scholar to China. She is co-director of Miami University's Center for Human Development, Learning, and Technology, and in that role has received numerous grants herself, as well as facilitated many external grants for Center Faculty Associates.

Marina U. Bers is an assistant professor at the Eliot-Pearson Department of Child Development and an adjunct professor in the Computer Science Department at Tufts University. She heads the interdisciplinary research group Developmental Technologies (DevTech). Her research involves the design and study of innovative learning technologies to promote children's positive development. Bers received the 2005 Presidential Early Career Award for Scientists and Engineers (PECASE), the highest honor given by the U.S. government to outstanding investigators at the early stages of their careers. She also received a National Science Foundation (NSF) Young Investigator's Career Award, a five-year grant to support her work on virtual communities, and the American Educational Research Association's (AERA) Jan Hawkins Award for Early Career Contributions to Humanistic Research and Scholarship in Learning Technologies. Over the past twelve years, Professor Bers conceived and designed diverse technological tools

Contemporary Perspectives on Science and Technology in Early Childhood Education, pages 183–186
Copyright © 2008 by Information Age Publishing

ranging from robotics to virtual worlds. She conducted studies in schools and after school settings, both nationally and internationally, as well as in Boston's Children's Hospital. She is the author of the book *Blocks to Robots: Learning with Technology in the Early Childhood Classroom* published by Teachers College Press. Bers is from Argentina. She received a Master's degree in Educational Media and Technology from Boston University and a Master of Science and Ph.D. from the MIT Media Laboratory.

Douglas H. Clements is Professor of Education at University of Buffalo, SUNY, where he was granted the Chancellor's Award for Excellence in Scholarship and Creative Activities. His primary research interests lie in the areas of the learning and teaching of geometry, computer applications in mathematics education, and the early development of mathematical ideas. He has published over 90 refereed research studies, 6 books, 50 chapters, and 250 additional publications. Currently, Dr. Clements is Principal Investigator on a large scale research project, *Scaling Up TRIAD: Teaching Early Mathematics for Understanding with Trajectories and Technologies* funded by the U.S. Department of Education's Institute of Education Sciences In addition, Dr. Clements has directed or co-directed over 15 additional projects funded by IES, NSF, and others including *Building Blocks-Foundations for Mathematical Thinking, Pre-Kindergarten to Grade 2: Research-based Materials Development* (http://www.buildingblocks.org), and the, national *Conference on Standards for Preschool and Kindergarten Mathematics Education* (co-funded by NSF and ExxonMobil Foundation, http://www.gse.buffalo.edu/org/conference/index.htm), which resulted in a book, Clements, D. H., Sarama, J., & DiBiase, A.-M. (Eds.). (2004). *Engaging young children in mathematics: Standards for early childhood mathematics education.*

Ithel Jones is an Associate Professor of Early Childhood Education at the Florida State University. A native of Wales, Ithel earned his bachelor's degree from the University of Wales, master's degree from the University of Wisconsin, and doctoral degree from the University of Georgia. He was an early childhood teacher and school principal in Wales for several years. He was also an Assistant Professor at the University of Wisconsin-Milwaukee before coming to Florida State University in 1998. He has produced publications in leading academic journals in the area of early education and cognate fields.

Vickie E. Lake is an associate professor of Early Childhood Education at The Florida State University. She earned her B.S. in Teachers of Young Children from Texas Tech University, M.Ed. in Elementary Education from Peabody College for Teachers at Vanderbilt University, and Ph.D. in Curriculum and Instruction from The University of Texas. As a former teacher, math specialist, staff developer, and early childhood district coordinator, she has worked to further the efforts of curriculum integration for young children. Her primary areas of research interest are moral and character education, development of innovative approaches to the education of young children, teacher education, and qualitative research methodology.

Miranda Lin is a doctoral student of Education at Florida State University. She has worked as an early childhood teacher/director in Taiwan, China, and America. Her areas of research include anti-bias curriculum, parent-child relationship, teacher education, and curriculum development.

Julie Sarama is an Associate Professor of Mathematics Education at the University at Buffalo (SUNY). She conducts research on the implementation and effects of her own software environments in mathematics classrooms, young children's development of mathematical concepts and competencies, implementation and scale-up of educational reform, and professional development, published in more than 35 refereed articles, 15 chapters, and 50 additional publications. She has been Principal or Co-Principal Investigator on five projects funded by the National Science Foundation. She has taught secondary mathematics and computer science, gifted math at the middle school level, preschool and kindergarten mathematics enrichment classes, and mathematics methods and content courses for elementary to secondary teachers. She designed and programmed microworlds for the National Science Foundation-funded *Investigations in Number, Data, and Space*.

Eliane Segers studied both Language, Speech & Computer Science and Cognitive Science at the Radboud University in Nijmegen. After graduation, she worked as a PhD student in Social Sciences on the study and development of an educational software program for kindergartners, which is now widely used in schools in the Netherlands. She has written several articles and book chapters about learning and ICT. and is now assistant professor at the Behavioural Science Institute at the same University. Her research focuses on multimedia learning, reading problems, specific language impairment and ICT interventions.

Grady Venville is Professor of Science Education at the University of Western Australia. Grady is a teacher and researcher with experience across the primary, secondary and tertiary levels in Australia, England and Japan. Grady has published widely on curriculum integration and conceptual change and is co-editor of two books titled, *The Art of Teaching Science*, (Allen & Unwin, 2004) and *The Art of Teaching Primary Science* (Allen & Unwin, 2007).

Anne Vermeer studied Dutch and General Linguistics at the University of Amsterdam. His main teaching and research activities deal with first and second language acquisition of children. His main research focus is development in growth of vocabulary and the relation with rule-governed and/or associated-pairs learning behavior of morphological complex words, with cognitive abilities and with textual abilities with respect to cohesion and coherence. He wrote several books on second language acquisition, vocabulary acquisition, and second language teaching. He developed diagnostic instruments of Dutch language proficiency for Dutch and ethnic minority children from 5 to 12 years old, and (second) language curriculum materials, folio as well as cdrom materials.

Michalinos Zembylas is Assistant Professor of Education at the Open University of Cyprus and Adjunct Professor of Teacher Education at Michigan State University. His research interests are in the areas of curriculum theory, philosophy of education, and science/technology education. His work focuses on exploring the role of emotion and affect in curriculum and pedagogy. He is currently involved in a longitudinal ethnographic project on the emotions of peace and reconciliation education in divided Cyprus. He is the author of the book *Teaching With Emotion: A Postmodern Enactment* (Information Age Publishing, 2005).